T0320038

The Political Economy of the New Deal

The Political Economy of the New Deal

Jim F. Couch
Associate Professor of Economics,
University of North Alabama, USA

William F. Shughart II
Professor of Economics,
University of Mississippi, USA

THE LOCKE INSTITUTE

Edward Elgar
Cheltenham, UK • Northampton, MA, USA

Published by
Edward Elgar Publishing Limited
Glensanda House
Montpellier Parade
Cheltenham
Glos GL50 1UA
UK

Edward Elgar Publishing, Inc.
6 Market Street
Northampton
Massachusetts 01060
USA

A catalogue record for this book
is available from the British Library

Library of Congress Cataloguing in Publication Data

Couch, Jim F., 1959–
    The political economy of the New Deal / Jim F.
Couch, William F. Shughart II.
    Includes bibliographical references and index.
    "The Locke Institute."
    1. United States—Economic Policy—1933–1945. 2. United States–
–Politics and government—1933–1945. 3. Depressions—1929—United
States. 4. New Deal, 1933–1939. I. Shughart, William F.
II. Locke Institute. III. Title.
HC106.3.C748   1998
338.973'009'043—dc21   98–27149
                                                  CIP

ISBN 1 85898 899 3

Printed and bound in Great Britain by
Biddles Ltd, Guildford and King's Lynn

TO my parents, my wife, Gina, and my daughter, Reagan

JFC

TO Hilary, Willie, and Frank, with love

WFS

Contents

List of Tables

List of Figures

List of Abbreviations

AAA   *either* Agricultural Adjustment Act
      or Agricultural Adjustment Agency
CCC   *either* Civilian Conservation Corps
      or Commodity Credit Corporation
CWA   Civil Works Administration
EHFA   Electric Home and Farm Authority
FCA   Farm Credit Administration
FERA   Federal Emergency Relief Administration
FHA   *either* Farmers Home Administration
      or Federal Housing Authority
FSA   Farm Security Administration
FSRC   Federal Surplus Relief Corporation
HOLC   Home Owners' Loan Corporation
NIRA   National Industrial Recovery Act
NRA   National Recovery Administration
NYA   National Youth Administration
PWA   Public Works Administration
RA   Resettlement Administration
RFC   Reconstruction Finance Corporation
TVA   Tennessee Valley Authority
USHA   United States Housing Authority
WPA   Works Progress Administration

Preface

The Great Depression is without doubt the most studied economic episode of the twentieth century; it may well be the most studied event in all of American economic history. Grainy, black-and-white photographs of beaten men standing on seemingly endless soup-kitchen lines and of pinched-faced children selling apples on street corners are engraved on the national conscience. The years which followed the stock market's crash in October 1929 became a defining moment for a generation hardened by economic crisis and soon to be bloodied by world war. In a very real sense, the decade of the 1930s whetted America's appetite for big government; the modern welfare state was born.

Countless books and articles have explored the depression era in all of its sorrowful details. What can possibly be left to say about a time so well documented and so finely dissected? Isn't it beyond dispute that Herbert Hoover's *laissez-faire* attitude toward the impending collapse was both callous and irresponsible? Didn't Franklin Roosevelt's swift and massive response to the economic emergency he inherited not only bring relief to the stricken masses but save American capitalism?

Such is the conventional wisdom. Like most superficial descriptions of complex events, however, the conventional wisdom about the New Deal is seriously incomplete. While the federal government greatly expanded its regulatory control of the private economy and spent money as never before, the manner in which the Roosevelt administration distributed the emergency relief funds appropriated by Congress by and large remained a mystery to contemporary observers. Some states, especially those located in the South, complained loudly of being unfairly shortchanged. The administration's opponents charged that the New Dealers responsible for allocating funds across states and across sectors of the economy had their eyes on more than simple economic 'need', but pressure to reveal the distribution formulas they used was steadfastly resisted.

Absent any empirical basis for testing these suspicions, questions about possible political influences on New Deal spending largely fell from scholarly discourse until 1969, when Leonard Arrington reported his discovery of a set of documents prepared by the Roosevelt administration in 1939 to showcase its economic policy accomplishments. Don Reading, Gavin Wright, and a number of other economists subsequently began exploiting Arrington's data set, which provides detailed information on New Deal spending by program by state by year from 1933 through 1939. These efforts produced the first solid evidence that New Deal spending was driven at least in part by political considerations: other things, including economic conditions, being the same, electorally rich states received proportionately more federal emergency relief dollars than states less critical to FDR's reelection campaigns of 1936 and 1940.

Rather than settling the issue for good, the new research on the political economy of the New Deal provoked attempts to find empirical support for alternative explanations for the seemingly perverse distribution of funds, which saw harder-hit states receiving fewer dollars than others where the depression's effects were less severe. One of the most noteworthy challenges was raised by John Joseph Wallis, who, while led by his own analysis of the evidence to acknowledge that politics played a significant role in the distribution of federal largesse, contends that states with lesser economic need were able to attract disproportionately more relief funds because of the 'matching' requirements of many of the New Deal programs. States with healthier economies were able to supply more matching funds and were therefore able to secure more aid from the federal government. Wallis reported some limited empirical evidence supporting the matching hypothesis based on an analysis of Works Progress Administration (WPA) expenditures.

The possibility that programmatic matching requirements channeled proportionately more New Deal dollars to states and regions where the depression's effects were less severe begs the question of why such an upside-down funding formula was adopted in the first place. It raises anew questions about the roles played by politics and by economic need in explaining the responses formulated by the New Dealers to the unprecedented crisis. It offers an opportunity to revisit the political economy of the New Deal.

This book, which began life as the first-named author's Ph.D. dissertation at the University of Mississippi, exploits Leonard Arrington's data set at a level of detail not probed hitherto. While previous research has almost always examined the cross-state distribution of New Deal funds aggregated across all programs and pooled over all years, we conduct detailed analyses of the monies spent by major federal emergency relief programs and agencies. In addition to reporting new econometric evidence supporting the idea that President Roosevelt used the New Deal to buy electoral votes, we analyze information discovered by us on WPA sponsor contributions by state to test the matching hypothesis directly. Contrary to Wallis's contention, our analysis suggests that the matching rates demanded of poorer states were in fact proportionately greater than those of their better-off neighbors. States whose citizens were in greatest economic need apparently were required to bear more of the cost of financing WPA projects. The New Deal's promise of relief, reform, and recovery seems to have rung hollow and was, perhaps, rotten at its core.

Pork barrel is commonplace in modern legislative processes. In a geographically based representative democracy, politicians and policy-makers realize higher personal payoffs from supporting programs and policies that channel benefits to narrow electoral constituencies than they do from tending to the public's interest. Evidence that ordinary interest-group politics helped shape the federal government's responses to the century's greatest economic crisis should help dispel the myths underpinning demands for collectivist solutions to more prosaic perceived plights. While we do not pretend to have answers for all of the questions raised by the New Deal, we hope to move the debate several steps forward.

We are grateful for the generous assistance we received as *The Political Economy of the New Deal* evolved into a book-length project. Dissertation committee members William Chappell, Jon Moen, and Michael Cain invested considerable time in reading the manuscript and made innumerable invaluable contributions to the final product. Portions of the manuscript were presented at the 1997 meetings of the Public Choice Society, where we were benefited from the insightful comments of Robert Young. Charles Rowley, the general editor of the Locke series, was likewise lavish with suggestions that were unfailingly helpful. Hilary Shughart focused her critical (but supportive!) eye on every chapter and helped prevent myriad expositional blunders. None of these unselfish readers should be held responsible for any remaining deficiencies, of course. We also express our gratitude to historian Michael Namorato, who guided us to some useful literature on the New Deal in the South, to J. G. Chen, who helped us put the finishing touches to Chapter 8's econometric models, and to Pete Williams, who came to the rescue when it was time to add the illustrations. Kudos to indexer Shirley Kessel.

Last, but certainly not least, Shughart once again acknowledges the financial support provided by the Self family of Marks, Mississippi, without which the time available for writing books would be appreciably more scarce.

Acknowledgments

We are grateful for permission to use the following copyrighted material.

'Song of the South.' Written by Bob McDill. Copyright © 1980 PolyGram International Publishing, Inc. and Ranger Bob Music. Used by permission. All rights reserved.

'The Sower.' © 1938, *The Washington Post*. Reprinted with permission.

'Anyway – The Little Fellow's in Line.' Reprinted with permission, *The Philadelphia Inquirer*.

'The Big-Check Suit That Was Hung on Harry.' Reprinted by permission of *The Kansas City Star*.

1. Introduction

Cotton on the roadside, Cotton in the ditch
We all picked the cotton, but we never got rich
Daddy was a veteran, a Southern Democrat
They ought to get a rich man to vote like that.

Somebody told us that Wall Street fell
But we were so poor that we couldn't tell.
Cotton was short, and the weeds were tall
But Mr. Roosevelt was gonna save us all.

Momma got sick, and Daddy got down
The county got the farm, and we moved to town.
Papa got a job with the TVA;
We bought a washing machine, and then a Chevrolet.
                                  – 'Song of the South', *Alabama*

While the Great Depression of 1929–41 is one of the most studied events in American economic history, numerous misconceptions about the period persist. Often seen as a sweeping collapse that sank all boats, the depression's impacts in fact varied considerably across geographic regions and sectors of the economy. Often praised for delivering relief to every needy man, woman, and child in the nation, the Roosevelt administration's responses to the unprecedented economic crisis were highly selective as well.

It is the purpose of this book to revisit the depression era and, in particular, to investigate the causes and consequences of the massive and unprecedented actions taken by the federal government during this historic economic downturn. These actions came to be known collectively as the 'New Deal', a moniker taken from Franklin Delano Roosevelt's 1932 speech accepting his party's nomination for the presidency: 'I pledge you, I pledge myself, to a new deal for the American people' (Williams 1994, p. 167).

During FDR's celebrated First Hundred Days, the nation witnessed an explosion of legislation designed, at least in theory, to assuage the human suffering visited by the economy's collapse and to put the country on the road to economic recovery. One does not have to read much of the history of the period to find considerable praise for the New Deal in general and for

1

President Roosevelt in particular. Writers who have reviewed the government's relief efforts during the depression have typically linked the policies pursued during the New Deal to the president's compassion for his fellow man.

Carl Degler (1959, p. 398), for example, has remarked that the good done by the government during the Great Depression reflected Franklin Delano Roosevelt's personal character. And that character was beyond reproach. Roosevelt, despite his New England patrician background, was said to have felt a genuine solicitude for the average person: 'Like the ordinary citizen, the President always demanded to know how a particular policy would affect the flesh-and-blood farmer, the worker in the factory, the housewife in the kitchen' (Degler 1970, p. 6). Paul Conkin (1975, p. 68) has written that FDR was for the little man, the exploited, the good, and unselfish; he was against bigness, unearned privileges, and economic selfishness. This same commentator goes on to say that Roosevelt was too powerful to be controlled by any interest group – a fact that made him incorruptible, 'perhaps as much so as any president in American history' (Conkin 1975, p. 75).

Glowing accounts of the New Deal's hagiographers notwithstanding, the theory of public choice teaches that normative models of government behavior based upon the untested assumption that politicians and policy-makers single-mindedly strive to promote the 'public interest' are seriously incomplete. Public choice theory insists that the same model of rational, self-interest-seeking behavior normally assumed to guide decision-making in ordinary markets be applied to the public sector as well. Thus, public choice scholars are skeptical of the enthusiastic accounts of the federal government's activities during the 1930s. Commenting on the New Deal, Anderson and Tollison (1991) note that while we have only lately come to understand how government transfer programs are often captured by and operated for the benefit of special-interest groups and self-interested politicians, pork barrel is far from new.

This book applies the public choice model to data produced by the Roosevelt administration itself in order to model New Deal spending decisions empirically. From this analysis, a more realistic appraisal of the government's actions during the depression will be gained. In particular, this study seeks to reassess the role played by politics in shaping the policies adopted by the New Dealers as they went about the business of distributing hundreds of millions of dollars worth of federal emergency relief funds across the states.

Previous research by Gavin Wright (1974) and by Gary Anderson and Robert Tollison (1991) leads to the conclusion that politics is central to explaining the cross-state allocation of New Deal largesse. Wright adduced evidence suggesting that Roosevelt's desire for reelection helped motivate the spending decisions, which targeted electorally rich states, while Anderson and Tollison extended Wright's analysis by taking congressional influence on the distribution of New Deal dollars into account. John Joseph Wallis (1984, 1987), on the other hand, has discounted these political explanations and, instead, has contended that matching requirements were responsible for producing the observed pattern of New Deal spending. Matching requirements meant that states with healthier economies attracted disproportionate shares of the federal government's emergency relief funds simply because they could afford to bear larger shares of the programs' costs. Ignoring the question of why such a funding formula was adopted in the first place, Smiley (1994, p. 133) agrees that politics was important but adds, 'Wallis restores some of the credibility of the traditional view of the New Deal.'

Unlike Wright and Anderson and Tollison, who were forced to pool the data over the entire New Deal period (1933–39), we disaggregate New Deal expenditures over time and across states. Because of the wealth of information contained in the primary data source uncovered by Leonard Arrington, we are also able to break expenditures down by program and by spending category, thereby gaining further insights into the relative importance of politics and economic need in explaining the distribution of New Deal spending. In addition, using previously unexploited data from the *Congressional Record*, we are able to test Wallis's matching hypothesis directly. We find it to be flawed: *poorer* states were in fact burdened with the heaviest matching requirements.

Historical context is important to our story. Although not by any means America's first economic crisis, the Great Depression presented the federal government with an unparalleled opportunity to prove that it could and should play an active role in the private market economy. To contend that special interests helped shape the government's relief programs, especially in light of the desperation to which millions were driven during the 1930s, is a serious charge. Hence, a knowledge of the causes and consequences of the Great Depression helps place the New Deal in proper context.

Chapter 2 supplies such historical perspective. It does so by describing the Great Depression – the stock market crash, the plight of the people, and the theories that have been advanced to explain the economy's free fall. Chapter 2 includes information about New Deal legislation and the New Dealers themselves; questions concerning whether the New Deal helped or hindered recovery are also addressed there.

Chapter 3 contains a detailed description of New Deal programs that targeted agriculture and rural relief. Many of the alphabet agencies of the New Deal are introduced and their activities are summarized. Confusing effect with cause, the administration believed that a return to parity prices for farmers was the key to recovery and prosperity and, hence, moved quickly to address this issue.

Chapter 4 examines the programs of the so-called First New Deal. Those of the Second New Deal are examined in Chapter 5. Information on how these programs worked, as well as their impacts on the economy, are provided. These chapters provide the background necessary to assess more adequately what the New Deal really accomplished.

Chapter 6 enlarges on the key aspect of the New Deal we seek to explain, namely the highly uneven distribution of relief funds across the country. The chapter makes the point that the severity of the downturn in economic activity differed greatly from region to region. Thus, as President Roosevelt himself claimed, additional aid would be expected to flow disproportionately into the hardest-hit states. Did the New Deal address economic need or respond to political influence?

Chapter 7 reviews the results of earlier studies that have explored the allocation of federal emergency relief spending across the states. Evidence indicating that political motives underlay the distribution of New Deal funds is summarized and critiqued.

The heart of our analysis is contained in Chapter 8. There we develop and estimate spending models to test empirically the hypothesis that politics motivated the pattern of spending adopted by the New Dealers. An unfavorable view of the federal government's role during the Great Depression is all but unavoidable. Our results suggest that while economic need imbued the rhetoric of action, political considerations dominated the distribution of the resources appropriated to allay those needs. Hence, the nation's most severe economic crisis was not exceptional in at least one respect: in emergencies, as well as in more ordinary times, private interests cannot be ignored in explaining the purposes and effects of public policies.

2.   A Concise History of the Great Depression

> Look, there's this particular fringe, and their one fundamental problem is they
> simply never accepted the New Deal. Didn't Franklin Roosevelt settle this
> issue once and for all? I mean, do we really have to go over it again?
> – Senator Daniel Patrick Moynihan

The Great Depression is to economics what the Big Bang is to physics (Margo
1993). The crisis itself, along with the far-reaching actions the government
took to reverse the economy's free fall, have been studied at length by
historians, economists, and political scientists. With good reason. While
certainly not the first American depression, the economic catastrophe that
unfolded in the wake of the October 1929 stock market crash was unprecedented both in its severity and scope. At the economy's trough, the Great
Depression left a quarter of the workforce unemployed. As the jobless millions
turned to Washington for succor, a desperate and hungry nation came to view
the government as an institution capable of mitigating the pernicious effects
of the economic collapse and, what is perhaps more important, equally
capable of preventing future crises.

With the inauguration of Franklin Delano Roosevelt on 4 March 1933, the
federal government's response to the economic emergency was both swift and
massive. Ultimately sustained by a compliant judiciary, the 'New Deal', which
the Democratic Party's nominee had promised would bring relief, recovery,
and reform, changed forever the powers of the executive and legislative
branches of government to regulate the affairs of the private economy. The
modern welfare state was born.

Succeeding a president who had seemed indifferent to the human toll
exacted by the economy's collapse, Roosevelt was extremely popular across
most of the country, particularly so in the South. He talked directly to the
people in a calm, convincing manner which did much to allay the nation's
fears. 'On the evening of March 12 Roosevelt made the first of his so called
"fireside chats" – reassuring the public regarding the banking crisis. "The
president took a complicated subject like banking," said Will Rogers, "and
made everybody understand it, even the bankers"' (Schlesinger 1958, p. 13).[1]

As the struggling nation embraced its magnetic leader, prominent members of FDR's 'brain trust' saw in the crisis a window of opportunity for greater government involvement in the economy that would bring an end to discredited *laissez-faire* policies. Harry Hopkins, who subsequently headed the largest of the New Deal agencies, the Works Progress Administration, said to his fellow New Dealers, 'Boys – this is our hour. We've got to get everything we want – a work program, social security, wages and hours, everything now or never. Get your minds to work on developing a complete ticket to provide security for all the folks of this country up and down and across the board' (Sherwood 1950, p. 65).

And work they did. 'New Deal legislation dealt with virtually all basic economic activity of the nation, such as banking, employment, unemployment, housing, agriculture, transportation, salaries and wages, credit, insurance, and regional economic development' (Hosen 1992, p. 8). 'Most of the legislation came in brief spurts in 1933, 1935, and, least important, in 1938. But the volume of important legislation so exceeded any earlier precedents, so overwhelmed the immediate capacity for full comprehension, that even today no one can more than begin to make sense out of the whole' (Conkin 1975, p. 20).

The first one hundred days of the Roosevelt administration were the most active of any executive in US history. As Arthur Schlesinger summarizes:

> On adjournment on June 15, 1933, the President and the exhausted 73rd Congress left the following record: March 9 – the Emergency Banking Act, March 20 – the Economy Act, March 31 – the establishment of the Civilian Conservation Corps, April 19 – abandonment of the gold standard, May 12 – the Federal Emergency Relief Act, setting up a national relief system, May 12 – the Agricultural Adjustment Act, establishing a national agricultural policy, with the Thomas amendment conferring on the President powers of monetary expansion, May 12 – the Emergency Farm Mortgage Act, providing for the refinancing of farm mortgages, May 18 – the Tennessee Valley Authority Act, providing for the unified development of the Tennessee Valley, May 27 – the Truth-in-Securities Act, requiring full disclosure in the issue of new securities, June 5 – the abrogation of the gold clause in public and private contracts, June 13 – the Home Owners' Loan Act, providing for the refinancing of home mortgages, June 16 – the National Industrial Recovery Act, providing both for a system of industrial self-government under federal supervision and for a $3.3 billion public works program, June 16 – the Glass–Steagall Banking Act, divorcing commercial and investment banking and guaranteeing bank deposits, June 16 – the Farm Credit Act, providing for the reorganization of agricultural credit activities, and June 16 – the Railroad Coordination Act, setting up a federal Coordinator of Transportation. (Schlesinger 1958, pp. 20–21)

This unprecedented growth in the activities of the federal government was not embraced by everyone. But the prevailing conditions made such massive legislative experimentation possible. Crisis spawned Leviathan (Higgs 1987). As Frederick Hosen (1992, p. 8) states, 'in 1933, in a social and economic situation which was bad and getting worse, action was called for, action that perhaps at another time would not have been acceptable.'

It was the magnitude of the crisis that made the unimaginable imaginable. The nation had never before experienced such an economic catastrophe – it faced 'an emergency more serious than war' (Higgs 1987, p. 159). As Richard Vedder and Lowell Gallaway (1993, p. 75) observe, of the last one hundred years for which data are available, the annual unemployment rate has reached double-digit levels on just 17 occasions. Ten of these bleak milestones occurred during the Great Depression.

Herbert Stein (1984, p. 30) emphasizes, however, 'words and statistics cannot convey to people who did not live through it and do not remember it anything like an adequate picture of the depression. In fact, most of the statistics with which we now measure the performance of the economy did not exist in the 1930s, but everyone present could see without the statistics that the condition was tragic.' Stein goes on to say that

> when twenty five percent of the labor force is unemployed, almost everyone is in or close to a family in which someone is unemployed. In the depression we all felt, or at least saw, the misery personally. We saw the unemployed, the breadlines, the foreclosed houses and the abandoned farms directly, and not through statistics or television film. When 25 percent were unemployed in 1932 there was no national unemployment compensation and few families with employed second workers. (Stein 1984, p. 30)

Simply obtaining adequate supplies of food became a priority for many, especially after they had exhausted all their sources of credit. 'In their desperation some urban folk actually tried to wring their food from the barren soil of the city. In Gary, Indiana, for example, 20,000 families were raising food on lots lent by the city' (Degler 1959, p. 380).

The depression represented a time of tremendous human suffering and massive economic displacement. While mere words cannot adequately capture the dispirit of the times, it is important to place the New Deal in its proper context. Because the stock market crash of 1929 stands out as the beginning of the end of the prosperity of the 1920s, that watershed event serves as the point of departure for the following overview of the Great Depression.

1 THE CRASH

Although it is conventional to trace the origins of the Great Depression to the stock market crash of October 1929, the economic downturn was well underway before Wall Street's monumental upheaval. Declines in output were being experienced in most industries by the middle of 1929 and, by September of that year, the economy was in recession (Williams 1994, p. 133). 'During the two months from the cyclical peak in August 1929 to the crash, production, wholesale prices, and [nominal] personal income fell at annual rates of 20 per cent, 7½ per cent, and 5 per cent, respectively' (Friedman and Schwartz 1963, p. 306). Hence, it may be more correct to say that the stock market crash was precipitated by bad economic news than that the falling economy was triggered by the crash. But the crash surely added fuel to the fire, inciting widespread fear and heightened uncertainty. Most observers agree that consumers and business firms were more hesitant about spending as a result of the calamity on Wall Street.

The Dow–Jones Industrial Average peaked at 381.17 on 3 September 1929, and thereafter experienced a series of ups and downs until 10 October when it reached 352.86. From this point on, the market began a continuous slide. On 24 October, 'Black Thursday', 13 million shares of stock were traded as compared with the usual 4 million (Williams 1994, p. 133).

Wall Street bankers, in an emergency meeting the following Friday, raised funds so that stock prices could be supported. Nevertheless, when trading opened on Monday, 28 October, the Dow dropped some 38 points – the largest one-day percentage decline in the history of the market (Williams 1994, p. 134). The downward trend continued until July of 1932, when the Dow bottomed out at 41.22 (Williams 1994, p. 134).

John Kenneth Galbraith (1988, p. 3) contends that the investors of the 1920s displayed 'an inordinate desire to get rich quickly with a minimum of physical effort'. According to his account of the crash, speculators imbued with Keynesian 'animal spirits' were interested only in profit-taking; all other aspects of stock ownership were unwelcome. Broker's loans or call loans, loans collateralized by the securities the borrower purchased, freed the speculator from the 'most grievous burden of ownership – that of putting up the purchase price – by leaving his securities with his broker as collateral for the loan that paid for them. The buyer gets the full benefit of any increase in value – the price of the security goes up, but the loan that bought them does not' (Galbraith 1988, p. 19).

Such call loans came to be regarded as a barometer of speculative fever, which banks fueled by expanding the funds available to investors: the volume of call loans grew from around $800 million in 1921 (Williams 1994, p. 124) to $4 billion on 1 June 1928, $5 billion on 1 November, and to $6 billion by year's end (Galbraith 1988, p. 21). Galbraith calls this series of transactions the 'most profitable arbitrage operation of all time'. The 'New York banks could borrow from the Federal Reserve Bank at 5 per cent and re-lend it in the call market for 12'. As stock prices climbed, business firms began to finance the speculation. Rather than produce real goods and services 'with its manifold headaches and inconveniences' (Galbraith 1988, p. 22), funds were diverted to the call market. Several corporations, including Cities Service, actually sold securities for the purpose of obtaining funds to lend in the stock market. Loans from non-banking sources increased to the extent that they equaled those from more traditional sources.

Another source of funds for speculation was the investment trust. 'The trust sold its own securities, stocks, and bonds to the public, using the proceeds to purchase other stock' (Hughes and Cain 1994, p. 438). According to their critics, such entities did not promote output, growth, or stimulate employment. Rather, the trusts 'merely arranged that people could own stock in old companies through the medium of new ones' (Galbraith 1988, p. 47).

The escalation of stock prices had to come to an end at some point, or so it seems evident to some market observers. When investors began to doubt that the bull market could continue and their confidence waned, profit-taking commenced and stock values weakened. The denouement was brutal. On 'Black Tuesday' (29 October 1929), prices fell so precipitously that the gains of the previous year were wiped out in a single day (Hughes and Cain 1994, p. 439).

1. Subsequent Declines in Economic Activity

The crash, by destroying consumer and business confidence, exacerbated the ongoing recession. According to Milton Friedman and Anna Schwartz, 'partly, no doubt, the stock market crash was a symptom of the underlying forces making for a severe contraction in economic activity. But, partly also, its occurrence must have helped to deepen the contraction' (Friedman and Schwartz 1963, p. 306). Issues of causation aside, the uncertainty resulting from the 1929 crash surely contributed to the severity of the Great Depression.

Confidence rocked, the economy continued its slide, with most measures of economic activity pointing sharply downward. The decline was dramatic: 'Net national product in current prices fell by more than one-half from 1929 to 1933 and net national product in constant prices by more than one-third' (Friedman and Schwartz 1963, p. 299). Money income adjusted for prices – real income – fell 11 percent between 1929 and 1930, 9 percent the next year, 18 percent between 1931 and 1932, and 3 percent the next year. As summarized by Friedman and Schwartz (1963, p. 301), 'These are extraordinary declines for individual years, let alone for four years in succession. All told, money income fell 53 percent and real income 36 percent.'

After peaking in June of 1929 at 125, the index of industrial production fell to 118 by October – the time of the crash – and continued to fall thereafter, reaching 88 by the following October (Williams 1994, pp. 138–39). Between 1929 and 1933, real output per capita decreased by 31 percent (Vedder and Gallaway 1993, p. 75). Prices decreased as well, making the real cost of borrowing extremely high and raising another roadblock to recovery.[2]

Coupled with the industrial sector's problems, falling farm commodity prices weakened bank loan portfolios so that financial institution failures escalated. Smaller banks in rural areas were the first to go:

> Larger urban banks tended to make more security loans, while more longer-term real-estate loans were made by country banks. For example, in 1930, New York and Chicago national banks had less than one percent of their loans in the form of real estate, compared with more than 13 percent for the country banks with national charters. With respect to bank investments, national banks kept fully 40 percent in the form of United States government bonds, compared with only 17 percent for the state banks. (Vedder and Gallaway 1993, p. 114)

The panic spread until more than one-fifth of the commercial banks in the country suspended operations. 'Voluntary liquidations, mergers, and consolidations added to the toll so that the number of commercial banks fell by well over one-third' (Friedman and Schwartz 1963, p. 299).

The end of 1930 brought the demise of the Bank of United States, at the time the largest bank ever to have failed. Because of the institution's size, this event further eroded the public's confidence in the banking system. The bank's name caused its collapse to generate more alarm than warranted since many mistakenly associated the bank with the US government (Williams 1994, p. 141).

2. Burgeoning Unemployment

For most people, the stock market crash and the growing number of bank failures were unnerving, but the extent of the crisis hit home as jobs were lost and unemployment escalated. Carl Degler (1959, p. 380) describes the fear generated by rising unemployment: 'No one knew whom it would hit next; the jobless were everywhere – in the cities, in the towns, on the farms. Their helplessness, their bewilderment, were often written in their faces, reflected in their discouraged gaits, and mirrored in their run-down dwellings.'

The sharp drop in employment came in four phases, according to Vedder and Gallaway (1993, pp. 76–79). About one-fourth of the increase in total unemployment occurred during the last half of 1929, while employment levels stabilized during 1930. The employment decline during the second phase was much more drastic. 'The rise in unemployment in November 1930 is almost certainly the largest single monthly increase in unemployment in the history of the nation. That surge in unemployment turned a recession into a depression.' The employment situation again stabilized over the first four months of 1931, but began to worsen thereafter. Stability was not to be achieved again until the economy had nearly bottomed out: unemployment increased during fourteen of the seventeen months between April 1931 and September 1932. 'The third phase was the biggest, the longest, and the one that made a depression into the Great Depression.' The final wave of accelerating unemployment occurred during the first quarter of 1933, peaking in March.

Widespread job loss was bad enough. But it was the length of time that individuals remained without work that proved to be the most dispiriting factor. 'Of unemployed men in Massachusetts at the beginning of 1934, a large majority (62%) had been unemployed for one year or more' (Vedder and Gallaway 1993, p. 75). Such unprecedented levels of unemployment triggered social unrest. The spreading fear caused an exception to be made to a proposed 10 percent across-the-board pay cut for government workers: 'President Hoover sent a secret message urging that the enlisted men of the Army and the Navy be excluded from such decreases so that in case of domestic troubles the federal government would not be compelled to rely upon disgruntled troops' (Degler 1959, p. 381).

2 WHAT CAUSED THE GREAT DEPRESSION?

The Great Depression paved the way for the New Deal. That much is clear. But what is not so clear is why an ordinary recession turned into the worst economic collapse in the nation's history. Before examining the Roosevelt administration's responses to the crisis, it is worth pausing to attempt to unravel some of the unsolved mysteries surrounding the historic downturn. Frederick Hosen suggests, however, that a complete explanation is not possible: 'The Depression, the decade . . . during which many people were impoverished in the United States as well as world wide, is in many ways still not fully understood. Not only are there numerous views of how it started, but there are various suppositions about how recovery was accomplished' (Hosen 1992, p. 7). While no culprit stands out as *the* cause of the Great Depression, numerous hypotheses have been advanced; some more entertaining than plausible.

1. Resumption

> In 1925, under the aegis of the Chancellor of the Exchequer, Mr. Winston
> Churchill, Britain returned to the gold standard at the old or pre-World War
> I relationship between gold dollars and the pound. There is no doubt that
> Churchill was more impressed by the grandeur of the traditional, or $4.86
> pound than by the more subtle consequences of overvaluation, which he is
> widely assumed not to have understood. (Galbraith 1988, p. 10)

England immediately became an unattractive place for foreigners to buy goods
and services, while foreign goods and services became more attractive to
British consumers. The pound's overvaluation created balance-of-payments
problems for England which resulted in gold reserves flowing out of the
country. 'On July 1, 1927, the ocean liner *Mauretania* arrived in New York
carrying two notable passengers, neither of whose names were on the
passenger list, Montagu Norman and Hjalmar Schacht. . .' (Williams 1994,
p. 122), the heads of England's and Germany's central banks.

They had come to persuade the Federal Reserve to adopt an easy money
policy. Such a policy would produce relatively lower interest rates in the
United States and provide incentives to convert dollars to gold rather than
pounds to gold (Williams 1994, p. 122). The mission was an apparent success,
for shortly thereafter the Fed began to expand the money supply. Some of the
additional money pumped into circulation was used to purchase stocks or was
made available to others for this same purpose which in either case served to
drive up share prices. Hence, according to this theory, Churchill's decision to
overvalue the pound set off a chain of events, begun clandestinely, which
ultimately fueled the speculation in the US stock market. The boom could not
go on forever and at some point the bears would be unleashed. Ironically,
Winston Churchill was among the thousands of people gathered on Wall
Street to witness the beginning of the disaster on Black Thursday, 24 October
(Williams 1994, p. 133).

Galbraith, for one, discounts this explanation because it 'obviously
assumes that people will always speculate if only they can get the money to
finance it. There were times before and there have been long periods since
when credit was plentiful and cheap – far cheaper than in 1927–29 – and
when speculation was negligible' (Galbraith 1988, p. 11). Galbraith seems to
have gotten the analysis right.

2. Business Cycle Theories

Other students of the period see the economic collapse as being almost
biblically ordained. In this view, the Great Depression was a necessary conse-

quence of the economy's rapid expansion during the Roaring 'Twenties.

> There will come seven years of great plenty throughout all the land of Egypt, but after them there will arise seven years of famine, and all the plenty will be forgotten in the land of Egypt; the famine will consume the land. . . . (Genesis 41: 29–30)

The theory goes that prosperity had run its natural course and the cyclical nature of the economy therefore demanded a downturn. But 'the twenties by being comparatively prosperous established no imperative that the thirties be depressed' (Galbraith 1988, p. 172). In short, no economic theory requires that the cost of a period of relative prosperity be a period of relative decline.

3. Monetary Policy Theories

As mentioned earlier, the economy had already been slowing down prior to the stock market's crash. A recession was underway by late summer of 1929. Christina Romer (1993, p. 26) attributes this slowdown to the tight money policy adopted by the Federal Reserve in 1928. By the spring of that year, the Federal Reserve had changed course – ending the easy money policy it had adopted in the wake of Britain's return to the gold standard and beginning to tighten the supply of money. As Williams (1994, pp. 125–26) points out, the monetary authorities became increasingly concerned with speculation in the stock market.

To rein in the bulls, the Federal Reserve Bank of New York raised its discount rate in a series of steps from 3.5 percent in February of 1928 up to 5 percent in July, the highest the rate had been since 1921. In addition, between January and July of 1928, the Fed's Open Market Investment Committee sold over $480 million worth of government securities and acceptances. Friedman and Schwartz assert that concern with the growing speculation shaped Federal Reserve policy during 1928 and 1929. Its initiatives were doubly lamentable: they 'clearly failed to stop the stock market boom. But they did exert steadily deflationary pressure on the economy' (Friedman and Schwartz 1963, p. 290).

The Federal Reserve's actions had predictable effects on interest rates. 'The real interest rate – calculated by subtracting the change in the producer price index over the following quarter from the commercial paper interest rate – rose from 5.6 percent in the fourth quarter of 1927 to 9.5 percent in the fourth quarter of 1928' (Romer 1993, p. 27). Romer suggests that this increase in interest rates provides an explanation for the moribund economy of the summer of 1929. Critics of the Federal Reserve's actions are numerous. As

Friedman and Schwartz (1963, p. 291) conclude, the Fed 'followed a policy which was too easy to break the speculative boom, yet too tight to promote healthy economic growth'.

4. Underconsumption Theories

Romer herself takes issue with the notion that a tight money policy was responsible for the Great Depression, however. The contraction of the money supply in 1928 was sizable, but not particularly large when compared with the other contractions that have occurred throughout history. According to Romer (1993, p. 29), the Great Depression which followed the stock market collapse was due to a spectacular fall in personal consumption expenditures. Insofar as it exceeded the declines recorded during either of the interwar period's other downturns, Peter Temin (1976, p. 65) agrees that the fall in consumption during 1930 was extraordinary. The most likely source of the decrease in consumption spending, Romer posits, is the crash itself. The dramatic tumble in stock prices destroyed consumer confidence, thereby triggering a sharp reduction in spending.

Temin identifies two ways in which the crash may have depressed consumption expenditures. By reducing personal wealth, the fall in stock market prices lowered disposable income and, *pari passu*, consumer spending. The crash may also have acted to change consumers' expectations in such ways as to lead them to curtail their purchases of durable goods (Temin 1976, p. 69).

Romer analyzes consumption patterns after the crash in search of evidence to support the hypothesis that the sudden drop in stock prices contributed to uncertainty which, in turn, led to the reduction in spending. According to her,

> the effect of this uncertainty was that consumers and producers immediately cut their spending on irreversible durable goods as they waited for additional information about the future. This effect is seen most clearly in the fact that department store sales and automobile registrations declined precipitously in November and December 1929, while grocery store sales and ten-cent store sales actually rose; this is exactly what one would expect if consumers were shying away from irreversible goods but had not substantially changed their point estimates of future income. (Romer 1993, p. 31)

While Romer explains the initial decline in consumption on the basis of the uncertainty generated by the stock market crash, a series of banking panics caused the contraction to continue. Bank failures had an impact on the supply of money in the economy. 'As depositors became nervous about the safety of banks, the ratio of deposits to currency fell dramatically. This greatly reduced the money multiplier, with the implication that a given stock of high-powered money could then support a much smaller total money supply' (Romer 1993, p. 32).

The Federal Reserve, apparently ignoring the problem, failed to act to increase the supply of high-powered money. M1 (currency plus demand deposits) thus declined and real interest rates soared. Friedman and Schwartz (1963, p. 413) attribute the central bank's inaction to a leadership void. Until 1928, they note, Benjamin Strong was Governor of the New York Federal Reserve Bank and was clearly the Federal Reserve System's dominant personality. Strong's first wife had committed suicide and after his second wife left him, he turned almost all of his attention to his work. But with his health failing, Strong's dedication had waned by August of 1928, and he died that October. Apparently, no one was prepared to assume the leadership mantle, creating an intellectual vacuum at the Federal Reserve.

With the death of Benjamin Strong, the presidents of other Federal Reserve Banks were able to wrest power away from New York. This shifting of the center of influence had important consequences, according to Friedman and Schwartz. The absence of effective leadership and the bureaucratic infighting that followed resulted in a tendency toward 'drift and indecision'. As Friedman and Schwartz (1963, p. 419) acknowledge,

> Great events have great origins, and hence that something more than the characteristics of the specific persons . . . that happen to be in power is required to explain such a major event as the financial catastrophe in the United States from 1929 to 1933. Yet it is also true that small events at times have large consequences, that there are such things as chain reactions and cumulative forces.

Personalities aside, when it comes to assigning blame for the Great Depression, these two influential economists hold the Federal Reserve's policy-making of the late 1920s and early 1930s culpable.

Not everyone accepts the premise that the Federal Reserve was merely incompetent. Anderson, Shughart and Tollison (1988) suggest that the monetary authorities were well aware of the consequences of the actions they took. The tight-money policy adopted by the Fed put much greater pressure on non-member banks, which were typically smaller and held less secure assets.[3] In fact, as the authors note, between 1930 and 1933, non-members accounted for 80 percent of the bank failures. The result was greater profits for the larger member banks as well as greater control over the banking system for the Fed.

Temin nonetheless rejects a monetary explanation of the Great Depression and offers an alternative:

A recession started in 1929 due to some combination of factors which cannot be disentangled. Financial markets were tight as a result both of the expectations built up around the stock market boom and the efforts of the Federal Reserve to arrest that boom. There was a variety of imbalances in particular markets, of which the apparent oversupply of housing at current prices was the most obvious. (Temin 1976, p. 170)

He also blames the depressed farming sector for placing additional downward pressure on the economy. Poor crop yields in 1929, coupled with better than average yields in foreign markets that traditionally imported agricultural products from the United States, deflated domestic farm incomes.

These observations help account for part of the reduction in consumption that took place during the early stages of the Great Depression. However, as Temin (1976, p. 172) admits, 'at the current stage of our knowledge, the unexplained fall in consumption is larger than the part we can explain, but the magnitude of the total fall is incontrovertible.' While rejecting monetary forces, Temin offers little in the way of a robust alternative explanation for the depression.

5. Other Theories

According to Michael Bernstein, it was the timing of the recession that produced such an unprecedented collapse: 'What in principle might have been a relatively brief panic became, by virtue of the delicate condition of the economy at the time it occurred, a prolonged major slump' (Bernstein 1987, p. 27). The economy of the interwar period was beset by major structural changes – in employee skill requirements, in production technologies, and in the composition of investment and consumption demand. New capital-intensive production methods were developed that reduced the manufacturing sector's demand for labor, generating widespread structural unemployment. The introduction of new products likewise altered consumer spending patterns, leaving the economy particularly vulnerable to financial shock.

Thus, 'recovery was lacking in the thirties because at the same time that long-run potentials for growth were shifting under the influence of a secular transformation to sectors whose presence in the aggregate economy was still relatively insignificant, short-run obstacles to a smooth transition emerged' (Bernstein 1987, p. 27). Shifts in the distribution of income and standards of living had altered consumption patterns. As investment activity responded to these new demands, labor skill requirements were transformed and large pockets of structural unemployment emerged. Hence, according to Bernstein, fundamental economic changes coincided with a garden-variety cyclical downturn to set the stage for the Great Depression.

Offering yet another explanation, Vedder and Gallaway (1993) explain the downturn as follows. In late 1929, price and productivity shocks resulted in reduced levels of output and employment. Under ordinary circumstances, such a labor market disequilibrium would be short-lived because the plethora of job seekers would bid down wages and thereby stimulate employment. Instead, money wages fell roughly 2 percent but consumer prices fell about 2½ percent, so that real wages actually increased. At this same time, output per worker declined some 4 percent, making labor even more expensive. These same trends continued into 1931. 'The 1931 price shocks, accompanied by a failure of money wages to adjust to either it or the previous year's productivity decline, seemed to be the root cause of the rise in unemployment to over 15 percent in 1931' (Vedder and Gallaway 1993, p. 81). Continuous increases in the real cost of labor made recovery impossible. In fact, at the height of the collapse (1933), real wages per hour were almost 13 percent higher than they had been in 1929, 'despite the fact that fully one-fourth of the labor force was unemployed' (Vedder and Gallaway 1993, p. 82).

The failure of the neoclassical model to predict wage behavior accurately during the depression may be attributable to the labor market intervention of the government. Both the Hoover and Roosevelt administrations adhered to a high-wage strategy in an effort to maintain purchasing power and thereby restore consumption spending to pre-crash levels. Hoover, meeting regularly with business leaders, 'jawboned' them into maintaining high wages. He coupled these efforts with protective tariffs which insulated labor from foreign competition. The Davis–Bacon Act of 1931, which required that workers on federally financed construction projects be paid the 'prevailing wage', put additional upward pressure on labor costs. The Roosevelt administration followed this same strategy under the auspices of the National Industrial Recovery Act (NIRA), which established minimum wages, and by pushing through other legislation which strengthened the hands of labor unions.

Williams (1994, p. 154) describes the flaw in this strategy:

Although wage income is a source of purchasing power, wages are also a cost of production. It is profitable for a business firm to hire an additional worker so long as the market value of the additional output exceeds his wages. For business firms to maximize profits, the optimal level of employment is that at which the increase in revenue produced by hiring one extra worker (marginal revenue product of labor) equals the wage rate. If wage rates are maintained in the face of falling prices, the marginal revenue product of labor will no longer justify the current level of employment.

For the wage-maintenance policy to succeed, domestic workers had to be protected from foreign competition. Thus, in June of 1930, President Hoover signed the Smoot–Hawley Tariff Act. 'Tariffs insulate the owners of both labor and capital resources from foreign competition, allowing them higher prices for their output and, in the case of labor, higher wages' (Vedder and Gallaway 1993, p. 95). By restricting import competition and preventing a market-equilibrating reduction in wages, the tariff at the very least contributed to the burgeoning rates of unemployment.

Vedder and Gallaway (1993, p. 131) in fact contend that 'government failure, not market failure, was the problem'. Although its intentions may have been noble, intervention in labor markets pushed wages higher and higher at the very time that wages should have been falling. In short, the federal government's own actions may well have prolonged and deepened the Great Depression, adding greatly to the misery and deprivation.

3 THE NEW DEAL AND THE NEW DEALERS

The Great Depression afforded the New Dealers an unprecedented opportunity to intervene in the private economy. *Laissez-faire* evidently had failed. Government could now regulate industry and replace 'ruinous' competition with more rational forms of business cooperation. The New Dealers could build model garden communities where people would live happy, prosperous lives under their benevolent direction. This group of compassionate and wise public servants was prepared to direct the whole economy if given the chance. Unlike the greedy business leaders of the time who thought only of personal gain, the New Dealers were not burdened with self-interest. These generous government officials would right all wrongs, correct all inequalities, hold fast to egalitarian principles and, with equanimity, distribute federal funds to the most deserving.

Such was the stated purpose of the New Deal. Its work would be directed by a collection of the best and brightest people ever to descend on the nation's capital:

> The New Dealers themselves were articulate, humane, and on occasion profound. Among them were the 'brain trust' (Adolph Berle, Raymond Moley, Rexford Guy Tugwell), the cabinet members (Henry Wallace, Frances Perkins, Harold Ickes, and others), and the administrators of the alphabetic agencies (Harry Hopkins, David Lilienthal, and others). And above them all was Franklin D. Roosevelt himself. They had no clearly defined set of goals, beyond that of extricating the nation from the depression of 1929–1932. (Zinn 1966, p. 15)

Experienced bureaucrats were somewhat suspicious of the new administration. 'A plague of young lawyers settled on Washington,' said George Peek, the first head of the Agricultural Adjustment Administration. 'I never found out why they came, what they did, or why they left' (Irons 1982, p. 3). Others have offered nothing but praise for the New Dealers: 'They brought with them an alertness, an excitement, an appetite for power, an instinct for crisis and a dedication to public service which became during the thirties the essence of Washington' (Schlesinger 1958, p. 17).

The 1930s were indeed heady times along the banks of the Potomac River. As Herbert Stein (1984, p. 36) writes:

> When Roosevelt came into office there was a considerable body of opinion that the trouble with the American economy was that it was 'unplanned'. There was no central authority to see that the various branches of industry produced the right amount of output and sold the output at the right prices, with the result that production became unbalanced, gluts appeared, and unemployment then developed.

Not lacking in confidence, these mostly Ivy League trained members of the Roosevelt administration set out to manage farming through the Agriculture Adjustment Act (AAA), to manage industry through the National Industrial Recovery Act (NIRA), and to provide employment opportunities through the Works Progress Administration (WPA), the Civil Works Administration (CWA), and the Federal Emergency Relief Administration (FERA), among other agencies. The New Dealers were in truth a very able and highly motivated group of individuals.

The agency established to administer the AAA, for example, attracted Thurman Arnold and Abe Fortas of Yale Law School; Adlai Stevenson of the University of Chicago; and, from Harvard Law School, Alger Hiss, Lee Pressman, John Abt, and Nathan Witt (Schlesinger 1958, p. 50). Despite the intricacies associated with organizing and managing something as complex as American agriculture, these individuals remained undaunted. Lack of knowledge did not stop them, but did leave them embarrassed from time to time. 'Lee Pressman, attending a meeting to work out a macaroni code, asked belligerently what the code would do for the macaroni growers' (Schlesinger 1958, p. 51). Another story has it that 'an AAA lawyer on a field trip to the countryside saw his first firefly and exclaimed, "Good God! What's that?"' (Schlesinger 1958, p. 51).

Trying to summarize the plethora of New Deal legislation in some orderly fashion has proved to be difficult. Upon closer examination, there appears to be neither rhyme nor reason for some of the measures adopted during the 1930s. 'In 1936, two agricultural programs existed side by side – the AAA and the RA [Resettlement Administration] – one trying to limit production within the system, the other trying to increase it while reforming the system'

(Conkin 1975, p. 83). The AAA sought to take acreage out of cultivation by paying farmers not to plant; at the same time the Bureau of Reclamation attempted to bring water to arid sections of the nation for the purpose of expanding arable farmland. An undistributed profits tax was placed on corporations in 1937 which was designed to stimulate consumption by forcing firms to distribute more of their earnings to shareholders; the social security legislation adopted during the New Deal had the opposite effect of reducing consumers' disposable incomes. A new agency, the Reconstruction Finance Corporation, was created to do basically what the Federal Reserve System was designed to do. Confusion and lack of direction were common to New Deal efforts.

In an effort to organize the mass of New Deal legislation into some sort of logical pattern, historians have divided the administration's programs into two parts – the so-called First and Second New Deals.

> According to this view, during the First New Deal Roosevelt worked closely with business to raise prices and regularize economic activity with the National Industrial Recovery Act being the key measure. The Second New Deal began in the summer of 1935 when FDR was disappointed with and chagrined at the lack of cooperation and even hostility shown by business toward his program. As a result, he then turned to measures to help the disadvantaged, abandoning his efforts at cooperation between government and business. (Degler 1970, p. 17)

Treating 1935 as a policy watershed, this method of grouping the programs of the New Deal is adopted when the various agencies and bureaus are examined in greater detail in later chapters.

For our present purposes, however, the federal government's spending programs can be arranged chronologically to provide a useful bird's eye view of the New Deal. A set of documents prepared by the Roosevelt administration in 1939 provides expenditure totals for the New Deal agencies, making such a summary possible. These reports – one of which was generated for each of the 48 states for each of the years 1933 through 1939 – were produced by the Statistical Section of the Office of Government Reports. The documents were designed to garner support for FDR in the 1940 presidential election by showcasing, state by state, the administration's efforts to respond to the economic crisis.

Utilizing this data source, a time line of the various programs of the New Deal is shown in Figure 2.1. Information on when individual programs originated, how agencies and programs were later combined or eliminated, and how much was spent each year is presented. While most of the enabling legislation was enacted during 1933 and 1935, the figure amply demonstrates

Figure 2.1 New Deal programs over time

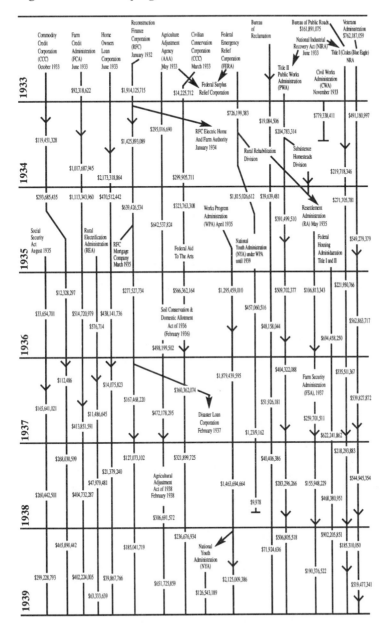

the complexity of the New Deal.

The reports break New Deal spending down into various expenditure categories. These categories are grouped and displayed in Table 2.1. The broad classifications are similar to those used by Reading (1972, pp. 12–14). Figure 2.2 then shows the percentage of total expenditures accounted for by each of the general spending categories, so that the relative importance of the administration's efforts in addressing various sectors of the economy can be seen.

Owing to the overlapping nature of many of the emergency relief programs launched during the 1930s, the classifications are somewhat arbitrary. As Reading (1972, p. 11) explains, 'many programs, of course, were intended by New Deal planners to achieve more than one purpose, and thus logically could be placed in more than one classification.' For example, Reading places the National Youth Administration (NYA) and the Civilian Conservation Corps (CCC) under the heading 'Youth Programs' while they fall under 'Work Programs' in Table 2.1. (By themselves, the youth programs would account for roughly 4 percent of total New Deal spending.)

Figure 2.2 shows that work programs accounted for the largest share of total New Deal spending – almost 35 percent. Total agricultural spending, including both direct expenditures and loans, contributed another 21 percent. Nineteen percent of the expenditures was allocated to relief and social welfare programs. About $45 billion was spent altogether. The resources commanded by the New Dealers were almost as great as the nation's entire Gross National Product (GNP) in 1933 ($56 billion) and nearly half of pre-crash 1928 GNP, which amounted to $97 billion (Hosen 1992, p. 268). Federal expenditures grew by 136 percent between 1932 and 1940 (Wallis 1984, p. 142).

Such massive outlays were controversial at the time, and questions about their effectiveness have been debated ever since. Did FDR's emergency relief measures help or hinder recovery? Speaking in 1939, Senator Everett Dirksen of Illinois stated that, 'It is with some fear and trepidation and a spirit of uncertainty that I approach increased spending, because it has not solved the problem' (US House of Representatives 1939a, p. 7267). The next section explores this issue in greater detail.

4 DID THE NEW DEAL SUCCEED?

The efficacy of the New Deal's economic prescriptions remains a subject of considerable controversy. As Hosen (1992, p. 8) observes, 'to what extent New Deal legislation hastened or slowed recovery will likely remain a question for continued discussion'. Some observers have concluded that the Roosevelt administration's swift and sure actions saved both democracy and free-market

Table 2.1 New Deal spending by program classification, 1933–39

SOCIAL WELFARE PROGRAMS
   Social Security Act
   US Employment Service
   Veteran's Administration
AGRICULTURE EXPENDITURES
   Agricultural Adjustment Administration
   Farm Security Administration
   Soil Conservation Service
   Research, Extension, and Agricultural Education
   Forest Service Funds
AGRICULTURE LENDING
   Farm Credit Administration
   Commodity Credit Corporation
   Farm Security Administration
   Rural Electrification Administration
OTHER LENDING
   Reconstruction Finance Corporation
   Public Works Administration
   Home Owners' Loan Corporation
   Disaster Loan Corporation
   US Housing Authority
INSURANCE PROGRAMS
   Insured loans by Federal Housing Authority (Titles I and II)
RELIEF
   Federal Emergency Relief Administration
WORK PROGRAMS
   Youth Programs
      Civilian Conservation Corps
      National Youth Administration
   Bureau of Public Roads
   Bureau of Reclamation
   Public Works Administration
   Civil Works Administration
   Works Progress Administration
   Schools and Emergency Relief Administration
      Vocational Education and Rehabilitation
      Books for the Blind
      Emergency Relief Administration Office of Education Funds

Table 2.1 (continued)

Schools and Emergency Relief Administration (continued)
    State Marine Schools
Other Expenditures
    Mineral Lease Act
    Federal Water Power Act payments
    Federal Surplus Commodities Corporation activities
    National Guard
    State Homes for Soldiers and Sailors

Figure 2.2 Spending percentages by category

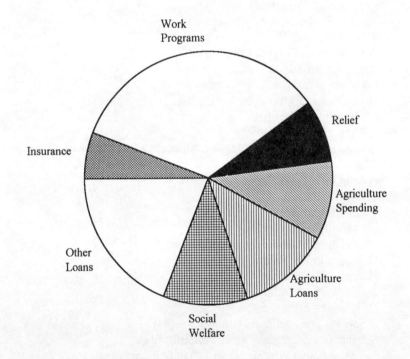

capitalism. According to one of the era's many hagiographers, the New Deal proved that 'the state could hasten the glorious era of abundance'. To do so, 'it had to discipline the sinful, aid the righteous, provide the mechanisms of a fair and stable market, and broaden the opportunities for all' (Conkin 1975, p. 26). On the other hand, commentators predisposed to view the world through Marxist lenses see the New Deal as merely helping those rich and powerful groups traditionally helped by the government: 'There was no significant redistribution of power in American society, only limited recognition of organized groups, seldom of unorganized peoples' (Bernstein 1968, p. 264).

Insofar as it took the Japanese bombing of Pearl Harbor finally to bring the depression to an end, the reality is that the New Deal delivered less than it promised. Still others go further, though, arguing that government intervention both deepened and prolonged the economy's tribulations. 'The tragedy of the New Deal era was that well-intentioned programs undertaken in the name of relief (unemployment insurance) or reform (the Wagner Act and old-age insurance under social security), so retarded the second "R" of the New Deal program, namely recovery' (Vedder and Gallaway 1993, p. 145).

Senator Everett Dirksen summarized the government's early efforts to restore full employment in the following terms:

Under the Hoover administration they followed the philosophy of meeting the farm problem and the unemployment problem by making generous loans to durable goods industries, to insurance companies, to railroads, and to banks, and employing institutions, believing that that was the place to start employment. I am going to admit, as a Republican, that it failed. (US House of Representatives 1939a, p. 7267)

The New Deal, according to Dirksen, was equally impotent in bringing an end to the Great Depression. According to him:

Under the Roosevelt administration they placed emphasis at the consumer end, the spending of money on the consumer side, in the hope that it would dribble through the retailer, through the jobber, on to the manufacturer, and then be translated in terms of employment and increased farm prices. I think the record, without any argument on my part, would indicate that it has substantially failed (US House of Representatives 1939a, p. 7267).

While opinions about the New Deal's effectiveness vary considerably, the critics of the administration's policies nevertheless seem to be in the minority. Even some of the faultfinders believe that any mistakes made were innocently motivated. Perhaps the New Deal failed to end the depression because the

New Dealers were utilizing the federal government's powers in wholly new ways, navigating the Ship of State in uncharted waters: 'Winston Churchill observed at the time that Roosevelt was an explorer who had embarked on a voyage as uncertain as that of Columbus' (Charles 1963, p. 44).

It is safe to say that most accounts, even modern ones, give high marks to the federal government's efforts to respond to the emergency. A statement offered by an 'envious Canadian' summarizes the conventional wisdom:

> In Canada we had no New Deal, no AAA, or other measures designed to give agriculture a parity with urban industry, no Wagner Act for the trade unions, no great public housing schemes, no CCC camps for unemployed youth, no TVA [Tennessee Valley Authority] to reconstruct a vast blighted area, no Federal Writers or Federal Artists Projects, no new parkways about our big cities and no new recreational camps among our lakes and forests; and – last but not least – no fireside chats. (Degler 1959, pp. 24–25)

The usually unreported sequel is that while the Great Depression was world-wide in scope, beginning about the same time across the globe's industrialized nations, dates of national recovery differed substantially, with the United States being among the last on the list (Romer 1993). Recovery 'occurred in 1932 for New Zealand; 1933 for Japan, Greece, and Romania; 1934 for Chile, Denmark, Finland, and Sweden; 1935 for Estonia, Hungary, Norway, and the United Kingdom; 1936 for Germany; and 1937 for Canada, Austria, and Italy. The United States . . . did not recover before the end of the sample in 1937' (Romer 1993, pp. 23–24).

Hence, the assertion that the New Deal helped to bring about recovery does not seem consistent with the available evidence. In spite of the large number of new federal programs and the massive increase in government spending, the economy continued to perform sluggishly. GNP in 1958 prices remained below its 1929 level until 1939, and started to climb noticeably only after the United States began shipping arms to the Allied forces opposing Adolph Hitler. The misery continued for more than a decade. Whatever else may be said, the bottom line is that the New Deal failed to end America's Great Depression.

1. The New Deal Did Not Go Far Enough

In fact, some critics contend that the New Deal failed to take advantage of a golden opportunity for institutionalizing economic reform. Rather than checking the many excesses of the unfettered free market, the administration merely helped those special interests that have usually been aided by the government – and ignored those that were usually ignored.

Barton Bernstein, for one, has argued that the New Deal's many proponents have overstated its accomplishments. The goal of creating a permanent command economy was never attained because the New Dealers who favored displacing the market system 'had too much faith in representative institutions and in associations to foresee perils – of leaders not representing their constituents, of bureaucracy diffusing responsibility, of officials serving their own interests' (Bernstein 1968, p. 270).

According to such critics, New Deal legislation neither significantly redistributed wealth nor encouraged recovery. Rather, ordinary politics remained at the forefront with the administration seldom risking antagonizing powerful special interests that might oppose them at election time. Bernstein (1968, p. 277) summarizes the government's failures in the following terms: 'the sad truth was that the heralded reforms were severely limited, that inequality continued, that efforts at recovery had failed. Millions had come to accept the depression as a way of life.'

Recovery might have come faster had the government adequately 'primed the pump' with larger appropriations targeted at those truly in need. Instead, the Roosevelt administration consistently catered to politically powerful groups, protecting the interests of the middle and upper income members of society. Groups with little political clout – sharecroppers, unskilled labor, blacks, and consumers – rarely benefited and were, in fact, frequently harmed by the legislation. The share of wealth controlled by the wealthiest 1 percent of the nation actually increased during the New Deal years (Bernstein 1968, p. 275).

The New Deal, according to this view, stopped far short of reaching many of its hoped-for goals and did not demonstrate government's true capabilities. Instead, the Roosevelt administration let political motivations steer it off course. As Bernstein (1968, p. 282) concludes, 'for some this would constitute a puzzling defect of liberalism; for some, the failure to achieve true liberalism.'

2. The New Deal Went Too Far

As noted previously, other critics contend that the New Deal blocked recovery and prolonged the depression by preventing the economy's natural return to full employment. Pressured by both Hoover and Roosevelt to maintain high wages in order to stimulate consumption – and protected from foreign competitors by higher tariffs – firms resisted cutting wages. This high-wage philosophy short-circuited the economy's self-correcting forces by artificially inflating labor costs.

Real wages in fact increased more during the first four years of the Great Depression than they had during the Roaring 'Twenties – a time of exceptional economic growth. Vedder and Gallaway (1993) construct a model in which unemployment rates can be simulated. Their results suggest that if money wages had fallen as rapidly as prices, the unemployment rate in the third quarter of 1932 would have been slightly less than 15 percent, some 12 percentage points less than the unemployment rate the economy by most accounts actually experienced.

The National Industrial Recovery Act (NIRA), Roosevelt's chief legislative initiative addressing the non-agricultural sectors of the economy, encouraged businesses to adhere to approved codes of 'fair' competition. Among the codes' provisions was a minimum wage which pushed up workers' pay considerably – 'the floor of forty cents an hour established as a general minimum was nearly 90 percent of the average hourly wage prevailing in mid-1933' (Vedder and Gallaway 1993, p. 137). Along these same lines, section 7(a) of the NIRA and the National Labor Relations Act of 1935 gave labor unions additional bargaining strength and contributed to the upward pressure on wages.

Using their model to assess the New Deal's labor legislation, Vedder and Gallaway estimated that absent these policies the unemployment rate would have fallen below 10 percent by 1937, rather than not reaching this level until 1941. Thus, the two economists contend that the misguided intervention of the federal government exacerbated the collapse of the economy and impeded recovery. Indeed, their results suggest that the Great Depression might have been avoided altogether if the government had refrained from interfering with private labor markets.

At the very least, there is little doubt that the New Deal alarmed business leaders and contributed to uncertainty. The erosion of confidence, brought on in part by the administration's anti-business rhetoric, pushed the economy deeper into recession. Many industrialists viewed the New Deal as a serious threat to the private sector and feared socialism. As Conkin (1975, p. 65) admits, their fears may not have been entirely unfounded: 'several new advisors [to Roosevelt] . . . seemed more concerned with penalizing big business than with achieving recovery.'

Those who had prospered during the 1920s were especially disliked by Secretary of the Interior Harold Ickes. Ickes attended a meeting of the US Chamber of Commerce and later wrote about the experience in his diary. Degler states that Ickes 'could sense the pitiable impotence to which the nation's industrial leaders had sunk. "The great and the mighty in the business world were there in force," he rather gleefully noted in his diary, "and I couldn't help thinking how so many of these great and mighty were crawling to Washington on their hands and knees these days to beg the Government to run their businesses for them"' (Degler 1959, p. 382).[4]

One report from business leaders stated unambiguously that the loss of confidence resulting from the New Deal led firms to postpone normal business activities. Conkin (1975, p. 71) asserts that the 'opponents of Roosevelt misconstrued the direction of the New Deal. Many believed Roosevelt's class language. They really thought America was losing its free capitalist soul to some type of socialism.'

Testifying before the Senate Special Committee to Investigate Unemployment and Relief in January of 1938, Lamont DuPont of E. I. du Pont de Nemours and Company stressed the importance of restoring business confidence and reassuring industry that the government did not pose a threat:

> I believe that business will recover only in an atmosphere of confidence in private industry, a wider understanding that the main burden of reemployment must fall on industry, not on Government. That recovery only comes about by a greater production and consumption of goods and services. The dissemination of this atmosphere should be fostered. Business must reassure the public that its services are essential, that it is in the aggregate, simply the way in which almost all of us make a living, and that farming, manufacturing, commerce, finance, and labor are interdependent. Government and business should take counsel together in a spirit of forbearance and cooperation. (US Senate 1938, Vol. 1, p. 275)

What was considered by policy-makers and social engineers to be bold experimentation appeared as reckless incertitude to business leaders and investors. As Smiley (1994, p. 136) writes, 'the New Deal, with its new laws, altered the environment within which business firms operated.' Private decision-makers were stranded on shifting sands and this climate of uncertainty more likely than not delayed recovery.

Creating what he calls 'regime uncertainty', Robert Higgs (1997) in fact contends that the New Deal led investors to fear the erosion of private property rights. These concerns became especially widespread beginning in 1935, when both the legislative initiatives of the Second New Deal and the administration's rhetoric took on a decidedly anti-capitalist tone. According to Higgs (1997, p. 586), the collapse in private investment that contributed to the economic crisis was triggered by 'the unparalleled outpouring of business-threatening laws, regulations, and court decisions, the oft-stated hostility of President Roosevelt and his lieutenants toward investors as a class, and the character of the antibusiness zealots who composed the strategists and administrators of the New Deal from 1935 to 1941. . . '.

Polls taken at the time tend to support Higgs's interpretation. A nationally representative survey conducted by the American Institute of Public Opinion in 1939, for example, asked, 'Do you think the attitude of the Roosevelt administration toward business is delaying business recovery?' Fifty-four percent said yes, while only 26 percent said no. The same pollsters also asked, "Do you think that ten years from now there will be more government control of business than there is now or less government control of business?' A majority (56 percent) of the respondents expected greater government control of business by 1949, while just 22 percent thought there would be less. In short, the hostile business climate created by the New Dealers may well have both deepened and lengthened the depression by discouraging capital formation.

5 THE LEGACY OF THE NEW DEAL

While it is not entirely clear whether the Roosevelt administration's actions hastened or retarded recovery, there is little doubt that the New Deal has had long-lasting consequences. The relationship between the citizens and the state was fundamentally altered – perhaps for all time. Americans became much more receptive to a larger role for the federal government. As Degler (1970, p. 25) points out, 'until the Depression and the New Deal, even politically and socially liberal Americans thought government's proper role in the economy was limited and peripheral.'

Rugged individualism, long a source of pride to most people, gave way to the welfare state. Dependence was to become a way of life for many at the lower end of the income distribution as a social 'safety net' replaced self-reliance. President Hoover warned of the dangers of dependency on government when he spoke of individuals with no stake in the economy, who would be vulnerable to any demagogue that came along promising more and more welfare (Conkin 1975, p. 54).

But to suggest that only the poverty-stricken would become dependent on government is to ignore the evidence. In fact, poor people were perhaps the least effective of the interest groups that came to rely on the federal Treasury as a source of special favors. As the public choice model teaches, like its contemporaneous counterpart, the government of the 1930s was, in the words of Barton Bernstein (1968, p. 270), 'generally the servant of powerful groups'.

The Roosevelt administration bestowed its largesse selectively on a wide variety of coalitions able to mobilize effective political influence. Industry benefited from the National Industrial Recovery Act, which relaxed the antitrust laws in favor of allowing firms to collaborate in writing codes of 'fair competition'. Farmers benefited from price supports and other income-increasing agricultural programs. Organized labor also gained from many of the measures adopted during the 1930s. By so effectively responding to the demands of special-interest groups, the New Deal did much to lay the foundations of the modern welfare state. Bernstein (1968, pp. 280–81) asserts that the New Deal also bought off, regrettably in his view, the groups most likely to have tipped the balance in favor of socialism:

> by assisting labor, as well as agriculture, the New Deal started the institutionalization of larger interest groups into a new political economy. Joining business as tentative junior partners, they shared the consensus on the value of large-scale corporate capitalism, and were permitted to participate in the competition for the division of shares.

Quickly grasping the benefits of rent seeking under FDR, self-interested lobbying activities by well-organized pressure groups would come to dominate the American economy and American politics. While it might be an overstatement to blame 'demosclerosis' entirely on the New Deal,[5] to ignore the role played by the Roosevelt administration in contributing to the growth of the transfer state would be equally inaccurate. In return for political support, the New Dealers and their congressional patrons delivered benefits to both farmers and industrialists at the expense of consumers and taxpayers. 'Farmers gained new effectiveness in political organization and thus worked through farm-state congressmen to dramatize their problems and to mute their economic successes' (Conkin 1975, p. 37).

The lobbying occasionally took more primitive forms. To illustrate:

> On April 27 over five hundred farmers crowded the courtroom in Le Mars, Iowa, to demand that Judge Charles C. Bradley suspend foreclosure proceedings until the state courts had passed on recently enacted legislation. When Bradley turned the farmers down and rebuked them for wearing hats and smoking in the presence of the court, a sullen murmur rose from the crowd. (Schlesinger 1958, pp. 42–43)

The group dragged the judge from the bench, beat him and blindfolded him.

> Then a mile from the city, they stopped, tossed a rope over a telegraph pole, fastened one end about his neck and tightened the knot till he nearly lost consciousness. Someone removed a hub cap from the truck and put it on his head, while others pushed him to his knees and told him to pray. Crowned with the cap, grease running down his face, thrust to the ground, he looked at the angry men around him and prayed: 'Oh Lord, I pray thee, do justice to all men.' And still he refused to pledge himself not to foreclose mortgages on their farms. They threw dirt on him, then tore off his trousers and smeared

them with grease and dirt, till, weary and perhaps abashed, they went away. (Schlesinger 1958, pp. 42–43)

Most transfer seekers were not met with such intransigence. Consider the silver interests. 'Concentrated in seven western states, the silver industry commanded a band of fourteen senators' (Schlesinger 1958, p. 249). At a meeting of the Economic and Monetary Conference in June of 1933, Senator Key Pittman demonstrated his support for silver:

> Pittman, clearly the most colorful of the American delegates, regarded the conference as a well-deserved respite from prohibition and remained drunk for the duration. Despite his constant state of inebriation, he was a forceful, and sometimes violent, spokesman for the silver interests. On one occasion, he chased an American adviser through the halls of Claridge's Hotel with a bowie knife because the gentleman had failed to show enough enthusiasm for silver. On another occasion, Pittman was found sitting naked in the kitchen sink at Claridge's, convinced that he was a statue in a fountain. (Williams 1994, p. 176)

Although little was accomplished at the meeting, Pittman eventually got all that he wanted. A subsequent agreement limited the sales of silver of India and China and committed the United States to purchase virtually all domestically produced silver. 'Roosevelt surrendered to political blackmail on the part of the silver hawks. He had reason to fear that a silver filibuster might hurt his legislative program, or that a silver veto might damage congressional prospects in the fall' (Schlesinger 1958, p. 252).

> The silver policy represented the most remarkable – as well as the least remarked – special interest triumph of the period. A minor industry, employing in 1939 less than five thousand persons, the silver industry, in effect, held the government ransom, extorting nearly a billion and a half dollars in the fifteen years after 1934 – a sum considerably larger than that paid by the government to support farm prices over the same period. (Schlesinger 1958, pp. 251–52)

Thus, one consequence of the New Deal that is still felt today is the increased influence of special-interest groups and the role of the government in transferring wealth among them. The part that politics played in determining just who received New Deal dollars will be explored at length in later chapters.

The economic legacy of the New Deal may be open to question, but no one can doubt its political success. As Stein (1984, p. 63) points out, 'no other President before or since has dominated the political scene as Roosevelt did.'

The New Deal prompted long-lasting changes in the voting habits of various groups. Agricultural interests quickly aligned themselves with the Democratic Party as did organized labor. Their loyalties to Roosevelt are certainly understandable. However, even some of those whose plight was largely ignored by the administration joined the Roosevelt coalition as well. Although FDR's appeal to low-income groups and minorities is puzzling in light of his actual legislative priorities, Bernstein (1968, p. 281) speculates that

> by the power of rhetoric and through the appeals of political organization, the Roosevelt government managed to win or retain the allegiance of these peoples. Perhaps this is one of the crueller ironies of liberal politics, that marginal men trapped in hopelessness were seduced by rhetoric, by the style and movement, by the symbolism of efforts seldom reaching beyond words.

Roosevelt, the consummate politician, brought various interest groups into the party where they have remained, for the most part, loyal members to this day.

To some of its critics, the New Deal represented little more than a grand vote-buying scheme. The administration's programs brought about 'the revitalization of the Democratic party; it was the political manifestation of that new spirit of reform which was stirring among the ranks of labor and the Negro people' (Degler 1959, p. 411).

Indeed, the shift of black votes from the Republicans to the Democrats perhaps represents the greatest political somersault by a voting group in history. One possibly apocryphal story tells of a previously loyal black Republican who turned Abraham Lincoln's picture to the wall, stating that his debt to the party had been paid. By 1936, black voters were firmly in the Democratic camp, to which they have been loyal ever since. Whether the allegiance of blacks to the New Deal and to FDR was justified by the pattern of emergency relief spending will be taken up later.

In sum, the New Deal helped assemble a powerful bloc of voters that translated into reelection victory for the Roosevelt administration. The support of numerous special-interest groups was galvanized and came to make up the core support of the Democratic Party. Big labor, urban voters, large farming interests, blacks, and residents of the South were to become the party's loyal foot soldiers.

In the runup to the 1936 election campaign, voters living below the Mason–Dixon Line so heavily favored the Democrats that their support could be considered solid. As Robinson (1970, pp. 19–20) explains, 'Democratic managers knew that Southern states do not ordinarily figure in any national strategy as planned by the Republican national organization.' Along with a strong showing in major urban areas, Roosevelt would be competitive in 1936 with this region's all-but-guaranteed votes. For victory to be assured, though, Roosevelt needed to carry a number of swing states.

FDR also needed the support of big labor to quell a possible third-party challenge led by the populist Louisiana firebrand, Huey Long. Such support was far from assured. Labor was increasingly disenchanted with the president, charging that the National Recovery Administration, which workers were calling the 'National Run Around', had sided with anti-union employers. Indeed, an article published in the *New York Times* on 3 February 1935 carried the headline, 'Labor Unions Break with the New Deal', and reported that labor leaders were 'almost in despair of making headway toward union recognition in the face of powerful industrial interests and an unsympathetic administration' (Hofstadter [1948] 1976, p. 437). Hence,

> Roosevelt, looking forward to 1936, now found himself in a difficult position. The Court had torn up his entire program for labor and industry. Labor seemed on the verge of withdrawing political support. Huey Long's popularity showed the dissatisfaction of a large part of the electorate. And no sigh of a really decisive turn toward business recovery had yet come. (Hofstadter [1948] 1976, p. 438)

The president's political work was evidently cut out for him. While FDR publicly attempted to make the 1936 election a referendum on himself personally – 'There's one issue in this campaign. It's myself, and people must be either for me or against me' (Hofstadter [1948] 1976, p. 436) – questions remain about whether the president privately exploited the New Deal to help achieve his political goals.

6   WHY REVISIT THE NEW DEAL?

This chapter opened with Senator Moynihan's observation that the New Deal is long since a settled issue. The conventional wisdom is that government was indispensable during the Great Depression and is equally capable of fixing what is 'broke' in the modern economy. Indeed, supporters of an activist public sector nowadays frequently point to the New Deal as a blueprint for intervention: responding to an historic economic emergency, a benevolent federal government came to the aid of its citizens and in the process prevented free-market institutions from crumbling. Merely accepting this version of the events of the 1930s, as some wish, opens the door to further government intrusions.

The New Deal demands additional scrutiny because it is perhaps the most misunderstood period in modern economic history. The conventional wisdom regarding the New Deal misses the mark widely – a misinterpretation that has triggered an explosion in the scale and scope of government.

The chapters to follow present theory and evidence showing how the federal government's relief efforts were shaped more by political consider-ations than by economic conditions in the states. An analysis of President Roosevelt's electoral strategy offers a much better explanation for the programs of the New Deal than alternative models based on benevolent government responses to the economic hardship visited by the Great Depression.

A New Deal pork barrel hypothesis is advanced – and tested against the empirical evidence – which suggests that political variables, including certain characteristics of state congressional delegations (legislative seniority, membership on key committees of the Congress, and so on) as well as the individual states' importance to FDR's reelection hopes, are critical to understanding how the federal government responded to the massive economic dislocations of 1929–41.

In sum, while the New Deal is often conceived of as being purposefully designed by a public-spirited government to alleviate the economic suffering caused by the Great Depression, it is argued herein that political forces, which are now widely recognized to influence today's spending priorities under the many big government programs and policies enacted during the 1930s, were in fact present at the creation. Greater appreciation of the role played by politics in the birth of the modern welfare state holds important lessons for students of contemporary public policy.

This chapter has presented an overview of the Great Depression and the New Deal. The next three chapters describe the specific bureaus and agencies created by the Roosevelt administration to respond to the economic crisis. We begin by examining the programs targeting agricultural interests and rural relief.

NOTES

1. Not everyone was so enamored: 'Most noted for his personal charm, his unprincipled propensity to play politics, and his lack of intellectual acuity, he was, in Walter Lippman's eyes, a "kind of amiable boy scout . . . a pleasant man who, without any important qualifications for the office, would very much like to be President"' (Higgs 1987, p. 170).
2. Declining prices can cause the real rate of interest to rise dramatically. This is precisely what happened during the first few years of the Great Depression. For example, suppose that the price level declines by 10 percent over some time period and the nominal rate of interest is zero. The real cost of borrowing would then be 10 percent. During the years 1931 through 1933, the real interest rate on US Treasury bills was higher than at any other time during the next forty years (Mishkin 1989, p. 545). This, of course, made the cost of borrowing extremely high, depressing business investment expenditures and consumer expenditures for durable goods.

3. Prior to the National Banking Act of 1863, all commercial banks were chartered by the states (State Banks). The law created a new system of federally chartered banks (National Banks). Thus, the US has a dual banking system composed of both state and federal institutions. When the Federal Reserve System was created in 1913, national banks were required to become members. State banks could join but most did not because of the costs associated with Fed membership (Mishkin 1989, p. 187).

4. Ickes's low opinion of American businessmen was later echoed by John Maynard Keynes. As quoted by Barber (1996, p. 108), Keynes wrote to FDR in 1938 that

    > business men have a different set of delusions from politicians; and need, therefore, different handling. They are, however, much milder than politicians, at the same time, allured and terrified by the glare of publicity, easily persuaded to be 'patriots', perplexed, bemused, indeed terrified, yet only too anxious to take a cheerful view, vain perhaps but very unsure of themselves, pathetically responsive to a kind word. You could do anything you liked with them, if you would treat them (even the big ones), not as wolves and tigers, but as domestic animals by nature, even though they have been badly brought up and not trained as you wished. . . . If you work them into the surly, obstinate, terrified mood, of which domestic animals, wrongly handled, are so capable, the nation's burdens will not get carried to market.

5. The term 'demosclerosis' was coined by Jonathan Rauch (1994) in reference to the paralytic effects of rent seeking and interest-group influence on the public policy process.

3.   The Farm Crisis and Rural Relief

One of the clichés of Populism was the notion that, whatever the functions of the other vocations, the function of the farmer was pre-eminent in importance because he fed, and thus supported, all the others. Although it has been heard somewhat less frequently of late, and a counter-ideology of urban resentment has even begun to appear, our national folklore still bears the heavy imprint of that idea. In reality something like the opposite has become true – that the rest of us support the farmer. . . . (Hofstadter 1955, p. 8)

One of the first economic problems addressed by the Roosevelt administration upon taking office was agriculture. For the new president, restoring farmers' purchasing power was the key to bringing the economy back from the depths of depression. Propping up farm commodity prices would give the farmer a 'fair' share of national income and, hence, help spur recovery. These sentiments were echoed by many contemporary observers, including New York mayor Fiorello LaGuardia, who contended that, 'Bringing agriculture to a parity with industry by fixing prices according to actual cost of production will establish in this country a new era of prosperity, enjoyed not by a small class but by all the real producers of wealth' (Zinn 1966, p. 229). 'Hence arose the anomalous but widely supported policy proposal to cure the depression, itself a catastrophic decline of real output and employment, by cutting back on production' (Higgs 1987, p. 174).

Farmers claimed that their economic position had been weakening before the depression began. 'Even in the supposedly prosperous 1920's, the farmer in the United States was in constant economic difficulty. Surpluses grew and prices fell, but the payments the farmer had to make to the banker, the railroader, and the middleman remained high' (Zinn 1966, p. 227).

Conkin (1975) doubts that these assertions of poor agricultural performance were well founded. But farmers, complaining that they had not shared in the decade's prosperity, blamed callous Republicans for not coming to their aid. As their economic positions deteriorated, the sector became more vulnerable to a recession. According to this interpretation, reduced agricultural purchasing power may have exacerbated the effects of the stock market crash, increasing the severity of the downturn. Farmers had a clear incentive to see that this reasoning became the prevailing view. But 'the reality never matched the myth. Overall farm prices in the twenties remained close to parity, or to the levels of the prosperous base period of 1909–1914. But all farmers did not share in the moderate prosperity, and almost none realized the profits of the lush war years' (Conkin 1975, p.37).

While the economic plight of the farmer during the 1920s is a matter of debate, there is widespread agreement that the agricultural sector became much better organized politically during the period. Farmers mobilized for personal gain and used their newfound political clout to lobby for legislative favors from Washington. Overstating their problems and understating their successes, farmers pushed their congressional delegations to promote their interests (Conkin 1975, p. 37).

The calls for federal farm aid, which had been intensifying during the 1920s, were legitimized by the Great Depression. The agricultural sector fell faster and harder than any other (Conkin 1975, p. 39):

> Farm income in 1932 was less than one-third of the already depressed 1929 figure. The parity index showing the relative level of prices farmers received compared to prices for what they bought (1910–1914 = 100) fell from a bad 89 in 1929 to a disastrous 55 in 1932. (McElvaine 1984, p. 147)

More than a quarter of US farm income came from exports – a fact which devastated American agriculture as the depression spread around the globe (McElvaine 1984, p. 36). Many farmers lost their homes and their land, while others slipped closer and closer to financial ruin.

This chapter examines the policies of the New Deal that targeted the agricultural sector of the economy as well as those aimed at providing more general rural relief. The programs that addressed agriculture (the Agricultural Adjustment Acts, the Commodity Credit Corporation, and the Farm Credit Administration) are described first. The legislative histories of these programs are rehearsed and the stated purposes of the measures are summarized. The 'unintended' consequences of the administration's early farm programs – rising numbers of displaced farm laborers and rural poor – are then explored. The activities of two New Deal agencies created to alleviate these problems (the Resettlement Administration and the Farm Security Administration) are examined next. Finally, these programs are evaluated in terms of their impact on rural poverty.

1 THE AGRICULTURAL ADJUSTMENT ACT OF 1933

The new administration pushed quickly for an emergency farm program. The agricultural adjustment bill sent to Congress soon after President Roosevelt's inauguration included many of the ideas advocated by those favoring greater government intervention into the economy – subsidized loans, price supports, and production controls. The central purpose of the legislation was to reduce agricultural output. 'Farm prices would be raised by government-subsidized scarcity. The executive branch was permitted to choose the means it thought best to achieve this end' (McElvaine 1984, p. 148). The bill sailed through the House but stalled in the Senate. After some debate, the latter chamber passed the measure 64 to 20 on 12 May 1933 (Schlesinger 1958, p. 44).

The Agricultural Adjustment Act of 1933 began with the following 'Declaration of Emergency':

> That the present acute economic emergency being in part the consequence of a severe and increasing disparity between the prices of agricultural and other commodities, which disparity has largely destroyed the purchasing power of farmers for industrial products, has broken down the orderly exchange of commodities, and has seriously impaired the agricultural assets supporting the national credit structure, it is hereby declared that these conditions in the basic industry of agriculture have affected transactions in agricultural commodities with a national public interest, have burdened and obstructed the normal currents of commerce in such commodities, and render imperative the immediate enactment of title I of the Act. (Hosen 1992, p. 61)

Title I gave the secretary of agriculture authority to negotiate voluntary agreements with producers to limit acreage or to reduce the actual production of basic agricultural commodities, and to make rental or benefit payments to the participating producers in amounts that seemed fair and reasonable to the secretary (Hosen 1992, pp. 64–65).

Section nine of Title I authorized a processing tax to fund the program. 'The processing tax shall be at such rate as equals the difference between the current average farm price for the commodity and the fair exchange value of the commodity' (Hosen 1992, p. 66). The 'fair exchange value' was defined as the price of the commodity that yielded the same purchasing power relative to goods purchased by farmers as the commodity commanded during selected base years (Hosen 1992, p. 67). The base period adopted for all commodities except tobacco was 1909–14. The years 1919–29 served as the base period for tobacco products (Hosen 1992, p. 62).

Henry Wallace was named Secretary of Agriculture and Rexford Guy Tugwell Assistant Secretary of Agriculture. A new bureau, the Agriculture

Adjustment Agency (AAA), was created within the Department of Agriculture to administer the new farm program. George Peek headed the organization. Because the administration sought to put its policies in place as quickly as possible, existing county agricultural agents were called upon to implement the crop-reduction scheme at the local level. 'In a whirlwind drive, the county agents now signed up hundreds of thousands of farmers for the . . . plow-up campaign' (Schlesinger 1958, p. 60).

Under this program, almost a third of the 1933 cotton crop was destroyed, with planters receiving in return more than $100 million (Schlesinger 1958, p. 61). Poor yields resulting from unfavorable weather made the destruction of existing wheat crops unnecessary, but incentives were given to wheat growers for the reduction of future crops (Schlesinger 1958, p. 62). 'In 1934, 35,768,000 acres were diverted and 30,337,000 acres were diverted in 1935. As of June 30, 1939, total rental and benefit payments under this program amounted to $1,357,969,394.00' (Office of Government Reports 1939, p. 2).

While the destruction of existing crops was controversial – even the mules pulling the plows were supposedly hesitant about plowing under the cotton crop – the public was outraged by the AAA's policy on hogs. Despite the hunger that existed throughout the nation, the government called for the destruction of between 5 and 6 million young pigs. Other complainers thought the administration was mistreating the pigs. Secretary Wallace was unimpressed. He remarked that, 'People seem to contend that every little pig has the right to attain before slaughter the full pigginess of his pigness' (Schlesinger 1958, p. 63).

The Federal Surplus Relief Corporation (FSRC) was created in an effort to mollify some of the critics. The project was initially placed under the Federal Emergency Relief Administration (FERA), but was transferred to the AAA in 1935. The agency acquired surplus commodities and distributed them to the poor (pork was one of the first commodities supplied to families in need). The surplus distribution program did not enjoy much success and elicited considerable opposition from businessmen. The private sector, whose markets were disappearing rapidly, saw the handouts as an unwelcome source of competition. The FSRC also took over surplus cattle and proposed that they be converted to canned beef and shoes for distribution to those on relief. Business interests again reacted negatively; shoe manufacturers refused to rent the necessary equipment to the government (Schlesinger 1958, p. 278).

The AAA's farm programs were mostly administered at the local level. Participating farmers became members of county associations and about 3,000 such associations came into being (Office of Government Reports 1939, p. 5). Local administrative responsibilities were delegated to committeemen elected by each of the associations, giving member farmers a strong voice in the programs' implementation (Office of Government Reports 1939, p. 5). County production-control committees 'helped persuade farmers to sign up and also determined, fairly or unfairly, the allotments and the base for the payments' (Conkin 1975, p. 40).

While the AAA wanted crop reductions to be voluntary, many farmers pushed for mandatory enforcement. A group of governors, led by Floyd Olson of Minnesota, proposed 'compulsory production control and price fixing for basic farm commodities, to be enforced by licensing all farmers and processors' (Schlesinger 1958, p. 66).

In 1934, acreage controls were placed on two crops, tobacco and cotton, by the Bankhead Cotton Control Act and the Kerr–Smith Tobacco Control Act. Again, the purpose was to create artificial scarcity and, thus, drive up the prices of the commodities. Processing taxes were used to enforce compliance (Schlesinger 1958, p. 73). In the case of cotton, transferable certificates were distributed to individual planters based on their respective shares of the total crop. The certificates could then be used to pay a government-imposed ginning tax. Those farmers with cotton in excess of their allotment found themselves with no certificates and had to pay a tax of 50 percent of the crop's market price (Whatley 1983, p. 916).

The processing tax which funded the payments to farmers was declared unconstitutional in 1936 (McElvaine 1984, pp. 150–51). However, 'the fundamental idea of curtailing production and subsidizing the farmer was maintained in the Soil Conservation Act of 1936 and the Agricultural Adjustment Act of 1938' (Zinn 1966, p. 232).

The Soil Conservation and Domestic Allotment Act was passed in February of 1936. The legislation was designed to promote conservation by 'encouraging a shift of acreage from the production of unneeded soil-depleting crops to soil-conserving crops, and the adoption of soil-improvement practices to check soil erosion and maintain and build soil fertility' (Office of Government Reports 1939, p. 2). Total payments to farmers under this program reached $369,288,006 by July of 1939 (Office of Government Reports 1939, p. 2).

2 THE COMMODITY CREDIT CORPORATION

The Commodity Credit Corporation (the other CCC of the New Deal) was the second major program the Roosevelt administration put in place to aid farmers. The program's father was Oscar Johnson, an officer of the AAA as well as the overseer of the Delta and Pine Land Company of Scott County, Mississippi – the largest cotton plantation in the United States at the time (Tindall 1967, p. 395). Under the CCC, the government was empowered to make loans to planters in amounts exceeding the market values of their crops. The commodity – cotton in this example – would be held by the government as security for the loan; this would in turn help prop prices up by keeping supplies off the market. If the commodity's price increased, the grower was allowed to redeem the cotton. Otherwise, the government kept the cotton in storage (Schlesinger 1958, p. 51).

As one observer puts it:

> Farmers had the choice of either letting the government keep the commodity and not repaying the loan or repaying the loan and reclaiming his crop for sale on the open market. This was popularly known as a 'non-recourse loan'. The loans for products were made at a flat rate per unit for each product included under the program. Due to the fact that the farmer would only reclaim his production if he could sell it for a higher price than received on the loan, this flat rate amounted to a price support for the commodity. (Reading 1972, p. 116)

The CCC was initiated by Administrative Order on 16 October 1933; it continued to operate after portions of the Agricultural Adjustment Act of 1933 were declared unconstitutional in 1936. The program subsequently was incorporated under Title III of the Agricultural Adjustment Act of 1938 (Reading 1972, p. 117).

The Department of Agriculture funded the CCC initially, but its financing was taken over eventually by the Reconstruction Finance Corporation. 'The Corporation made loans to producers of cotton, corn, wool, mohair, rye, and tobacco and to certain cooperative associations on tobacco, peanuts, figs, dates, prunes, hops, naval stores, raisins, and butter' (Office of Government Reports 1939, p. 8). Local lending agencies were utilized as conduits for these loans, but direct loans were also made when no local facilities were available (Office of Government Reports 1939, p. 8). Table 3.1 shows the loan amounts on the various commodities as of 30 June 1939. Non-recourse loans totaled $1,160 million from 1933 to 1939 (Reading 1972, p. 117).

3 THE AGRICULTURAL ADJUSTMENT ACT OF 1938

The Agricultural Adjustment Act of 1938 established an enduring national farm policy. 'The AAA of 1938 refined, made constitutional, and made permanent the types of programs developed during the previous six years' (Reading 1972, p. 30). The law established crop storage mechanisms to ensure more stable supplies of corn, wheat, cotton, tobacco, and rice. The new agri-

Table 3.1 Aggregate Commodity Credit Corporation loans as of 30 June 1939

Commodity	Disbursements	Loans Outstanding
Cotton	$867,489,922.42	$562,327,759.84
Corn	301,735,862.92	145,331,403.88
Tobacco	9,632,966.00	3,574,681.86
Turpentine and rosin	21,841,658.68	14,717,564.76
Figs	208,813.32	52,096.78
Peanuts	12,467,984.04	50,995.79
Prunes	2,742,193.14	182,337.17
Raisins	3,757,085.69	2,396,199.25
Wheat	48,971,216.33	12,689,593.69
Butter	31,029,292.05	8,972,332.25
Pecans	440,648.58	405,565.82
Hops	1,456,708.52	1,417,176.97
Wool and mohair	3,724,333.54	1,468,245.11
Totals	$1,305,498,785.23	$753,585,953.17

Source:
Office of Government Reports (1939, p. 9).

culture bill was signed by FDR on 16 February 1938. Secretary Wallace, in a radio address to the nation, described the act and promised that it would bring an abundance of agricultural products. Emphasizing the act's simplicity, he suggested that both farmers and consumers would benefit (Zinn 1966, p. 232). The act called for an 'ever-normal granary' which would even out the peaks and troughs of supply, thereby ensuring adequate prices for farmers and abundant supplies for consumers (Wallace [1939] 1966, p. 235).

As described in Office of Government Reports (1939, p. 3), the principal methods used under the 1938 law included:

1. Acreage allotments.
2. Payments to assist farmers in meeting the costs of practices which prevented erosion and maintained soil fertility.
3. Parity payments to equalize farm incomes.

4. Loans on crops stored in the ever-normal granary.
5. Marketing quotas when needed and approved by the farmers themselves.

The acreage allotments provided for a specified total output for each farm commodity, and farmers growing that crop were apportioned accordingly. In an effort to push prices up, non-recourse loans were utilized to encourage farmers to store surplus crops rather than bring them to market. When made necessary by excess production, however, mandatory marketing quotas could be put into place if approved by two-thirds of the producers (Office of Government Reports 1939, p. 3). The marketing of commodities in excess of the established limits resulted in a substantial penalty. With the cotton crop, for example, 'a prohibitive tax of fifty percent on all cotton sold beyond the allotment' was imposed (Tindall 1967, p. 396).

An estimated five million producers took part in the 1938 AAA program, covering 320,693,000 acres and accounting for roughly 72 percent of the nation's cultivated land. 'As of June 30, 1939, conservation payments under the 1938 program totaled $409,074,847' (Office of Government Reports 1939, p. 3). Producers of cotton, corn, wheat, and rice who planted in compliance with their 1939 acreage allotments received, in addition to the conservation payment, $212,000,000 in price adjustment or parity payments (Office of Government Reports 1939, p. 4).

The program worked as follows. National goals were set for

> wheat, 55 to 60 million acres; cotton, 27 to 29 million acres; corn, 94 to 97 million acres; potatoes, 3,100,000 to 3,300,000 acres; peanuts, 1,550,000 to 1,650,000 acres; rice, 850,000 to 880,000 acres; tobacco, burley, 375,000 to 410,000 acres; flue-cured, 860,000 to 900,000 acres; fire-cured and dark air-cured, 160,000 to 170,000 acres; cigar-filler and binder, 85,000 to 90,000 acres; Georgia-Florida Type No. 62, 2,000 to 3,000 acres. (Office of Government Reports 1939, pp. 3–4)

By imposing these restrictions, the government attempted to limit output in various commodities so that the quantities consistent with farm price targets were produced.

Farmers adhering to their assigned allotments were rewarded with payments if the prices of their crops fell below 75 percent of parity. 'Participating cotton growers in 1939 were able to earn conservation payments of 1.8 cents per pound and parity payments of 1.6 cents per pound on their crops; wheat growers could earn 17 and 11 cents per bushel in conservation and parity payments respectively; corn growers, 9 and 6 cents per bushel; and rice growers, 9 and 12 cents per hundredweight' (Office of Government Reports 1939, p. 4). Tobacco prices remained high enough that no parity payments were made. However, those tobacco producers who complied with the program received conservation payments of between 0.8 and 1.26 cents per pound. Conservation payments of $3 per ton were also made to peanut growers, and potato growers were paid 3 cents per bushel (Office of Government Reports 1939, p. 4).

As we have seen, the Agricultural Adjustment Act of 1938 also established the so-called ever-normal granary. The Commodity Credit Corporation accordingly made loans on the 1938 crop, with surplus commodities serving as collateral. Farmers could store their produce on their own farms or in commercial storage facilities. Loans were extended on more than 84 million bushels of wheat at prices averaging 60 cents per bushel. About 250 million bushels of corn were in storage with a loan rate of 57 cents per bushel. Loans averaging 8.85 cents per pound were made on almost 5 million bales of the 1938 cotton crop (Office of Government Reports 1939, p. 5). By September of 1939, the CCC had assumed title to both the 1934 and 1937 cotton crops under its loan programs, with the result that approximately 11 million bales of cotton from the 1934–35, 1937–38, and the 1938–39 crops were ultimately under loan. The federal government also made loans on tobacco, wool and mohair, turpentine, peanuts, and hops.

Cotton production reached levels in 1938 that triggered a referendum on the producers' application for a mandatory marketing quota. The quota was put in place on 1 August 1939, following the measure's approval by more than two-thirds of the planters. Tobacco farmers defeated an AAA-prescribed referendum that would have imposed similar restrictions (Office of Government Reports 1939, p. 5).

'Total expenditures under AAA for the 1933 through 1939 period were nearly $2.9 billion. This included both the 1933 and 1938 acts and amounted to $25.57 per person for the seven year period' (Reading 1972, p. 31). Calculating state AAA expenditures on a per-capita basis, Reading (1972, p. 31) reported that North Dakota and South Dakota received the most AAA funds and, moreover, that these were the only states in which AAA spending exceeded $100 per capita.

Rather than utilizing total state populations in the denominator, Table 3.2 shows the cross-state allocation of AAA funds on a per-farmer basis. (The number of farmers in each state was taken from the 1937 *Statistical Abstract of the United States*.) The term 'farmers' includes all persons living on farms regardless of occupation in 1935. As can be seen, 14 of the top 15 recipient states are located west of the Mississippi River. The most interesting finding

Table 3.2 Total AAA expenditures per farmer, by state, 1933–39

North Dakota	$271.32	South Carolina	$71.43
Kansas	255.47	Georgia	68.50
Montana	252.83	Alabama	68.50
South Dakota	240.05	Maryland	63.18
Nebraska	212.92	Ohio	57.55
Iowa	200.53	Nevada	55.12
Wyoming	157.58	North Carolina	52.01
Texas	156.58	Wisconsin	50.82
Colorado	151.37	Tennessee	45.10
Idaho	139.28	Kentucky	44.45
Oklahoma	133.89	Delaware	44.07
Illinois	129.01	Michigan	43.73
Minnesota	99.13	Florida	35.59
Arizona	97.83	Connecticut	29.61
Washington	96.75	Massachusetts	28.33
Louisiana	90.09	New York	25.55
Indiana	87.75	New Jersey	24.86
Arkansas	86.35	Virginia	21.42
Oregon	83.99	Maine	19.53
Mississippi	82.77	Pennsylvania	16.99
Missouri	81.65	Vermont	16.99
California	80.14	New Hampshire	13.09
Utah	77.98	Rhode Island	8.83
New Mexico	73.79	West Virginia	8.79

is that southern states – states with economies that were dominated by agriculture – received relatively few AAA dollars.

The Agricultural Adjustment Act of 1933 contained three parts. Title I established the Agricultural Adjustment Agency and provided for acreage reductions, while Title III was concerned with monetary issues. Title III was known popularly as the Thomas amendment, named after the head of the pro-inflation bloc, Senator Elmer Thomas of Oklahoma. 'He had incessantly urged inflationary remedies from the start of the depression' (Schlesinger 1958, p. 42). The Thomas amendment was attached to the agriculture bill and called for currency devaluation. Title II, which was designed to provide more adequate sources of credit to the nation's farmers, is described next.

4 THE FARM CREDIT ADMINISTRATION

Title II of 1933's Agricultural Adjustment Act was called the 'Emergency Farm Mortgage Act'. It was designed to extend credit to farmers on the brink of foreclosure. In particular, 'it provided for refinancing, reduction of interest rates on land loans, extension of time obligations, and direct loans along with financing aid to farmers' (Reading 1972, pp. 28–29). These emergency measures were later extended by the Farm Credit Act passed in June of 1933. The latter act established the Farm Credit Administration (FCA) and placed all existing agricultural lending agencies under its direction. Henry Morgenthau, Jr, headed the new agency (Reading 1972, p. 112).

In addition to taking charge of the existing farm loan apparatus, the FCA organized 12 Production Credit Corporations and an equal number of Banks for Cooperatives – one for each city where a Federal Land Bank was located. Production Credit Associations and a Central Bank for Cooperatives were also chartered (Hosen 1992, p. 228).

The farm credit system thus incorporated some existing agencies and created some new ones. The nation was divided into 12 Farm Credit Districts, which included the Land Banks that made mortgage loans to farmers and the Intermediate Credit Banks that made production loans to cooperatives. The Production Credit Corporations were established to link individual farmers with the Intermediate Credit Banks. Finally, the Central Bank and the 12 regional Banks for Cooperatives provided loans to farmers' cooperatives (Reading 1972, p. 112).

The Federal Land Banks financed first farm mortgages. Farmers obtained these mortgages through local branches of national farm loan associations. Nearly 3,900 of these local mortgage-credit cooperatives existed nationwide (Office of Government Reports 1939, p. 10). Attempting to ameliorate the farm foreclosure problem, the federal government made emergency funds available to the Federal Land Banks. Due to the severity of the crisis, another subsidized loan – known as the Land Bank Commissioner Loan – was created for the purpose of financing both first and second mortgages at higher rates of interest (Office of Government Reports 1939, p. 11). All told

> there were 1,061,000 Federal Land Bank and Land Bank Commissioner loans, aggregating $2,626,400,000 outstanding on September 30, 1939. This represented about 37 percent of the total farm mortgage debt in the United States. From 1933 to 1935 more than 90 percent of all Land Bank and Commissioner loans were used to refinance existing mortgages and other debts. (Office of Government Reports, p. 10)

The national farm credit system also included 532 production credit associations. These organizations, created by the Farm Credit Act of 1933, made short-term loans to farmers which typically matured when crops and livestock were ready for market. As mentioned, the act established production credit corporations in each of the 12 Farm Credit districts. The corporations were created 'for the purpose of organizing, capitalizing in part, and supervising the operations of local production credit associations' (Office of Government Reports 1939, p. 11). From the time of their establishment through 30 September 1939, approximately $1,347,000,000 had been loaned while $1,173,000,000 had been repaid, leaving some $174,000,000 in outstanding loans on the associations' books (Office of Government Reports 1939, p. 12). The 12 Federal Intermediate Credit Banks sold bonds to the public and used the proceeds to extend credit to the production credit associations (Office of Government Reports 1939, p. 12).

The 12 district Banks for Cooperatives and the Central Bank financed farmers' cooperatives. 'The initial capital of the banks for cooperatives was subscribed by the Federal Government as provided by the Farm Credit Act of 1933' (Office of Government Reports 1939, p. 13). These banks made loans totaling $458,000,000 to 2,400 farmers' cooperatives (Office of Government Reports 1939, p. 13). Loans were made 'to finance or refinance the purchase, construction, or lease of needed physical facilities, such as creameries, fruit-packing plants, or warehouses' (Office of Government Reports 1939, p. 13).

The Farm Credit Administration also made emergency production loans to farmers unable to secure financing from other sources. These loans were funded by special congressional appropriations. Additional funds were supplied to the land banks by the Federal Farm Mortgage Corporation created by Congress on 31 January 1934. Government-guaranteed bonds were issued to raise the necessary capital (Office of Government Reports 1939, p. 13).

Altogether, nearly $4 billion was loaned to the nation's farmers during the New Deal years. Table 3.3 provides a summary of the Roosevelt administration's agricultural lending programs. Like the price support payments of the AAA, agricultural loans exhibited substantial variation across the states. 'The wide dispersion of allocations among states is evident when one finds that Massachusetts received $4 per capita while North Dakota was allocated $212 per capita. On a regional basis the Mountain states were allocated $103 per person while the Northeastern states received $6 per capita' (Reading 1972, p. 112).

Table 3.3 Numbers and amounts of agricultural loans, 1 May 1933–30 September 1939

Loaning Agency (by type of loan)	Number	Amount
Farm mortgage loans		
Federal land banks	351,288	$1,381,845,505
Land bank commissioner	532,118	987,889,084
Short-term credit		
Federal intermediate credit banks	N/A	695,489,286
Production credit associations	1,265,907	1,346,949,144
Regional agricultural credit associations	115,753	430,059,082
Emergency crop loans	1,712,487	189,272,276
Drought relief loans	300,614	72,008,540
Loans to cooperatives		
Federal intermediate credit banks	N/A	139,780,070
Banks for cooperatives	6,596	489,746,211
Totals	4,284,763[a]	$5,702,039,198

Note:
a. Excluding federal intermediate short-term loans and loans to cooperatives.

Source:
Office of Government Reports (1939, p. 9).

5 THE IMPACT OF NEW DEAL FARM POLICY

The administration's hopes of bringing about overall economic recovery through its agricultural policies fell far short of the mark. New Deal farm policy redistributed wealth, but did little to encourage its creation. While commodity prices increased somewhat as a result of government-sponsored scarcity, other New Deal programs acted to offset these gains. For example, 'the farm implement manufacturers and the mail order houses, responding to the National Recovery Administration drive, started to put their prices up' (Schlesinger 1958, p. 64).

Gene Smiley (1994, pp. 45–46) argues that FDR's farm program was not effective in restoring the agriculture sector, much less the whole economy. 'If successful, the programs would have largely maintained the existing farm population. However, . . . the long decline of the agricultural sector required a reallocation of resources out of agriculture.' There is substantial evidence to support this contention. Lee Alston (1983, p. 889), for instance, reports that the farm foreclosure rate per 1,000 farms was 18.7 in 1931, had climbed to 38.8 by 1933, but only fell to 18.1 in 1937. The government was battling trends it simply could not stop – let alone reverse.

The farm program's sharpest critics have highlighted its disparate effects on certain segments of the population. In particular, while the planter class benefited the rural poor were, in some cases, made worse off by the New Deal. The AAA 'gave the most help to those who needed it least, the biggest producers among the nation's six million farm families. The rural poor, those two million families who received less than ten per cent of the total income, received the least aid from the Act' (Zinn 1966, p. 239). Conkin (1975, p. 40) also noted the seemingly unfair distribution of the funds adding, 'basing payments on production instead of need inevitably aided most generously the already large and prospering farmers.' Bernstein (1987, p. 270) goes further, contending that 'in assisting agriculture, the AAA . . . sacrificed the interests of the marginal and the unrecognized to the welfare of those with greater political and economic power.'

6   THE DISLOCATION OF FARM TENANTS AND SHARE-CROPPERS

An analysis of the New Deal's farm programs would be seriously incomplete without investigating their impact on the rural poor. Certainly the least influential among the rural population were the sharecroppers and the tenant farmers. Tenant status is defined as follows:

> Wage Hand – An individual who lives on the plantation and has a definite agreement with the operator to work for a more or less definite number of months at an agreed upon wage.
> Cropper – A family which has a definite agreement with the operator whereby the family furnishes only labor in cultivating an agreed upon

acreage and receives in return a specified share of the crop, usually one-half share or less.

Share Tenant – A family which has a definite agreement with a landlord whereby the family furnishes some or all of the work stock and implements in cultivating an agreed upon acreage and receives in return a share of the crop, usually more than one-half. (Holley, Winston and Woofter 1940, p. 7)

Because of their poverty, the tenants often depended on the planters to 'furnish' them with various necessities, such as seed, fertilizer, and farm tools. The so-called furnish came with a price, however. 'In 1934 interest charges on these advances in three cotton counties of Texas and Mississippi ranged from 16.1 to 25.3 percent' (Tindall 1967, p. 410).

The plight of the tenant farmer during the Great Depression was well-documented and made popular through such works as John Steinbeck's *The Grapes of Wrath*. One New Deal field representative described them as follows: 'An illiterate, wretched people, undernourished, with standards of living so low that, once on relief, they are quite willing to stay there the rest of their lives' (Mertz 1978, p. 4). According to Assistant Secretary of Agriculture Rexford Tugwell, 'Tenants are everywhere; they are, in fact, nearly half of our farmers, about three million in number and well distributed' (Degler 1970, pp. 177–78). The 1937 *Statistical Abstract of the United States* indicates that, in 1935, almost 70 percent of the farms in Mississippi were operated by tenants, 37 percent in Kentucky, and 60 percent in Arkansas. For the most part, the percentages of farms operated by tenants across the deep South fell within this range. Tenants operated nearly 50 percent of all the farms in South Dakota, Nebraska, and Iowa; they operated 45 percent in Illinois, 40 percent in Colorado, and were distributed, albeit more thinly, across the remainder of the nation.

Despite their obvious need, the federal government's pump-priming activities largely bypassed the rural poor. The AAA's plow-up program provides an excellent example of the 'unintended' consequences of New Deal farm policy. It was the landlords who signed the agreements to reduce agricultural production and who therefore received the allotment checks. They were required to distribute the funds to tenants according to their interests in the crop, with sharecroppers entitled to roughly half and share tenants roughly two-thirds of the total (Mertz 1978, p. 23). But as Mertz (1978, p. 23) notes, 'a landlord holding the check was in a position to make any settlement he wished.'

Many tenants received less than their fair shares of the plow-up money. Some landlords kept all of the payments, applying the money toward the 'furnish' debts incurred by their tenants. Croppers, vulnerable to being exploited due to their lack of education and frequent illiteracy, were not completely fooled. A folklore existed among the croppers about landlords who 'kept books with a crooked pencil' (Tindall 1967, p. 410).

The incentives created by the government's farm policy left the tenant farmer with few places to turn for relief. As Schlesinger (1958, p. 376) points out, 'The landlords dominated not only local administration of AAA but the sheriffs at the county courthouse and the congressmen in Washington.'

The crop-reduction contracts of 1934 and 1935 gave the planters the lion's share of the payments, just as the 1933 plow-up had done. The government paid 4.5 cents per pound of the average yield for acres taken out of production. Of this amount, 3.5 cents went to the landlords as 'rent'. The remainder was known as the 'parity payment' and was to be divided between landlord and tenant, with tenant status determining the precise split. Sharecroppers received one-half cent and share tenants received three-fourths of a penny, on the average (Mertz 1978, p. 24). Commenting on their reportedly meager payments, 'the croppers aptly called their share the "poverty payment"' (Zinn 1966, p. 241).

Even this small share was contingent on the honesty of the landlord because, once again, they received the checks and redistributed the funds. Tenants often received no benefits or saw their payments applied toward debts. Frequently, a tenant's status was downgraded so that the planter could keep a larger share of the AAA funds (Mertz 1978, p. 28).

Whether landlords systematically denied benefits to their tenants is not known, but some evidence supporting the charge does exist. Members of the Progressive Southern Club – a group of southerners living in New York – wrote to then-Governor Bibb Graves of Alabama in June of 1936 urging him to 'see to it that parity checks are distributed equitably in Alabama'. A particular case had been brought to the group's attention, namely that of Fab Caldwell of Waverly in Lee County, Alabama. Mr Caldwell had apparently been 'threatened with death because he reported to the AAA investigator that his landlord had kept his parity check'.[1]

The most serious problem for tenant farmers was eviction. New Deal farm policy created incentives that led to the displacement of thousands of tenants. Often, 'plantation owners evicted their tenants in order to collect AAA payments for taking the land out of production' (McElvaine 1984, p. 150). Indeed, in a survey of southern farms, 'croppers showed a decrease of 63,000 or nearly a ten percent' reduction between 1930 and 1935 (Holley, Winston and Woofter 1940, p. 49).

Although the practice of evicting tenants was clearly in conflict with the spirit of section 7 of the AAA's standard-form cotton contract, the section was largely ignored. Written in part by Oscar Johnson, manager of the largest plantation in the United States, the contract allowed landlords to evict a tenant who had become a 'nuisance'. This provision supplied a loophole for planters wishing to take sharecropper acres out of production in order to obtain full plow-up benefits.

Secretary Wallace, faced with internecine fighting within the Agriculture Department over the AAA's treatment of the tenant farmers, sided with the planters. Commenting on Wallace's stance, Arthur Schlesinger (1958, p. 81) noted that, 'Washington had developed new appetites in Wallace. The Secretary of Agriculture was dominated by the mounting ambition to be the successor to the President.'

The policy thus continued and, as Whatley (1983) points out, the landlord's return from displacing tenants increased over time. 'On an acre yielding 350 lbs. of cotton the return from displacing a sharecropper increased from $1.78 in 1934 to $16.78 by 1939. Over the same period the return from displacing a share tenant increased even more – from $2.62 to $19.16 per acre.' Whatley goes on to say that, 'A once "fair" landlord, responding to his tenants' pleas for "fairness" may soon have to reply "I'm sorry, but the cost has simply become unbearable"' (Whatley 1983, p. 919).

The extent of the damage done to the rural poor by the AAA program was made clear in a study funded by the Rockefeller Foundation. It concluded that 'the AAA cotton program had been an "unforeseen calamity" for sharecroppers and tenants, reducing and even destroying the minimal security afforded by the crop lien system. Landowners now found it profitable to reduce the number of tenants and demote those remaining to wage laborers' (Mertz 1978, p. 95).

Pressure mounted from both within and without the administration to do something about rural poverty. Tugwell expressed disgust with the status quo and requested new responsibilities. He complained that 'If we have no intention of attacking poverty at its source . . . the administration ought not to have credit for helping really forgotten families; only for doing what democracies have usually done – helped those who needed help less because those who needed it more did not count politically' (Degler 1970, p. 176).

Disgruntled sharecroppers blamed the administration for their troubles. 'Too often he [Roosevelt] has talked like a cropper and acted like a planter' (Schlesinger 1958, p. 379). Responding to the criticism, FDR established the Resettlement Administration (RA) on 1 May 1935, as a separate agency to be headed by Rexford Tugwell. 'The RA would relocate people affected by the retirement of submarginal lands and would have charge of several types of rural and suburban planned communities, as well as land-planning undertakings' (Mertz 1978, p. 124).

7 THE RESETTLEMENT ADMINISTRATION

Receiving the second largest share of the monies apportioned under the Emergency Relief Appropriation Act of 1935 (the Works Progress Administration received the largest amount), the Resettlement Administration – the forerunner of today's Farmers Home Administration (FHA) – was a mixture of old and new programs with divergent goals. 'The striking feature of the Resettlement Administration was the combination of purposes. Its administration was rendered extraordinarily difficult by the diverse sources and differing objectives of these aims' (MacMahon, Millet and Ogden 1941, p. 81).

The agency's head, Rexford Tugwell, wanted to remove the rural poor from their infertile land, resettle them on good land, and provide them with access to tools, seed, and expert farming advice. The RA primarily made loans and grants to farm families in need (MacMahon, Millet, and Ogden 1941, p. 131). As Tugwell ([1937] 1970, p. 172) described it,

> One of the achievements the Resettlement Administration set for itself this year in Alabama was to see the last of its clients graduated from bulls to mules as farm motive power. This seems like a small gain, perhaps, but it is really a very great one in percentage.

Unfortunately for Tugwell, the RA's reach seems to have exceeded his grasp. 'Tugwell had more plans than funds' (Conkin 1975, p. 58). But even the modest amounts of aid provided to the rural poor were no doubt gratefully received.

It was the agency's activities in the area of housing assistance that were best known, however. Tugwell inherited the rural housing projects the administration had already launched. The RA took over the activities of the Subsistence Homestead Division of the Department of the Interior and the Rural Rehabilitation Program of the Federal Emergency Relief Administration (FERA). These agencies had both tackled essentially the same problem by working to relocate 'urban slum dwellers in autonomous garden cities and submarginal farmers in new, productive farm villages' (Conkin 1975, p. 58). The model farm villages were less appealing to Tugwell, but he fully supported the planned suburban communities. 'So ambitious was the early plan that there was talk of such projects on the fringes of every city of one hundred thousand inhabitants or over' (McMahon, Millet and Ogden 1941, p. 83). The federal government thereby began encouraging the flight from the inner cities to the suburbs – a trend it later came to discourage.

FERA's Rural Rehabilitation Division, one of the agencies absorbed by the Resettlement Administration, was devoted to relief of the rural poor. 'Its most useful efforts went to what was known as rehabilitation in place – that is, loans to farm families for seed, fertilizer, livestock, or farm tools" (Schlesinger 1958, p. 267). Along with providing such loans, the Rural Rehabilitation Division experimented with planned farming communities. Pine Mountain Valley, near Warm Springs, Georgia, was one of President Roosevelt's favorites (Tindall 1967, p. 423).[2]

The projects of the Subsistence Homestead Program were also shifted to the Resettlement Administration. This program's chief advocate was Senator John H. Bankhead of Alabama. Soon after the new administration took office, Senator Bankhead began trumpeting the merits of such a program. 'The back-to-the-land movement, Bankhead said, offered "a new basis for American society, in the restoration of that small yeoman class which has been the backbone of every great civilization"' (Schlesinger 1958, p. 363).

With White House support, Bankhead was able to attach an amendment to Title II of the National Industrial Recovery Act which appropriated $25,000,000 for subsistence homesteads. The act was passed on 16 June 1933, with section 208 of the legislation describing the program's purposes:

> To provide for aiding the redistribution of the overbalance of population in industrial centers $25,000,000 is hereby made available to the President, to be used by him through such agencies as he may establish and under such regulations as he may make, for making loans for and otherwise aiding in the purchase of subsistence homesteads. The moneys collected as repayment of said loans shall constitute a revolving fund to be administered as directed by the President for the purposes of this section. (Hosen 1992, p. 207)

The RA's Subsistence Housing Division was headed by M. L. Wilson. Wilson was chosen because of his ideological commitment to rural as opposed to urban living. He once remarked that the residents of the Mormon villages of Utah perhaps enjoyed the country's highest quality of life (Schlesinger 1958, p. 363). The idea was indeed superficially appealing:

> Placid communities made up of small white houses with green shutters in which families stranded by urban or rural poverty would find shelter and peace, engaging in hand-weaving or woodworking or small manufacturing, and growing their own food on their own garden plots. (Schlesinger 1958, p. 364)

Projects were to be established where needs were most urgent and the chances of success greatest. Several types of communities were envisaged: houses situated around small industries in rural settings where further decentralization was deemed likely; projects near large urban centers; and homesteads for the rural poor stranded on submarginal land.

The government developed the projects 'with reference to a sound long-range plan for the economic and social development of the community or region' (Wager 1945, p. 8). Typically, the communities were designed to accommodate from 25 to 100 families with individual sites ranging in size from one to five acres. Homesteaders were to acquire ownership of their individual housing units through long-term purchase contracts, but long-term leasing was also possible.

The Federal Subsistence Homestead Corporation was organized within the Subsistence Homestead Division to make loans for the initiation, development, and operation of the various projects. Local non-profit corporations were set up at the community level to serve as conduits for the funds. The homesteaders were persuaded that it was impractical for each of them to personally own livestock and tools. Thus, cooperative ownership arrangements were encouraged and substantial financial assistance was made available to finance such activities.

Not surprisingly, the lion's share of the dollars earmarked for subsistence homesteads was delivered to the Birmingham, Alabama area – near Senator Bankhead's home. 'Five projects, involving an expenditure of about $6,000,000 were initiated in Jefferson and Walker Counties' (Wager 1945, p. 15).

While the idea captivated the back-to-the-land movement's supporters, in practice the subsistence homestead venture was unsuccessful. One historian, commenting in particular on the Alabama projects, noted that 'The experience of the government with cooperatives in these several communities has been an unhappy one' (Wager 1945, p. 123).

The history of Palmerdale, one of the planned communities located northeast of Birmingham, provides a good example. In 1936, the Palmerdale Cooperative Association applied for and received a loan of $19,742.50. The proceeds were used to finance a cooperative farm service as well as a store and a gasoline station. A barn was constructed, working stock purchased, and farm implements obtained.

The farm service experienced financial difficulties from the start and was liquidated in 1941 (Wager 1945, p. 109). The store fared no better. 'The overhead costs were excessive; the management was inexperienced and bought unwisely; there was allegedly some pilfering; and most of all, there were few among the members who had a thorough comprehension of what cooperation involves' (Wager 1945, p. 110). Although management was replaced, inventories reduced, and other efforts made to salvage the operation, the enterprise was forced to close in February of 1943. After liquidation, the cooperative still owed $15,927.27.

The Bankhead Community, located just north of Jasper, Alabama, organized a cooperative association in 1937 to operate a farm service, provides another useful example. A loan was obtained and a tractor and equipment purchased for $6,594.50. In addition, mules and equipment worth $8,330.50 were bought by the cooperative.

Homesteads in the Bankhead Community were much larger than usual, averaging some 20 acres each. Nevertheless, on 21 March 1949, the association was forced to liquidate its assets. The cooperative had been troubled from the start, with residents voicing displeasure with the sharing of equipment. After selling the tractor, equipment, mules, and so on, the debt was reduced to $6,256.21.

The Bankhead Community also organized a Homestead Industrial Company for the manufacture of 'full-fashion hosiery' (Wager 1945, p. 121). After obtaining $310,000 from the government, a site was purchased, a brick building constructed, and the factory equipped with modern machinery. Like the other cooperative ventures, the factory did not prosper.

Wager (1945) defends the cooperatives, stating that the stores often faced stiff and sometimes unfair competition. He lists some of these allegedly 'unfair' practices: competitors from the private sector responded to the organization of the cooperatives by lowering their prices, improving the quality of their merchandise, and improving the appearances of their stores. In some cases they offered to sell on credit and, hence, took more business away from the cooperatives.

As of 31 August 1944, the five Alabama cooperatives were behind in their obligations by $66,451.29 (Wager 1945, p. 123). Upon liquidation, the average homestead in the Bankhead Community sold for $1,940, though costing an average of $7,220 to build (Wager 1945, p. 181).

The cooperatives' backers were disappointed by their failure but stubbornly clung to the merits of the idea. They blamed the residents of the communities for the lack of success. Wager (1945, p. 125) argues that, 'There was no thorough understanding by the members of the principles of coopera-tion or deep devotion to those principles.' Rexford Tugwell 'held the participants culpable for the failure because of their lack of community spirit and adherence to individualism and competition' (Schlesinger 1958, p. 373). Indeed, responding to questions from a New Dealer about the communities, one resident exclaimed, 'I believe a man could stay around here for five or six years and save enough money to go out and buy him a little hill farm all his own' (Tindall 1967, p. 423).[3]

Unfortunately for the New Dealers, the homestead movement caught the eye of First Lady Eleanor Roosevelt. She became involved in an incident that caused her husband great embarrassment. When the administration's critics wanted a particularly good example of policy failure, they mentioned Reedsville, West Virginia.

Reedsville was the location of one of the RA's planned communities and was to serve as a model for similar projects. Some 50 prefabricated houses were ordered and shipped to the West Virginia site. While they were quite attractive, the houses were designed for summers on Cape Cod and were completely unsuitable for the harsh winter months at Arthurdale – Reedsville's new name. Unwilling simply to replace the inadequate units, Mrs Roosevelt brought in a team of New York architects to retrofit the structures for the local climate. Complaining to the president about wasted resources, Secretary Ickes noted that the project was hardly a model for low-cost housing. FDR 'agreed, but added, a little helplessly, "My missus, unlike most women, hasn't any sense about money at all"' (Schlesinger 1958, p. 366). Commenting on the project to his colleagues, Senator Vandenberg of Michigan likewise remarked that, 'public money was poured lavishly into this enterprise. It is as yet scarcely one year old. But already we are told that half a million dollars has been irretrievably lost to the Government . . . in this Reedsville enterprise' (US House of Representatives 1935a, p. 2020).

The rural rehabilitation activities of the FERA and the Subsistence Homestead Division of the Department of the Interior were both brought into the Resettlement Administration on 30 April 1935. Tugwell endeavored to shape the programs more to his own liking. In particular, he had little faith in the Subsistence Homestead Program. The back-to-the-land movement did not enable the rural poor to compete with the planters. Technological changes demanded large-scale mechanized farming practices – methods unavailable to poor farmers working small plots of land. Through the RA, Tugwell set up several large cooperative communities with the intention of enabling the residents to take advantage of superior equipment and managerial talent.

Tugwell preferred to locate the planned communities just outside large cities rather than in rural areas. Greenhills, near Cincinnati, and Greendale, near Milwaukee, were two such locations, accommodating around 1,000 families (MacMahon, Millet and Ogden 1941, pp. 12–13). Once again, these projects were not particularly successful. And while they provide some interesting insights into the philosophy that guided the administration's agricultural policies, planned communities in fact played a relatively minor role in Tugwell's overall strategy for the Resettlement Administration. As Tindall (1967, p. 423) notes, 'Far more effort was made to salvage farmers by rehabilitation loans and grants than to settle them in communities. The aid went for supplies, equipment, tools, and debt adjustments to keep farm families off relief.'

Despite the efforts of Tugwell and others, the widespread poverty of the nation's rural population continued to be a thorn in the administration's side. A committee investigating tenancy 'recommended as a successor to the RA a new program which sought to provide low interest loans designed to enable tenants to buy their own farms' (Tindall 1967, p. 424).

The original legislation proposing long-term, low-interest loans for tenants was sponsored by Alabama's Bankhead, the administration's point man on agricultural matters in the Senate. The bill was reported out of the Agriculture and Forestry Committee on 11 April 1935, but faced much opposition.

Opponents, including the planters, argued that the proposal would, by increasing agricultural production, undermine the intentions of the AAA. Commenting on the contradictory nature of New Deal farm policy, Huey Long noted that one program was designed to take land out of production while another program was designed to put land back into production: 'We have two agencies of farm relief, one to hire a man not to raise, and the other to [enable] him to buy land on which to raise' (Mertz 1978, p. 137).

Southern congressmen had little interest in a piece of legislation which might help the non-voting poor and anger the planter. Roosevelt himself reportedly lost interest in the measure following Huey Long's assassination, concluding rightly that the South would now be solidly behind him in the upcoming presidential election.

Even Tugwell opposed the so-called Bankhead Bill, believing that poverty, not tenancy, was the chief problem. Small-farm owners, he said,

> carry the weight of a mortgage and consistently sacrifice to the god of interest; they face foreclosure with every fall in prices; their management suffers from the same or greater disabilities than that of tenants. One trouble with tenancy is landlordism; one trouble with ownership is the mortgage. Neither yields security, efficiency, or conservation. (Tugwell [1937] 1970, p. 174)

The bill's supporters eventually convinced its opponents that the legislation would benefit not only the South but other regions of the nation as well, and the Bankhead Bill finally passed in July of 1937. The Resettlement Administration was transferred to the Department of Agriculture and given responsibility for implementing the legislation. Tugwell resigned on 1 July 1937, to be replaced by Will Alexander. Shortly thereafter, the RA was renamed the Farm Security Administration (FSA). The new agency was charged with carrying out the RA's existing responsibilities and for administering the tenant-purchase programs of the Bankhead Bill. The FSA fought rural poverty on three fronts.

8   THE FARM SECURITY ADMINISTRATION

The FSA provided farmers with technical advice on farming practices and with help in negotiating more favorable payment schedules with creditors. Cash grants were made to those families in extreme distress. From 1935 to 1939, 771,067 families received such grants, which averaged less than $20 per month (Office of Government Reports 1939, p. 17). The FSA also made rehabilitation loans maturing in from one to five years at interest rates of 5 percent. Over the same period (1935–39), 772,315 families obtained FSA loans averaging approximately $350 per month (Office of Government Reports 1939, p. 17).

The FSA carried on the homestead projects begun by other New Deal agencies. All told, the FSA 'operated 146 homestead projects helping more than 11,000 low-income families attain security on good land' (Office of Government Reports 1939, p. 19).

While these responsibilities were simply inherited from the RA, the tenant-purchase programs were unique to the FSA. Farm tenants, certified by local committees, were given the opportunity to purchase small farms through loans repayable at interest rates of 3 percent and maturing in 40 years (Office of Government Reports 1939, p. 18). 'Each borrower was required to keep business-like records and meet with an FSA rehabilitation supervisor who would help work out a program for sound home and farm management' (Reading 1972, pp. 34–35). 'By June 30, 1939, 6,179 tenant purchase loans had been made during the two years in which they were available, aggregating $33,339,684' (Office of Government Reports 1939, p. 18).

The Farm Security Administration's impact on the rural poor can once again be gauged by examining a somewhat unusual, but nevertheless instructive, case in Alabama. Gee's Bend, near Camden, Alabama, was selected as an FSA project site. The area sits on an isolated peninsula – bounded on three sides by the Alabama River – with the closest town located on the opposite bank. By and large, the residents of the Bend were descendants of slaves purchased by Mark Pettway in 1845 in Halifax, North Carolina. After they were freed, most of the former slaves adopted the Pettway surname, but unique Christian names were apparently more difficult to come by. To take care of this problem, vowels were added to the names to distinguish individuals from one another. Ergo, Tom Pettway, Tom-o-

Pettway, and Tom-i-Pettway, were three residents who lived at the Bend at the time of the Great Depression.

After Mark Pettway's death, his son, John, ran the plantation until he died in 1900. With the white owners gone, the former slaves ran the operation and maintained the plantation. At the time of the Great Depression, some of the residents spoke an African dialect completely unintelligible to outsiders. Isolated, the community developed and prospered, with some families living there during the World War I era reportedly earning yearly incomes as high as $1,000 (Graves 1937, p. 15).

According to contemporary observers, the homes in Gee's Bend were simple but well maintained with clean yards and picket fences. The residents were reportedly hard working and the Sheriff of Wilcox County stated that no one from his office had made an arrest at the Bend in more than 30 years.

Declining cotton prices, resulting from the economic slowdown, brought hardship to the Bend. But for three years a local merchant agreed to advance the residents supplies against unsold cotton. When the sympathetic business-man died, his operation was liquidated and the residents of Gee's Bend lost everything as well.

The federal government purchased the Bend for $125,000 in 1937 and turned it into one of its resettlement projects. A community manager was appointed to provide technical assistance and to supervise the project. A cooperative was established that operated a retail store. A farming cooperative was set up to provide equipment, to purchase seed and fertilizer, and to market the crops grown by the families. A cotton gin, grist mill, and warehouse were also constructed and operated collectively.

New homes and outbuildings on five-acre plots were sold to the coopera-tive's members at favorable rates of interest. Each family was also given the option of leasing an additional 95 acres of farm land. 'The intent was for each household to become self-sufficient through farming, stock raising, and truck gardening' (Trend and Lett 1985, p. 6).

Although the setting of this effort was rather unusual, the results were not. The community store soon ran into trouble with 'dangerously high accounts receivable' (Trend and Lett 1985, p. 8); low inventory turnover was apparently at the heart of the problem. The farming component of the cooperative enterprise was headed toward bankruptcy as well. Before that point was reached, however, the organization had to be liquidated as a result of a fire that destroyed the community cotton gin.

Trend and Lett (1985) perform a cost–benefit analysis of the govern-ment's relief and reform efforts at the Bend. The results are clearly unfavor-able. 'From an efficiency point of view, Gee's Bend Farms was not a worthwhile investment for the government or for society. Even at [a] three percent rate of discount, the project loses two dollars for every one advanced' (Trend and Lett 1985, p. 19).

While the government probably did not waste any more of the taxpayers' money at Gee's Bend than it did on similar New Deal projects, the long-run consequences of the program are disturbing. Modern Boykin, Alabama, the new name recently given to the community, in no way resembles the area that existed prior to the Great Depression. 'A review of the 1980 Wilcox County public assistance rolls indicates that it is now likely that a majority of Boykin area households receive public assistance in the form of SSI payments, AFDC benefits, or subsidized work programs' (Trend and Lett 1985, pp. 22–23). To be sure, the New Deal's contribution to modern-day welfare dependency is debatable, but the history of Gee's Bend suggests that government attention did little to encourage the kind of self-reliance the residents once exhibited.

9   THE DISTRIBUTION OF RURAL RELIEF

Although their reasoning differs, most observers agree that the administration's overall efforts at alleviating rural poverty were ineffective. As Zinn (1966, p. 251) notes, 'the scale of operations was far too small to do more than attack the edge of the huge problem of rural poverty.'

Tables 3.4 and 3.5 show the distributions of RA and FSA loans and expenditures on a state-by-state basis. Dividing FSA funds by the states' respective farm populations in 1935 suggests that southern states received relatively few dollars from a program that was putatively directed at the South. Table 3.6 catalogs RA and FSA spending by census region. As shown, expenditures and loans in the Mountain Region were substantially higher than those in the other regions and, based on a statistical test of the differences between mean regional and national average FSA loans and expenditures per farmer, the difference is significant at a 99 percent level of confidence. No other region of the country exhibits FSA activity that differs significantly from the national average.

As will be seen in subsequent chapters, this pattern is typical of many New Deal programs. Certain regions of the country – particularly the Mountain and Pacific states – seem to have benefited disproportionately from the policies adopted by the Roosevelt administration to address the national economic crisis. Our goal is to identify the economic and political factors that underlie the observed distribution of New Deal funds.

The prevailing view is that the emergency measures adopted during the 1930s, which were implemented by somewhat imperfect but basically well-intentioned public servants, represented sincere efforts to provide relief. Mistakes may have been made, but the motives of the New Dealers were be-

Table 3.4 Total FSA expenditures per farmer, by state, 1933–39

South Dakota	$63.18	Maine	$6.85
Montana	62.63	Utah	6.77
Maryland	60.95	West Virginia	6.56
North Dakota	59.99	Missouri	5.96
New Jersey	26.52	Michigan	5.29
Wyoming	23.26	South Carolina	5.24
Rhode Island	22.54	Delaware	4.59
Arizona	21.87	New York	4.28
Wisconsin	18.57	North Carolina	4.16
Colorado	16.91	Louisiana	3.95
Florida	16.31	Illinois	3.87
New Mexico	16.10	Tennessee	3.82
Oregon	16.08	Indiana	3.71
Nebraska	14.93	Georgia	3.51
Ohio	14.37	Virginia	3.50
California	10.85	Pennsylvania	3.39
Nevada	10.72	Kentucky	3.43
Kansas	10.32	Mississippi	3.32
Idaho	8.74	Texas	3.33
Oklahoma	8.51	Connecticut	2.69
Alabama	8.12	Iowa	1.43
Washington	7.95	New Hampshire	0.89
Arkansas	7.93	Vermont	0.55
Minnesota	7.41	Massachusetts	0.43

yond reproach. However, a review of the Roosevelt administration's farm programs plants seeds of doubt about a model of government behavior which assumes that politicians and bureaucrats seek only to serve the public interest. Well meaning or not, these programs operated at cross-purposes, working to cut agricultural production on the one hand and to increase it on the other. These same programs displaced thousands of tenant farmers and sharecroppers; they encouraged the formation of resource-wasting cooperative enterprises and orchestrated agricultural cartels; and they distributed funds in ways that benefited those who needed it least.

Table 3.5 FSA loans per farmer, by state, 1933–39

Wyoming	$91.01	California	$11.99
Montana	46.83	Georgia	11.45
Nevada	42.46	South Carolina	10.65
Colorado	42.04	New Jersey	9.95
Utah	35.85	Minnesota	9.91
South Dakota	35.08	West Virginia	9.52
Idaho	28.72	Iowa	9.25
Maine	28.06	Rhode Island	9.08
North Dakota	24.37	Wisconsin	8.83
Nebraska	22.47	Illinois	8.30
New Mexico	18.51	Indiana	8.05
Florida	18.30	Vermont	7.95
Washington	17.65	Ohio	7.03
Kansas	17.61	Michigan	6.97
Oregon	17.23	North Carolina	6.56
Arizona	16.61	New York	5.40
Oklahoma	15.30	Tennessee	4.22
Arkansas	14.83	Virginia	4.13
New Hampshire	14.07	Massachusetts	4.06
Alabama	13.32	Kentucky	3.82
Louisiana	13.25	Connecticut	3.64
Texas	13.17	Pennsylvania	3.40
Mississippi	12.71	Maryland	2.70
Missouri	12.04	Delaware	2.36

An alternative approach to analyzing public policy was articulated in its modern form by George Stigler (1971). He insisted that the true intentions of a policy be uncovered by ignoring the stated goals and instead focusing on the actual effects. The next chapter begins following Stigler's lead by exploring the so-called First New Deal with an eye toward looking 'as precisely and carefully as we can, at who gain[ed] and who los[t], and how much' (Stigler 1975, p. 140).

Table 3.6 FSA loans and expenditures per farmer, by region, 1933–39

Region	Dollars	Z-Score[a]
New England	$15.39	0.53
Middle Atlantic	10.23	0.90
East North Central	17.27	0.41
West North Central	30.70	0.55
Pacific	25.80	0.20
South Atlantic	15.69	0.52
East South Central	13.33	0.69
West South Central	19.36	0.26
Mountain	59.54	2.60[b]

Notes:
a.   Difference in mean regional and national average per farmer FSA loans and expenditures.
b.   Significantly different from zero at the 1 percent level.

Source:
Office of Government Reports (1939).

NOTES

1.   Letter from the Progressive Southern Club to Governor Bibb Graves, Alabama Department of Archives and History, P. O. Box 300100, Montgomery, AL 36130 USA.
2.   Warm Springs was, of course, the location of FDR's 'Southern White House' and the place of his death.
3.   Because they create incentives much different from those created when property rights are well defined, economic theory predicts that collective ownership arrangements will be less efficient by market standards than private ownership arrangements. Whenever the rewards of collective effort are shared, rational individuals tend to engage in free-riding behavior – they seek to capture their share of the benefits produced by cooperation without contributing their share of the costs. When large numbers of the group free-ride, the quantity or quality of the group's output falls. Free-riding and overutilization of common-pool resources (the 'tragedy of the commons') dissipate the gains cooperation would otherwise yield.

4. The First New Deal

Our task is not discovery or exploitation of natural resources, or necessarily producing more goods. . . . It is the soberer, less dramatic business of administering resources and plants already in hand, of seeking to reestablish foreign markets for our surplus production, of meeting the problem of under-consumption, of adjusting production to consumption, of distributing wealth and production more equitably, of adapting existing economic organizations to the service of the people. The day of the enlightened administration has come.

           – Franklin Delano Roosevelt

We have reached the end of the pioneering period of go ahead and take. We are in the age of planning for the best of everything for all.
           – Harold Ickes

Why should the Russians have all the fun of remaking a world?
           – New Dealer Stuart Chase

The Great Depression opened a window of opportunity for those in the Roosevelt administration disdainful of *laissez-faire*. The federal government would not only expand its role in the agricultural sector but would take on the job of curing many of the private market economy's other perceived ills as well. Poverty and unemployment, worker training and career counseling, industrial planning, and the regulation of business – these were all to become public responsibilities.

This chapter investigates the programs of the so-called First New Deal, which began in March of 1933, and lasted till the Supreme Court's 1935 *Schecter* decision consigned its legislative centerpiece, the National Industrial Recovery Act (NIRA), to history's dustbin. The discussion begins with a brief overview of the ideological foundations on which much of the administration's policy agenda rested. By way of introduction, the major programs utilized by the First New Deal to inject money into the economy, their chief objectives, and the total amount spent by each of them over the entire New Deal period are shown in Table 4.1. (Some of these programs, such as the Reconstruction Finance Corporation, had been launched before FDR took office; most continued to be funded beyond 1935.)

Table 4.1 Spending Conduits of the First New Deal

Program	Expenditures (1933–39)	Objective
Reconstruction Finance Corporation	$4,725,246,822.00	Made loans to banks, certain corporations, and other New Deal agencies.
Public Works Administration	3,935,112,403.00	Financed large-scale public works projects 'of lasting social value'.
Civilian Conservation Corps	2,181,515,868.00	Employed youths to conduct conservation activities.
Home Owners Loan Corporation	3,422,507,798.00	Purchased mortgages from note holders in financial distress and renegotiated terms.
Federal Housing Authority	2,687,284,051.00	Provided insurance to mortgage bankers on loans made for building repair or new construction.
Federal Emergency Relief Administration	3,017,454,557.00	Furnished direct relief and work relief to needy and distressed people.
Civil Works Administration	807,263,411.00	Provided work relief through the winter of 1933–34.
Bureau of Public Roads	1,612,468,019.00	Built and repaired roads and highways. (Was not a New Deal agency but was utilized to provide work relief.)
Bureau of Reclamation	291,398,502.00	Engaged in construction activities to bring water to the arid West.

Table 4.1 (continued)

| Veterans Administration | 3,961,363,619.00 | Provided pensions to veterans, built and ran veterans' hospitals. |

Source:
Reading (1972).

1 THE IDEOLOGY OF THE FIRST NEW DEAL

While industrial production had fallen precipitously, President Roosevelt did not at first intend to respond to that important set of problems in the special legislative session he convened immediately after taking the oath of office. Rather, he thought that raising farmers' incomes and, hence, restoring the purchasing power of the agricultural sector would be sufficient to jump-start the economy. A bill sponsored by Senator Hugo Black of Alabama limiting hours worked to 30 per week, however, prompted the president to act more quickly. Preferring legislation that afforded him wider authority, FDR decided to push Congress to address industrial recovery more broadly (McElvaine 1984, p. 156).

In formulating this legislation, the administration was pulled in opposite directions by the advocates of two very different strategies. One of these groups, believing that excessive industrial concentration had precipitated the downturn, sought to promote competition by using the antitrust laws to break up America's giant corporations. The other group, convinced that large-scale enterprises were both inevitable and desirable for efficiency reasons, called for economic planning by the central government to control their excesses (Bernstein 1987, p. 186). 'When asked if he [Roosevelt] believed in Louis Brandeis' emphasis upon competition as the way to control business, he answered that Brandeis was "one thousand per cent right in principle – but at times government had to step in to regulate too"' (Degler 1970, p. 17).

The early legislative program, known to many scholars as the First New Deal, was largely shaped by the planners. The resulting 'strange brew of New Deal policy' (Bernstein 1987, p. 186) reflected the anti-market leanings of Rexford Guy Tugwell – an institutional economist from Columbia University. 'Tugwell is often considered the architect of the first New Deal' (Conkin 1975, p. 35).[1]

Tugwell's 'policies suggested enough varied controls to frighten almost everyone' (Conkin 1975, p. 36). He expressed little faith in the price system's ability to direct the allocation of resources:

> The truth is that profits persuade us to speculate; they induce us to allocate funds where we believe the future price situation will be favorable; they therefore have a considerable effect on the distribution of capital among various enterprises – an effect which seems clearly enough inefficient so that other methods might easily be better. (Tugwell 1932, p. 80)

Central planning was superior to the price system as a method of achieving efficient resource use in Tugwell's view. He stated that 'the deadliest and most subtle enemy of speculative profit-making which could be devised would be an implemented scheme for planning production' (Tugwell 1932, p. 83). Investment decisions by business firms in a free-market society were, according to Tugwell, made on the narrow basis of profit-seeking, an objective that left little or no room for overarching national interests. National goals could therefore only be achieved if investment decisions were coordinated by cadres of industrial planners.

Tugwell and the other advocates of central planning placed blame for the depression 'on the tendency of large firms to engage in distorted investment decision making' (Bernstein 1987, p. 190): 'Capital tied up in slowly growing industries did not necessarily move into industries with faster rates of growth, because privately based expenditure decisions were uncoordinated and often chaotic' (Bernstein 1987, p. 190).

Speculation, the impetus for which was greed and avarice, would be brought under control. 'The traditional incentives, hope of money-making and fear of money loss, will be weakened; and a kind of civil-service loyalty and fervor will need to grow gradually into acceptance' (Tugwell 1932, p. 90). Innovation, largely disjointed in a capitalistic economy, would be coordinated and planned. 'New industries will not just happen as the automobile industry did; they will have to be foreseen, to be argued for' and to hold the promise of 'desirable features of the whole economy before they can be entered upon' (Tugwell 1932, p. 90).

Embracing this anti-market ideology, the Roosevelt administration placed much hope in the central government's ability to produce favorable results, unlike the unregulated market-based economy which had, according to its critics, produced the worst depression in the nation's history. The New Deal – especially so the National Industrial Recovery Act – was heavily influenced by the nostrum of central planning, but the administration's legislative program was shaped by many other elements.

Core beliefs aside, in a representative democracy politicians must stand for reelection. As McElvaine (1984, p. 157) admits, 'most of the New Deal was the result of political and not economic thought'. No single philosophy or individual was responsible for all of the legislation passed during the 1930s.

> Some New Deal programs were established to meet a specific emergency; others were directed toward aiding depressed areas for the duration of the depression; still others were permanent and lasting. Some programs were the creation of New Deal planners; others were holdovers from the previous administration. (Reading 1972, p. 7)

Indeed, the Roosevelt administration utilized many existing programs – the Bureau of Public Roads and the Bureau of Reclamation, to name two – to provide employment opportunities for the millions who were unable to find work (Reading 1972, p. 7). The New Dealers also inherited two precursor pieces of legislation enacted during Herbert Hoover's term of office, namely the Reconstruction Finance Act and the Emergency Relief and Construction Act of 1932 (Hosen 1992, p. 9).

The following sections discuss these legislative initiatives along with other measures comprising the programs of the First New Deal which, for the most part, dealt with issues outside the agricultural sector. Other than Title I of the National Industrial Recovery Act, the administration's chief foray into the realm of central planning, the administration's regulatory policy agenda is avoided in this discussion.[2] Attention is focused almost exclusively on the New Deal's spending programs.

2 THE RECONSTRUCTION FINANCE CORPORATION

The Reconstruction Finance Corporation (RFC) was created on 22 January 1932, with authority to make loans to various types of financial institutions and, in some cases, to railroads engaged in interstate commerce (Hosen 1992, p. 2). It was hoped that the availability of additional credit would stimulate the business sector and, thus, increase output and employment.

The legislation establishing the RFC was supported by President Hoover and enacted during his administration's final year. With some modifications, the agency continued to operate under FDR. As noted by Herbert Stein (1984, p. 33), the formation of this emergency relief program represents 'an action so at odds with the cliché image of Hoover that most people forget it was Hoover who did it'. The program would utilize the private sector to channel additional funds into the economy, thereby restoring business confidence.

'Believing confidence to be central to recovery and credit to confidence, the President was sincere in his advocacy of the RFC' (McElvaine 1984, p. 89).

The purpose of the legislation was set forth in section 5 of the Reconstruction Finance Act:

> To aid in financing agriculture, commerce, and industry, including facilitating the exportation of agricultural and other products, the corporation is authorized and empowered to make loans . . . to any bank, savings bank, trust company, building and loan association, insurance company, mortgage loan company, credit union, Federal land bank, joint-stock land bank, Federal intermediate credit bank, agricultural credit corporation, livestock credit corporation, organized under the laws of any State or of the United States. . . . (Hosen 1992, p. 4)

Concern over the mounting federal deficit led the Hoover administration to establish the RFC as an off-budget item, so that its expenditures would not add to the government's current outlays (Williams 1994, p. 159). The RFC was bankrolled initially with a Treasury contribution of $500 million, with authority to borrow $1.5 billion more from it or from other lenders (Williams 1994, p. 159).

During its first year of operation, the RFC primarily made loans to railways, relieving 'some of the biggest banks of some of their most problematic assets – railroad bonds' (Todd 1992, p. 24). Thereafter, the agency extended credit to other industries in an attempt to encourage new construction and modernization (Todd 1992, p. 24).

The financial disarray triggered by the national liquidity crisis and the subsequent runs on bank deposits prompted the RFC to 'authorize loans in the aggregate amount of $1,334,822,736 to 5,817 banks, principally in the years 1932 and 1933' (Office of Government Reports 1939, p. 93). Loans amounting to some $1,339,457,524 were also made and distributed to the depositors of closed banks. It has been estimated that 20 million depositors benefited from this action, receiving, on the average, 65 percent of their deposits in failed financial institutions (Office of Government Reports 1939, p. 93). The RFC loans enabled the banks to compensate at least partially 'a multitude of families and small businesses who were in distress because their deposits were tied up pending liquidation or reorganization of these banks' (Todd 1992, p. 24).

But with little apparent improvement in the economy, Hoover supported and signed the Emergency Relief and Construction Act of July 1932. The measure provided $300 million to the RFC for extending credit to state and local governments (Charles 1963, p. 16). The loans were to be used 'in furnishing relief and work relief to needy and distressed people and in relieving the hardship resulting from unemployment' (Hosen 1992, p. 16).

The Emergency Reconstruction Relief Act is noteworthy in that it marked the beginning of the federal government's involvement in the relief picture in a major way. The funds advanced to the states were to be repaid through deductions from future federal highway grants (Office of Government Reports 1939, p. 73). The legislation authorized the RFC to provide funds for certain types of construction project in an effort to create employment opportunities (Hosen 1992, p. 24).

The inauguration of Franklin Roosevelt in March 1933 initiated a number of changes in the RFC's mode of operation. Among the most important of these was the cancellation of the requirement that the funds advanced to states be repaid. Jesse Jones, a businessman from Houston, Texas, was installed as the agency's chairman. Under Jones, the RFC began purchasing the preferred stock of banks in order to help alleviate their pressing capital needs. 'The Corporation authorized the purchase of preferred stock or notes and loans upon stock of 6,861 banks in the aggregate amount of $1,395,702,589' (Office of Government Reports 1939, p. 93). Presumably, 'this [action] increased the liquid capital of banks and thus indirectly permitted an increase in lending' (Reading 1972, p. 107).

The perception that the RFC revived the banking industry during the 1930s is most likely inaccurate. As McKenzie (1985, p. 86) notes, the additional funds made available to financial institutions during the depression 'were overwhelmed by the one-third contraction in the money stock engineered by the Federal Reserve between 1929 and 1933. The less than $1 billion lent by the RFC . . . was a drop in the bucket when compared with the 50 percent contraction in gross national product between 1929 and 1933.'

RFC loans were used by numerous other agencies in a multitude of ways. Loans amounting to $143,616,495 were made to more than 600 drainage, levee, and irrigation districts for the purpose of refinancing outstanding indebtedness (Office of Government Reports 1939, p. 94). The RFC helped finance myriad construction projects, including the San Francisco-Oakland Bay Bridge, an almost 250-mile-long aqueduct carrying water from the Colorado River to southern California, and a power line from Boulder Dam to Los Angeles (Office of Government Reports 1939, p. 94). Nearly $850 million was loaned to 84 railroads, and funds in excess of $500 million were made available to other business organizations (Office of Government Reports 1939, p. 94). Included among these were loans to insurance companies and mining interests. Other New Deal agencies also received RFC funds. The Rural Electrification Administration, for example, was loaned $146,500,000 (Office of Government Reports 1939, p. 95).

1. Subsidiaries of the RFC

The RFC established subsidiaries to provide credit to other sectors of the economy. These included the RFC Mortgage Company, the Electric Home and Farm Authority (EHFA), and the Disaster Loan Corporation. At the outset, the RFC made loans for the repairing of property damaged by such natural disasters as tornadoes, hurricanes, and floods. In February of 1937, the Disaster Loan Corporation was formed for the same purpose. The managers of this subsidiary corporation were appointed by the RFC.

The RFC Mortgage Company was organized on 14 March 1935 to help reestablish the market for mortgages on income-producing properties located in urban areas (Office of Government Reports 1939, p. 96). The company made loans, secured by first mortgages, on real property such as apartment houses, office buildings, and hotels if the venture was considered reasonably safe. In some cases, the company also financed new construction projects.

The EHFA was established on 17 January 1934. Its purpose was to encourage the purchase of modern appliances and other electrical devices. It purchased consumer credit contracts from retail appliance dealers and contracted with local utility companies to collect the payments. Attic ventilating fans, clothes ironers, washing machines, refrigerators, radios, ranges, vacuum cleaners, milking machines, and water heaters were among the items whose purchase was financed by the EHFA. Through similar arrangements, the agency financed the electrical wiring and re-wiring of thousands of homes and farms. Through June 1939, the EHFA had purchased in excess of 130,000 consumer credit contracts amounting to over $20,000,000 (Office of Government Reports 1939, p. 98).

2. The Economic Impact of the RFC

Chairman Jones embraced more of a free-market philosophy than most of the New Dealers and hoped to utilize the RFC in such ways as to produce 'outcomes roughly analogous to those that would have been expected had the markets been left alone' (Todd 1992, p. 26). However, by providing credit only to the customers of established firms, potential entrants were placed at a disadvantage. As such, 'from a normal, free-market, procompetitive perspective, the RFC was interventionist and anticompetitive, providing subsidized credit to existing businesses that was unavailable to new entrants into those lines of business' (Todd 1992, p. 27).

The RFC's purposes and effects have been criticized along other lines as well. First, requiring banks to use their most valuable assets to secure loans from the agency prevented these assets from being used as collateral to obtain funds from other sources. What is more important, the public came to view RFC loans to a financial institution as a sign of weakness and reacted by withdrawing their deposits from institutions obtaining such loans (McKenzie 1985, p. 86).

The RFC survived into the 1950s, when a number of scandals led to the agency's abolishment.[3] Many of the RFC's activities are nevertheless still being carried out by a variety of other government agencies – the Export-Import Bank and the Small Business Administration, to name two (McKenzie 1984, p. 90).

3 THE NATIONAL INDUSTRIAL RECOVERY ACT

As mentioned at the chapter's outset, FDR was pressured by a bill introduced by Senator Hugo Black into sponsoring legislation dealing with industrial recovery. The president broached the ideas of government aid for industry and economic planning during the second of his fireside chats on 7 May 1933 (Schlesinger 1958, p. 98).

The bill that followed was known as the National Industrial Recovery Act (NIRA), an 'ambiguous, catchall piece of legislation' (McElvaine 1984, p. 157). The measure took interventionist ideas from everyone:

> From business hopes for protection of prices and profits, from trade union hopes for protection of labor standards, from liberal hopes for creative national planning, from a collective revulsion against a competitive system which competed at the expense of human decency – opinion was converging on a broad approach to the problem of industrial recovery. (Schlesinger 1958, p. 94)

Passed on 16 June 1933, the National Industrial Recovery Act contained two major provisions. Title I proposed collectivist solutions to revive the US industrial sector while Title II established a public works agency to carry out construction projects. As Tindall (1967, p. 433) cogently explains, the legislation's 'purposes, briefly stated, were twofold: to stabilize business by codes of "fair" competitive practice, and to get more purchasing power into the market by assuring employment, defining labor standards, and raising wages'.

Title I of the NIRA opened with the following 'Declaration of Policy':

> A national emergency productive of widespread unemployment and disorganization of industry, which burdens interstate and foreign commerce, affects the public welfare, and undermines the standards of living of the American people, is hereby declared to exist. (Hosen 1992, p. 194)

Far from being a statement of the obvious, the preamble's language suggests that Washington had learned the lesson taught by World War I, namely that crisis conditions stifle opposition to expansions of government power (Higgs 1987). The legislation went on sweepingly to state that it was the policy of Congress to

> provide for the general welfare by promoting the organization of industry for the purpose of cooperative action among trade groups, to induce and maintain united action of labor and management under adequate government sanctions and supervision, to eliminate unfair competitive practices, to promote the fullest possible utilization of the present productive capacity of industries, to avoid undue restriction of production (except as may be temporarily required), to increase the consumption of industrial and agricultural products by increasing purchasing power, to reduce and relieve unemployment, to improve standards of labor, and otherwise to rehabilitate industry and to conserve natural resources. (Hosen 1992, p. 195)

Section 3(a) gave the president authority to 'approve a code or codes of fair competition for the trade or industry' (Hosen 1992, p. 195). Those industries whose codes won presidential approval were also granted exemptions from key provisions of the antitrust laws. Under section 3(b), the approved codes became the 'standards of fair competition for the trade' (Hosen 1992, p. 196), while section 3(f) declared code violations to be a misdemeanor and provided that, 'upon conviction thereof an offender shall be fined not more than $500 for each offense and each day such violation continues shall be deemed a separate offense' (Hosen 1992, p. 197). Section 7(a) was designed to win the support of organized labor; it called for collective bargaining, maximum hours of work, and minimum wages.

Authority to create a Federal Emergency Administration of Public Works (Public Works Administration, or PWA) was delegated to the president by Title II. Section 202 of the act specified the types of project the agency was empowered to undertake: construction and repair of public highways, public buildings and facilities, harbors, and low-cost housing; installation of electrical transmission lines; conservation of natural resources; and slum clearance (Hosen 1992, p. 202).

FDR appointed General Hugh Johnson to head the National Recovery Administration (NRA), the agency created to implement the NIRA. As Arthur Schlesinger notes, Johnson adopted the position that he should control all of the activities authorized by the law. He argued forcefully that the industrial planning provisions (Title I) and the public works provisions (Title II) of the NIRA complemented each other and should therefore be coordinated to encourage recovery.[4] The president, on the other hand, conceived of the PWA as a temporary agency that would last only as long as the economic emergency. He expected the NRA to become a permanent Washington fixture, though, forever altering the federal government's role in the free-market economy. Heeding the president's preference for dividing up the administrative responsibilities, Roosevelt's cabinet concurred wholeheartedly with that plan, 'happy at the chance to whittle down a noncabinet rival' (Schlesinger 1958, p. 104).

Although disappointed by the decision and harboring some reservations, Johnson agreed to head the NRA. The Secretary of the Interior, Harold Ickes, was directed to administer the public works program. Against Johnson's wishes, there was no coordination between the two agencies and, in fact, Ickes 'actually directed his subordinates not even to consult the General' (Schlesinger 1958, p. 109).

As mentioned earlier, the NRA exempted signers from the antitrust laws, enabling firms to engage in what otherwise would have amounted to illegal collusion. Johnson tirelessly negotiated codes of conduct with businesses and trade associations establishing maximum hours of work, minimum wages, and minimum prices. 'By February [of 1934], 557 "codes of fair competition", covering even the most trivial of industries were in use' (Williams 1994, p. 184).

Ever the promoter, Johnson wanted an eye-catching symbol to represent the program. He ultimately settled on the famous Blue Eagle and the slogan, 'We Do Our Part'. The Blue Eagle symbol was attached to products and displayed in store windows to signify support for 'fair competition'. The General hoped that non-participants – they were called 'slackers', a term apparently first applied during World War I to young men who were not anxious to discharge their patriotic duties in the mud of France – would thereby be identified and pressured into joining. Herbert Hoover was among the many who signed up (Schlesinger 1958, p. 115).

The General, aware of the benefits of good public relations and desiring to build additional support, assembled the largest parade New York City had yet seen in September of 1933. Nevertheless, the program was not approved by everyone. Asked about the Blue Eagle, Henry Ford remarked, 'Hell, that Roosevelt buzzard! I wouldn't put that on my car' (McElvaine 1984, p. 160).

There is a fairly broad consensus that the NRA codes of fair competition were nothing more than government-sanctioned price-fixing schemes.[5] By 1935, '568 out of the over 700 codes had one form or another of minimum-price provision' (Schlesinger 1958, p. 125). The most popular methods of establishing minimum prices were proscriptions on selling at prices below 'cost' (Williams 1994, p. 184). Five of the codes called for the basing-point system of calculating delivered prices (prices inclusive of shipping charges), which results in all sellers quoting the same price to any one customer and which is generally thought to be a strategy for maintaining higher prices (Schlesinger 1958, p. 125).[6] Production quotas were established by 'regulating hours of machine operation' or through 'imposed restrictions on new plant and equipment' (Schlesinger 1958, p. 125).

In general, larger business firms tended to praise the activities of the NRA while smaller firms began to question its purpose. As Bernstein (1987, p. 197) contends, because 'NRA code authorities were dominated by older firms within older industries, there was an inherent bias toward aiding slow-growth activities'. The NRA's advocates simply asserted that big business, by supporting the program, demonstrated greater sophistication and enlightenment.

However, the legislation clearly created winners and losers. Some industries and regions of the country benefited from the measures while others were placed at a disadvantage. Southern textile mills, for example, were more mechanized and more efficient than their rivals located in the Northeast. Controlled in large part by the latter interests, the codes wiped out many of the advantages enjoyed by the southern mills:

> The 80-hour limit on operations curtailed activity in the South while New England mills expanded their production. One mill at Easley, South Carolina, reduced its total operating hours from 128 in May to 80 in August. Its total payroll went from $10,131.40 to $11,889.40 but its working force dropped from 1,399 to 1,036. (Tindall 1967, p. 436)

As a result of the pressures the textile codes imposed on them, the southern mills eventually 'broke with the rest of the industry over the NRA and sought to pursue their own course' (Bernstein 1987, p. 201).

The petroleum industry provides another example of intra-industry redistribution at work. Large producers favored the NRA codes regulating output while their smaller rivals saw the codes as restricting their ability to compete (Bernstein 1987, p. 201).

The government's industrial policy during the Great Depression was predictably counterproductive. 'Governments are dreadful judges of commercial opportunities' (Kealey 1996, p. 204). They are too distant from the market, too short-sighted, and too vulnerable to pressure-group demands to be expected to allocate resources to their highest valued uses. 'Code authorities were ill-equipped to choose among alternative investments' (Bernstein 1987, p. 196). Far from directing resources toward new and dynamic market opportunities that would expand output and employment, inefficiency was rewarded. There is reason to believe that the codes actually hindered recovery.

The NRA became the subject of mounting criticism. 'Huey Long and some labor leaders began saying that the agency's initials stood for "National Run Around"; William Randolph Hearst's version was "No Recovery Allowed"' (McElvaine 1984, p. 160). Repeated complaints led the administration to establish a National Recovery Review Board (NRRB) to investigate the economic impact of the codes. One of the era's most famous lawyers, Clarence Darrow, was named as the NRRB's chairman and an unfavorable report was subsequently submitted by the board.

Lack of observable results and persistent attacks on the NRA eventually took its toll on Hugh Johnson. He 'became increasingly unstable psychologically disappearing for days on drunken binges' (Williams 1994, p. 186). Johnson nevertheless continued to defend his program and fought back, directing his ire at his most influential critic, Clarence Darrow, about whom he had this to say:

> Nobody in the world was ever more adept in convincing twelve men that another man who had bombed somebody, or poisoned somebody . . . or with psychopathic urge, had taken a little boy into the Michigan dunes and beaten the life out of him, hadn't either bombed, or poisoned . . . or beaten anybody. (Schlesinger 1958, p. 134)

The Darrow report generated a new round of attacks. Agricultural interests complained that their gains in purchasing power were being wiped out by increased prices for industrial goods (Williams 1994, p. 186). Even the PWA was critical of the NRA's impact on the construction industry, which raised the costs of public works projects (Schlesinger 1958, p. 135). Hugh Johnson resigned his position in September of 1934, to be replaced by a five-member board. The NRA was disbanded when the Supreme Court declared the National Industrial Recovery Act unconstitutional in its *Schecter* decision,[7] handed down in May 1935 (McElvaine 1984, p. 162).

History has not been kind to the NRA: 'By almost any reckoning, the NRA was a colossal failure' (McElvaine 1984, p. 161). Recently, however, scholars have begun reevaluating the program's effects. Several empirical issues remain unresolved. First, industrial output apparently rose before the codes went into effect. 'The index of factory production, which had hit a low of 56 in March, rose to 101 in July 1933' (McElvaine 1984, p. 160). One explanation for this unexpected finding is that firms anticipated the passage of the legislation and responded by building up their inventories before the NRA substantially increased labor costs. Second, although from July through December of 1933, the six-month period following the NIRA's passage, overall production dropped 25 percent (Williams 1994, p. 189), when other factors are controlled for, outputs in many of the code-dominated industries, especially those engaged in the manufacture of durable goods, boomed during the NRA era (Bittlingmayer 1995). This evidence is of course inconsistent with the idea that the codes of fair competition facilitated industrial cartelization.[8] The jury is still out, though.

4 THE PUBLIC WORKS ADMINISTRATION

Title II of the National Industrial Recovery Act gave President Roosevelt authority to 'create a Federal Emergency Administration of Public Works' (Hosen 1992, p. 201). This provision established the Public Works Administration (PWA) and provided \$3.3 billion in start-up funding. The PWA was placed in the Department of the Interior under the direction of Secretary Harold Ickes.

The underlying strategy was to attack the problem of chronic unemployment directly by coming to the aid of the many workers who had lost jobs in the highly cyclical construction industry. Such action, it was believed, would also stimulate hiring in the heavy manufacturing industries:

> Contractors and builders, workers in the building trades, and employees normally at work in factories fabricating building materials were widely unemployed. Construction was more severely depressed than any other major American industry. As an inevitable consequence, the heavy industries were also depressed. (Office of Government Reports 1939, p. 86)

In the early years of the New Deal, the PWA was on the front line of the administration's efforts to end the depression (McElvaine 1984, p. 152).

The agency was authorized to spend money in a variety of ways in order to jump-start the depressed construction industry.

> It could initiate its own projects as a construction agency. It could make allotments to enable other federal agencies to carry on construction work. It could offer a combination of loans and grants to states and other public bodies to stimulate nonfederal construction. And, for a time, it could make loans to certain private corporations. (Schlesinger 1958, p. 284)

In contrast to other New Deal work relief programs, the PWA did not hire unemployed workers directly – the monies were normally channeled through private contractors. In a bow to organized labor, workers were to be paid the 'prevailing wage' in the area of the project. Projects were supposed to be selected and administered 'in such a way as to relieve unemployment in areas where the employment situation had become serious' (Office of Government Reports 1939, p. 87).

Non-federal projects were funded through grants to state and local governments. The Public Works Administration initially contributed 30 percent of the projects' costs but that percentage was later raised to 45 percent. The remaining cost share (70 percent or 55 percent depending on when the project was begun) was the responsibility of the sponsoring agency (Office of Government Reports 1939, p. 87).

The projects, whether federal or non-federal, were ostensibly to be of lasting social value. Whether or not one agrees that the public works financed by the PWA met this criterion, the sponsored projects were frequently technically complex. And because of this, the PWA devoted more of its resources to purchasing materials and to employing skilled workers than subsequent work relief programs. 'Much of the PWA appropriation went for materials, architects, engineers, and skilled workers. All this was to the long-term good' (McElvaine 1984, p. 152). Maybe so; it was undoubtedly to the short-term good of the craftsmen and the materials suppliers.

The nature of the projects selected did contribute to one criticism of the program, though. The PWA was painfully slow in actually breaking ground. Complicated construction jobs of the sort undertaken by the agency required long lead times for surveys, blueprints, and procurement (Schlesinger 1958, p. 286).

The delays inherent in this type of work were exacerbated by the administrative style of Harold Ickes – methodical, by all accounts. He wanted public employment to be a permanent feature of the American economy and, thus, was perceived as being circumspect in spending the taxpayers' money. According to one admirer, 'Ickes required careful planning of projects, jealously guarded against waste and political influence, and eventually secured the maximum benefits from always too limited funds' (Conkin 1975, p. 32).

Despite its slow start, the PWA was ultimately responsible for a staggering array of public works projects. Some 70 percent of all new educational buildings constructed between 1933 and 1939 were built by the PWA (McElvaine 1984, p. 152). Numerous ships and submarines, including the aircraft carriers *Yorktown* and *Enterprise,* were PWA projects (Schlesinger 1958, p. 287). Many well-known structures and engineering landmarks were the work of the agency; among these are the 100-mile long causeway from the coast of Florida to Key West, the Grand Coulee and Bonneville dams, and the Triborough Bridge in New York City (McElvaine 1984, p. 153). The PWA was involved in urban renewal, slum clearance and low-cost housing construction (Office of Government Reports 1939, p. 88). In addition, the agency loaned over $200 million to railroads for 'modernization of trains and rails, electrification of through routes and the improvement of rolling stock' (Office of Government Reports 1939, p. 87).

From the program's beginning through 30 June 1939, some 34,476 projects were funded by the PWA – 17,819 federal and 16,657 non-federal (Office of Government Reports 1939, p. 87). Over the same period, the PWA's total expenditures, including both operating and administrative expense items, amounted to some $5,183,988,149. Wages contributed $1,464,911,460 to the total and materials costs accounted for another $2,823,375,990 (Office of Government Reports 1939, p. 88). Hence, though many of the PWA's projects were undoubtedly useful, they proved to be very expensive, costing more than $150,000 each, on the average.

Lack of additional appropriations in 1939 meant that the program came to an end. 'The 1938 PWA Act required that all projects allotted under the Act be completed by June 30, 1940 and the program was phased out' (Office of Government Reports 1939, p. 88).

Measured in absolute terms, the northeast region of the country received the most generous allocation of PWA funds while the southern states received the least. As with many other New Deal programs, however, the western states appear to have captured the lion's share when PWA spending is calculated on a per-capita basis. Montana, in particular, received more than twice the amount allocated to any other state (Reading 1972, p. 65).

5 THE CIVILIAN CONSERVATION CORPS

Relief programs targeting the nation's youth were among the most popular items on the New Dealers' policy agenda. The Civilian Conservation Corps (CCC) and the National Youth Administration were the administration's main efforts along these lines. The National Youth Administration – a program of the Second New Deal – will be discussed in the next chapter.

FDR is credited by his many admirers with believing strongly that the conservation of natural resources should be promoted by the federal government whenever possible. Coupled with the problem of widespread unemployment, this belief led the president to propose the Civilian Conservation Corps. Jobless, unmarried men between the ages of 18 and 25 were to be sent into the nation's forests to plant trees and to perform other conservation activities. Robert Fechner was appointed director of the Corps.

The bill establishing the CCC was passed in March of 1933. Other government agencies were to assist it in carrying out its work, with the Labor Department recruiting participants, the War Department constructing and running the camps, and the Department of Agriculture and the Department of the Interior jointly supervising the conservation projects (Schlesinger 1958,

p. 337). Directing the work programs from Interior were the National Park Service, the General Land Office, the Grazing Service, the Bureau of Reclamation, the Bureau of Biological Survey, and the Office of Indian Affairs. Among the bureaus of the Department of Agriculture involved were the US Forest Service, the Soil Conservation Service, and the Bureau of Entomology (Office of Government Reports 1939, p. 51).

As of April 1939, nearly 2.5 million young men had rotated through the CCC's camps. During its six years of operation, the agency claimed to have taught more than 75,000 illiterates to read and write and to have provided job training to 1,850,000 participants (Office of Government Reports 1939, p. 52). Each corpsman signed up for a period of 18 months and was paid, in addition to food and lodging, $30 per month – three-fourths of which was required to be sent to his family (Degler 1970, p. 125).

Despite its popularity, the program faced some opposition, especially from organized labor. Union leaders expressed concern that the relatively low pay offered to the participants would depress wages in the private sector. Some critics on the extreme left said that the CCC amounted to forced labor (Schlesinger 1958, p. 337). Others were frightened by the social consequences of massing armies of the unemployed in the nation's forests. In light of events taking place in Europe, the Assistant Secretary of War, Harry Woodring, did not do much to assuage these fears when he commented that he would organize the CCC into a system of 'economic storm troops' (Schlesinger 1958, p. 339).

The Roosevelt administration was quick to capitalize on widespread approval of the CCC by trumpeting its accomplishments. A contemporary description of a 'typical' CCC camp in northern Georgia was infused with bucolic charm:

> Buildings of unpainted wood, but the door and window frames are touched with color. Whitewashed stones border the road that comes to an end in this remote work settlement. Walks paved with stones taken from the hills connect most of the structures: infirmary, recreation hall, officers' quarters, garage. And there is a log schoolhouse built from the trees of the forest by the labor of the men. (Hill [1937] 1970, pp. 121–22)

Taking the government's own account at face value, the record of the CCC workers was indeed impressive: corpsmen planted 1,741,000,000 trees and acted to eradicate tree diseases and pests on 22,587,918 acres of land. To aid in protecting the nation's forests from fire, 104,000 miles of truck trails were blazed and over 4,000 fire towers were built. To control soil erosion, CCC workers fashioned over 22,000 miles of terraces. The Corps worked in 1,000 state and national parks, clearing footpaths and building bridges, cabins, and picnic areas (Office of Government Reports 1939, p. 53).[9]

The CCC not only took credit for its conservation activities, but also boasted of the beneficial changes wrought in the program's participants:

> The CCC considers one of its greatest accomplishments to be the physical and mental improvement apparent in the young men who have passed through its ranks. All youths in the camps have had the opportunity to learn how to work, the benefits of education and training that would otherwise have been denied them, the chance to be self supporting and to aid their families, and have received the benefits of regular hours, good food, shelter and splendid leadership, all of which have aided them in becoming more self reliant and better citizens. (Office of Government Reports 1939, p. 54)

According to the CCC's champions, the outdoor work was sometimes demanding, but it built up the men physically while the classroom learning opportunities provided further developed their mental skills and abilities. The popularity of the education and job training offered at the camps was demonstrated by the fact that over 60 percent of the workers participated in such programs (Hill [1937] 1970, p. 124).

The 'physical and mental improvement' of the participants is impossible to gauge, and was, most likely, overstated by the New Dealers. However, the overall cost of the program is known. It was expensive. In total, the CCC spent more than $2 billion between 1933 and 1939. Once again, the western states received the most generous allocations, measured absolutely and on a per-capita basis (Reading 1972, p. 54). Nevada, for instance, received almost twice as much as any other state (Reading 1972, p. 56). It must be pointed out, though, that not all of the money remained in the state to which it was initially distributed because participants were not necessarily residents of the state in which their camp was located. (Recall that a substantial portion of the CCC worker's pay had to be sent home to his family.) Nevertheless, the economic and political benefits of having a campsite in one's state were obvious and CCC facilities were competed for vigorously.

6 HOUSING SUBSIDIES

The New Deal addressed the problems of the nation's housing industry through a variety of programs offering guaranteed loans, grants, and mortgage insurance. As the depression deepened, the housing market was hit hard, variously being 'described as "frozen", "stagnant", "disappeared", "distressed", or "collapsed". As a result, it was reported that new home construction in 1933 represented only 10% of its 1925 level' (Lloyd 1994, p. 62). The crisis created by the near total drought in housing starts was reinforced by an alarming number of foreclosures. 'In early 1933, foreclosures were taking place at a rate of more than a thousand a day' (Schlesinger 1958, p. 297). Such a large number of mortgage defaults put heavy pressure on the financial institutions carrying the notes.

In response, the Reconstruction Finance Corporation (RFC) loaned over $350 million to private mortgage companies in an effort to prevent failure and to allow them to grant payment extensions to borrowers. Almost $120 million was disbursed to building and loan associations so that foreclosure rates might be reduced (Office of Government Reports 1939, p. 95). In addition, as discussed previously, the RFC Mortgage Company was set up to finance urban income-producing properties such as apartment buildings, hotels, and office buildings. The agency made loans to holders of first mortgage real estate bonds in financial difficulty; it purchased outright mortgages meeting certain criteria as well (Office of Government Reports 1939, p. 96).

The Public Works Administration (PWA) also intervened by engaging in slum clearance and low-cost housing construction activities. These projects, 51 in all, were transferred in October 1937 to the newly created United States Housing Authority (USHA), an agency authorized by the United States Housing Act of 1937 (Wagner–Steagall Bill). In addition to completing the projects begun by the PWA, the USHA made grants and loans to local public housing authorities. The purpose of these grants was 'to assist in the development, acquisition, or administration of low-rent housing or slum-clearance' and to promote 'the maintenance of the low-rent character of such projects' (Office of Government Reports 1939, p. 89). Local housing authorities were required to contribute sums equal to at least 20 percent of the funds they obtained from the USHA, and they were obligated to take steps to improve or remove unsafe dwellings in the area surrounding USHA-funded projects.

Additional housing legislation followed quickly on the heels of President Roosevelt's inauguration. The Home Owners' Loan Act was passed on 13 June 1933, creating the Home Owners' Loan Corporation (HOLC) and the Federal Savings and Loan Association (Hosen 1992, p. 144).

The HOLC purchased mortgages from note holders in financial trouble and then renegotiated the terms of the loans – lengthening repayment schedules and substantially reducing the rates of interest charged (Reading 1972, p. 126). Funds for financing home repairs and for paying delinquent property taxes were often included in the restructured loans. The agency adopted $14,000 as the maximum loan amount (Schlesinger 1958, p. 298) and repayment schedules were extended to 25 years (Office of Government Reports 1939, p. 102).

In short, 'the HOLC set out to provide for the urban home-dweller what the Farm Credit Administration provides for the farm dweller, namely a long term low interest rate amortized loan' (Office of Government Reports 1939, p. 101). When the agency's lending operations were terminated in June 1936, over 1 million homeowners had received loans amounting to more than $3 billion. 'This sum represented about one-sixth of the estimated urban home mortgage debt of the country' (Office of Government Reports 1939, p. 102). As of 30 June 1939, homeowners had saved an estimated $175 million in interest payments as a result of refinancing by the HOLC (Office of Government Reports 1939, p. 102).

The program was extremely popular, especially with middle-class voters, who were the chief beneficiaries of the loan subsidies. The program has been given much credit for strengthening the housing market during the 1930s. According to Schlesinger (1958, p. 298), the HOLC saved the real estate market by enabling banks to return to somewhat normal lending operations.

Regionally, the HOLC's expenditures followed the by-now familiar pattern. On both absolute and per-capita bases, the southeastern states received the smallest allocation of funds while midwestern states received the largest. Examining the per-capita allocation state by state, Utah ranked first at $56 per person and Mississippi last at $9 per head (Reading 1972, pp. 126–27). Table 4.2 summarizes the distribution of HOLC funds by census region. As shown, the amount allocated to the East North Central states was significantly greater than the national average.

Federal Savings and Loan Associations were chartered to provide citizens living in rural areas and small towns with access to thrift and home-financing services. These S&Ls were subjected to periodic examination by agents of the Federal Home Loan Bank Board and depositors' accounts were insured by the Federal Savings and Loan Insurance Corporation. Member institutions were required by law to qualify for the deposit insurance, which forced them to meet certain standards, namely 'sound financial condition, competent management, sage lending policies, ability to meet withdrawal demands, and satisfactory earning power' (Office of Government Reports 1939, pp. 100–101). By August 1939, there were 1,392 federal savings and loan associations in existence with assets of $1,472,900,000 (Office of Government Reports 1939, p. 100).

On another legislative front, the Federal Housing Administration (FHA) was established by the National Housing Act of 1934. The agency provided insurance protecting mortgage bankers on loans made for the repair of existing structures or for the building of new ones. According to its sponsors, the program would lift the ailing residential construction industry and aid homeowners as well. By assuming ultimate responsibility for repayment, the

Table 4.2   Home Owners' Loan Corporation expenditures per capita, by region, 1933–39

Region	Per-Capita Dollars	Z-Score[a]
New England	$25.81	0.05
Middle Atlantic	31.33	0.65
East North Central	45.25	2.15[b]
West North Central	20.84	0.48
South Atlantic	14.67	1.15
East South Central	12.73	1.35
West South Central	19.88	0.58
Mountain	28.71	0.37
Pacific	28.58	0.35

Notes:
a.   Differences in mean regional and national average Home Owners' Loan Corporation expenditures per capita.
b.   Significantly different at the 1 percent level of confidence.

Source:
Office of Government Reports (1940).

FHA made it possible for many individuals and families to buy homes at low rates of interest (Conkin 1975, p. 60).

In the words of the National Housing Act of 1934, the FHA's objectives were as follows (Office of Government Reports 1939, p. 103):

1. the drawing of fresh capital into the housing field,
2. the stimulation of new construction and the repair of existing buildings,
3. the reduction of mortgage interest and financing charges,
4. the promotion of long-term, amortized, single-mortgage financing, and
5. the setting of higher standards of construction and neighborhood stability.

Robert Lloyd (1994, p. 62) suggests that 'the "innovation" offered by the federal government in the National Housing Act was that FHA mortgage insurance provided for fully amortized loans on 80 percent of value, at 5 or 6 percent interest, with a term of up to 20 years.' This innovation was provided by Title II of the act. In addition, insured structures could not accommodate more than four families and mortgages could not exceed $16,000 (Office of Government Reports 1939, p. 104).

Financial institutions were protected on construction and improvement loans in amounts up to $2,500 through Title I of the National Housing Act (Property Improvement Plan). More than 2 million such notes were insured through the period ending 30 June 1939 (Office of Government Reports 1939, p. 103). During the same time, 442,964 mortgages valued at $1,869,290,000 were accepted for insurance (Office of Government Reports 1939, p. 104).

Yet another New Deal program targeting the housing market was the Federal National Mortgage Association. 'Fannie Mae' was organized by the Reconstruction Finance Corporation and authorized under Title III of the National Housing Act of 1934. The agency's chief purpose was to establish a market for FHA-insured first mortgages. It sold bonds to investors and used the proceeds to finance rental houses, apartments, and other multi-family dwellings (Office of Government Reports 1939, p. 98).

7 DIRECT RELIEF

The Great Depression years marked a period of great human suffering. The impression left by the era's empathetic writers and documentary film-makers is one of abject helplessness in the face of impersonal and uncontrollable economic forces. Many people seem to have simply given up.[10]

The protracted nature of the economic collapse provided the impetus for federal action targeting the hungry, poverty-stricken masses. The burgeoning numbers of poor people became a major problem to the nation's policy-makers. Opposed in principle to the idea of government handouts, President Hoover relied on the Reconstruction Finance Corporation to provide relief indirectly. Insisting that restoring business confidence and promoting individual responsibility were the keys to economic recovery, Hoover sealed his political fate by ordering General Douglas MacArthur to use troops to disperse the 5,000-member 'Bonus Army' that had camped on Washington's Anacostia Flats to await action on their demand for advance payment of amounts due in 1945 to veterans of World War I.

FDR subsequently acted to channel federal money directly into the hands of the millions who had fallen on hard times. These relief efforts were carried out through two key New Deal programs: the Federal Emergency Relief Administration (FERA) and the Civil Works Administration (CWA).

Prior to the Great Depression, public relief efforts in the United States were essentially patterned after the English poor laws of Elizabethan times. Localities assumed responsibility for the needy and assistance was typically provided in-kind, mostly in the form of groceries and coal supplies (Office of

Government Reports 1939, p. 72). Beginning in the early 1900s, some states increased their efforts by supplying 'categorical relief to such "worthy" poor as the aged, disabled, blind, and young mothers with dependent children'. The recipients of relief were required to take a pauper's oath and many of the states denied them the right to vote and the right to hold office (Kurzman 1974, p. 45).

The economic collapse of the 1930s overwhelmed local relief efforts and the states responded by creating emergency agencies to help localities deal with the problem. Further economic decline, reinforced by growing political pressure from the jobless, led President Hoover to sign the Emergency Relief and Construction Act into law on 21 July 1932. This legislation made $300,000,000 available to the Reconstruction Finance Corporation for distribution to the states to help finance their direct relief and work relief programs. The money was provided in the form of loans, with any unpaid balances to be deducted from future federal highway funds (Kurzman 1974, p. 61). This repayment requirement, as noted earlier, was subsequently relaxed by the incoming New Deal Congress.

1. The Federal Emergency Relief Administration

President Roosevelt quickly submitted new legislation targeting the needy and the unemployed. The Federal Emergency Relief Act passed the Senate in March 1933 by a vote of 55 to 17, and the House in April by a margin of 326 to 42 (Schlesinger 1958, pp. 264–65). Unlike the Hoover administration's appropriation, Federal Emergency Relief Act funds were grants rather than loans and they were to be distributed directly to the jobless (Patterson 1969, p. 50). The economic crisis again provided justification for sweeping government action:

> The Congress hereby declares that the present economic depression has created a serious emergency, due to widespread unemployment and increasing inadequacy of State and local relief funds, resulting in the existing or threatened deprivation of a considerable number of families and individuals of the necessities of life and making it imperative that the Federal Government cooperate more effectively with the States . . . in furnishing relief to their needy and distressed people. (Hosen 1992, p. 89)

Section 3(a) of the bill created the Federal Emergency Relief Administration (FERA) to implement the legislation (Hosen 1992, p. 90). Harry Hopkins was named the administrator. Shortly after taking command, Hopkins was instructed by FDR to distribute relief without regard to political considerations (Charles 1963, p. 5). Given a free hand, Hopkins rapidly rose to prominence;

he soon became, 'after Roosevelt, the most powerful man in the administration' (Reading 1972, pp. 16–17).

Section 2(a) of the law authorized the Reconstruction Finance Corporation to make up to $500,000,000 available to FERA in addition to the funds already provided under the Emergency Relief and Construction Act of 1932 (Hosen 1992, p. 89). Four main divisions were created within FERA. The Division of Research, Statistics, and Finance collected data in order more accurately to assess each state's ability to contribute to the relief effort. The Works Division sought to 'raise the caliber of work projects already in existence' (Charles 1963, p. 32) and to develop new projects after the Civil Works Administration was eliminated. The Division of Rural Rehabilitation was responsible for helping farmers. In addition to providing program supervision, the Division of Relations with States worked to coordinate state FERA operations with those of FERA's Washington headquarters (Charles 1963, p. 32).

Operating in an atmosphere that demanded haste, FERA chose to utilize existing state emergency relief organizations rather than setting up its own network of offices. This decision, along with other administrative considerations, led Roosevelt and Hopkins to adopt a grant-in-aid system (Kurzman 1974, p. 81). Thus, half of FERA's funds ($250 million) were distributed on a matching basis – 'one dollar of federal money for every three dollars spent by the state on relief programs during the previous three months' (Reading 1972, p. 17). The remainder of the money was distributed at Hopkins' discretion and, presumably, 'went where need was urgent' (Schlesinger 1958, p. 267).

Section 5 of the law specified how the states were to obtain their matching funds. Governors were required to submit applications to FERA which included the following information:

(1) the amounts necessary to meet relief needs in the State during the period covered by such application and the amounts available from public or private sources within the State . . . to meet the relief needs of the State, (2) the provision made to assure adequate administrative supervision, (3) the provision made for suitable standards of relief, and (4) the purposes for which the funds requested will be used. (Hosen 1992, p. 92)

The needy, in turn, applied to local public relief agencies for help. A so-called budgetary standard – the difference between the family's 'need' and its income – determined the amount of assistance received. Local relief agencies conducted investigations to make this determination (Charles 1963, p. 33). As already mentioned, FERA differed from previous relief efforts in that aid was given in the form of cash (Kurzman 1974, p. 84). According to Schlesinger

(1958, p. 268), 'Hopkins felt "more damage was done to the human spirit by loss of choice than by loss of vitamins."'

The matching requirement made it possible for relatively better-off states to attract the largest shares of the federal government's relief funds. With larger and more diversified tax bases than their poorer sister states, they could actually impose lower tax rates and still raise more revenue for matching purposes. Moreover, as Patterson (1969, p. 65) observed, 'most states of low per capita wealth were already taxing their residents more heavily than wealthy states'.

As would be anticipated, the rivalry for FERA grants led to considerable controversy about the agency's funding formula. Smaller and poorer states pushed for more discretionary spending and urged FERA to abandon the matching requirement. States with greater resources favored the continuation of matching.

After Texas collected the first of the discretionary grants on 27 June 1933 (Patterson 1969, p. 50), the matching requirement began to erode. Some states, unable or unwilling to raise large sums for matching purposes, were nevertheless able to obtain federal grants. For instance,

> Colorado legislators, convinced that the federal government would never cut off funds, earmarked only $60,000 for relief in their 1933 session – an amount intended to last until mid-1935. They guessed correctly, for Hopkins, aware of the urgent needs in the Dust Bowl of eastern Colorado, granted the state $330,000 per month plus additional sums for surplus commodities, care of transients, and aid to cooperatives. (Patterson 1969, p. 69)

Perhaps justifiable in normal economic times as a way of getting the states that could afford it to shoulder more of the burden, it was difficult during a collapse of the Great Depression's magnitude for the administration to defend a requirement that rewarded less hard-hit states with larger appropriations. Hence, 'in the fall of 1933, Hopkins obtained President Roosevelt's approval for expanding the discretionary basis for approving grants to the states' (Charles 1963, p. 35). This decision gave Hopkins much more control over the allocation of funds and, at least in the view of some, thereby 'assured a fairer distribution of relief funds by providing more support for the poor states' (Charles 1963, p. 35).

FERA also singled out specific groups for special relief efforts. The emergency education program, the college student aid program, the rural rehabilitation project, and the transient program focused on particular hardship cases. Transients, defined as individuals who had resided less than 12 months in the state in which they applied for relief, posed special problems because state residency requirements rendered them ineligible for many other

New Deal programs. In March 1935, at the program's peak, FERA had enrolled 5,493,358 active relief cases. 'Of these, 2,369,605 cases received work relief, 2,802,085 received direct relief only, and 321,668 were aided under the special programs, exclusive of transients' (Office of Government Reports 1939, p. 74). A survey conducted in March 1935 estimated that there were an additional 196,854 transient cases (Office of Government Reports 1939, p. 74).

Over the program's life (1933–35) total FERA expenditures from all sources amounted to $4,119,004,631. Because the program undertook work relief beginning in April of 1934, this figure includes the costs of supervising such activities along with the costs of materials. Over 70 percent of this total was financed by the federal government (Office of Government Reports 1939, p. 75).

FERA changed direction after the Civil Works Administration was eliminated in 1934. Prior to and during the CWA's existence, FERA aid was primarily in the form of direct relief rather than work relief. By all accounts, the work relief undertaken by the CWA 'had little emphasis on quality control, was hastily planned, and by Roosevelt's own admission, often of the "leaf-raking" variety' (Kurzman 1974, p. 80). Until 1934, FERA funds could not by used for the purchase of materials, thereby limiting the kinds of project that could be funded (Kurzman 1974, p. 89).

FERA began its second phase by continuing the CWA projects that had not yet been completed. These efforts furnished employment to many of its predecessor agency's participants – FERA wrapped up more than 240,000 existing CWA projects (Kurzman 1974, p. 80), spending $1,300,000,000 in the process (Charles 1963, p. 67). Although many of the activities were of dubious social value, there were visible accomplishments:

> FERA workers in 1934–35 built 5,000 new buildings; every three out of ten were school buildings. They repaired 200,000 miles of roads and . . . 44,000 miles of highways. They constructed 7,000 bridges. They laid 2,700 miles of sanitary and storm sewers; dug over 9,000 miles of drainage, irrigation, and other ditches; built over 2,000 miles of levees; laid 1,000 miles of new water mains; and constructed over 400 pumping stations. They provided Americans with 2,000 more playgrounds, 800 new small and large parks, over 350 new swimming pools, and over 4,000 new athletic fields. (Charles 1963, pp. 67–68)

The Federal Emergency Relief Administration was disbanded in the summer of 1935, with the emphasis of the administration's work relief efforts shifting to the newly created Works Progress Administration. A small group of individuals supervised the transition from FERA to WPA and, over a period of six months, gradually closed the agency's active case files (Kurzman 1974, p. 88). FERA's Rural Rehabilitation Program was transferred to the Resettlement Administration and the National Youth Administration took over the college aid program. Responsibilities for administering direct relief programs were shifted back to the states.

The FERA has its share of detractors as well as supporters. Patterson (1969, p. 71) offers high praise for the agency's emergency relief efforts: 'The FERA was efficient, remarkably free of scandal, and indispensably humane. Without it, deprivation would have been a great deal more serious.' On the other hand, the FERA's critics echoed Herbert Hoover's fears that such a program would cause a breakdown in American core values of individualism and self-reliance. One FERA field representative was 'alarmed when she heard little boys in Salt Lake City boasting about whose father had been on relief longer' (Schlesinger 1958, p. 275).

The cross-state distribution of FERA funds followed patterns observed before, with states in the Mountain Region receiving more FERA dollars per capita than the rest of the nation. 'All eight Mountain states ranked in the top ten per capita in FERA allocations'; South Dakota and North Dakota, which ranked first and third per capita, rounded out the top ten recipient states (Reading 1972, p. 18). The Mountain states received twice as much per capita from FERA as the southeastern states (Reading 1972, p. 18).

2. The Civil Works Administration

As the economy continued to deteriorate, the approaching winter of 1933–34 looked as 'dismal and bleak as any during President Hoover's tenure in office' (Charles 1963, p. 46). Realizing that Harold Ickes's Public Works Administration was coming together much too slowly to help, Harry Hopkins proposed that the administration respond with a federally sponsored work relief program that would focus on projects that could be started quickly. Utilizing FERA's staff, a new Civil Works Administration (CWA) would be created to repair and erect public buildings, especially schools, build new streets and highways, and construct new recreational facilities and playgrounds (Charles 1963, p. 47).

With FDR's blessing, the Civil Works Administration was launched on 9 November 1933, operating under Title II of the National Industrial Recovery Act. Harry Hopkins, the head of the FERA, also headed this organization (Kurzman 1974, p. 93). The goal was to employ 4 million persons in projects that were 'socially and economically desirable, and of such character that could be undertaken quickly' (Office of Government Reports 1939, p. 74).

Funding for the new program came from several sources. Roosevelt ruffled Ickes's feathers by transferring $400,000,000 from the PWA to the CWA – an action that 'secretly delighted Hopkins' (Kurzman 1974, p. 95). Hopkins supplied an additional $89,960,000 from FERA while Congress added $345,000,000 in a supplemental appropriation approved 'when the program's political popularity had been firmly established' (Kurzman 1974, p. 95).

The Civil Works Administration differed from the FERA in several respects. It was, by design, a temporary program lasting through what was expected to be a long, difficult winter. Unlike the FERA, which involved a state–federal cooperative relationship, the CWA was exclusively a federal program. In addition, the agency paid cash wages to recipients, rejecting the 'budgetary deficiency' standard of the FERA (Kurzman 1974, p. 94).

Hopkins appointed all state CWA administrators and these state officials in turn selected all local personnel. Thus, every CWA employee ultimately answered to Washington and to Hopkins (Charles 1963, p. 50). The program proved to be very popular with the states because of the source of the funds – the federal Treasury (Kurzman 1974, p. 95).

The Civil Works Administration accepted all able-bodied persons currently on the relief rolls of the FERA. The remainder of those on the CWA's payrolls, about half of them, were selected by the United States Employment Service. Recipients were required to be unemployed and not on other forms of relief. No means test was imposed (Office of Government Reports 1939, p. 74).

'Transfers of persons to Civil Works rolls was begun on November 16, 1933' (Office of Government Reports 1939, p. 74) and on 'November 22, 1933 payroll checks were issued for the first week's work to 814,511 workers in a total amount of more than $7,500,000' (Kurzman 1974, p. 93). The program, from its inception to its termination – a period of less than five months – spent over $900,000,000 (Charles 1963, p. 50).

The CWA was the first public relief program to pay the 'prevailing wage' to workers in the form of cash (Kurzman 1974, p. 98). Wage payments soon became one of the CWA's biggest problems, however. The minimum hourly rates were determined by geographic region and type of work (skilled or unskilled) and were in keeping with the codes set forth in the National Industrial Recovery Act. The hourly wage schedule is shown in Table 4.3. These wages proved to be too high in the South. 'I wouldn't plow nobody's mule from sunrise to sunset for 50 cents per day,' a Georgia farmer complained to his Governor, Eugene Talmadge, 'when I could get $1.30 for pretending to work on a DITCH' (Schlesinger 1958, p. 274).[11]

The CWA was put in place so quickly that administrative lapses were inevitable. Most of the projects were selected and sponsored by state and local

Table 4.3 Minimum hourly wages paid by the CWA

Skill Level	Southern Zone	Central Zone	Northern Zone
Skilled	$1.00	$1.10	$1.20
Unskilled	$0.40	$0.45	$0.50

Source:
Charles (1963, p. 52).

organizations. 'Because of the magnitude of the task and the shortness of time, state CWA officials spent very little time checking projects' (Charles, 1963, p. 51). Consequently, many of the projects chosen were of dubious value and most were not carried out in even a remotely efficient manner. As Charles (1963, p. 63) notes, 'there was no [public] need for leaf raking and similar projects.'

Nevertheless, there were demands for the program to be continued beyond winter's end. Politicians pushed the administration to support its extension, but the program, as set up, was far too expensive. The CWA did serve as a precursor to the Works Progress Administration, however, a work relief program that was to become the hallmark of the New Deal.

8 PRE-EXISTING PROGRAMS

Programs in existence long before the advent of the Great Depression were utilized to some extent by the New Dealers to channel money into the economy. The Bureau of Public Roads, created in 1893, and the first Federal Road Act, passed in 1916 to finance road improvements to speed the delivery of mail, represent examples along these lines. 'The New Deal administration continued expenditures to states through the Bureau of Public Roads, viewing the program, in part, as a works program' (Reading 1972, p. 61). Over $1.5 billion was spent by this agency during the New Deal era.

The Bureau of Reclamation of the Department of the Interior likewise served the New Deal's ends. Created for the purpose of financing irrigation projects that would open up the arid West to cultivation, the Federal Reclamation Act was signed by President Theodore Roosevelt in June of 1902. The Bureau played an enormous role in 'the widening of the agricultural base' in the western United States, and since 1933 the Bureau has received an added impetus in its work, and is now engaged in the greatest construction program in its history. Projects under construction will, upon completion, add approximately 2,300,000 acres to the watered area of the Western States. In addition, supplemental water will be provided for about 1,700,000 more acres which now have insufficient water to produce good crops. (Reading 1972, pp. 28–29)

In all, the New Dealers allocated almost $300 million to Bureau of Reclamation projects.

The Veterans Administration also helped prime the pump. Established well before the 1930s, the agency was used to distribute additional New Deal dollars nationwide. Pension payments, expenditures for veterans' homes and hospitals, and other spending by the Veterans Administration amounted to some $4 billion between 1933 and 1939.

Despite the massive activities of the federal government during the period of the so-called First New Deal (1933–35), the economy was still operating far below its potential. Unemployment rates remained at double-digit levels. Increased pressure from the left prompted FDR to consider alternative measures to ease the depression's effects and, it was hoped, to spur recovery. The rhetoric became increasingly more anti-business and the ensuing legislative proposals more radical. As the proponents of 'reform' gained the upper hand, the nation was to witness, in 1935, the launching of the 'Second New Deal'.

NOTES

1. See Namorato (1988) for a detailed narrative of the life and times of Rexford Guy Tugwell.
2. The 1930s witnessed an explosion of federal intervention into the private sector. For example, the Glass–Steagall Act of 1933 limited the scope of commercial banking, prohibiting the underwriting of securities issues. In 1934, the Securities and Exchange Commission was established to regulate capital markets. One year later, the Federal Deposit Insurance Corporation was set up. The Wagner Act (National Labor Relations Act) of 1935 altered the balance of power between labor and management, granting workers additional collective bargaining rights and establishing the National Labor Relations Board to arbitrate disputes. In addition, the Robinson–Patman Act of 1936 strengthened the law against price discrimination. The Fair Labor Standards Act was passed by Congress in 1938, granting the federal government authority to regulate wages, hours, and working conditions. The Civil Aeronautics Board and the Federal Power Commission were also created in 1938.
3. After World War II the mission of the RFC changed somewhat, with its responsibilities shifting toward providing smaller firms with credit. Large firms, it was said, enjoyed an advantage over smaller firms in credit markets and the RFC would act to correct this inequity. However, the lending record of the RFC reveals that over the two-year period, 1948–49, one single firm, the Kaiser–Frazier Automobile Company, received loans exceeding those provided to all small business applicants (McKenzie 1985, p. 88). More damaging and, in fact, striking the agency's death knell, was the publication of a report entitled *Favoritism and Influence: Interim Report of the Committee on Banking and Currency Pursuant to Senate Resolution 219*, 82d Cong., 1st sess. (Washington, DC: US Government Printing Office, 1951), which revealed evidence

that payments made to certain agency officials had influenced the outcomes of matters before the RFC.

4. The bureaucratic empire-building benefits to General Johnson personally of having charge of both of the law's provisions should not escape notice.

5. George Bittlingmayer (1995) disputes this conclusion, though. See below.

6. For alternative, pro-competitive interpretations of the purposes and effects of delivered pricing systems, see Haddock (1982) and Carlton (1983).

7. *Schecter Poultry Corp.* v. *United States*, 295 U.S. 495 (1935).

8. Bittlingmayer (1995) suggests that the antitrust law exemptions provided by the NRA codes allowed firms in industries characterized by relatively high ratios of fixed costs to variable costs collectively to solve the 'integer problem', a problem that exists when minimum average cost can only be achieved at integer multiples of the economically efficient plant size. A competitive industry equilibrium may not be sustainable in such cases, with every bit of excess production capacity triggering price wars and ruinous, cutthroat competition. Under the NRA, however, firms in high-fixed-cost industries were jointly able to rationalize the utilization of their existing production capacities, thereby lowering costs and expanding output without precipitating the antitrust challenges such inter-firm collaboration would normally provoke.

9. Not all of the work performed by the Civilian Conservation Corps was appreciated. Kudzu, the only living thing known to grow more rapidly than government bureaucracy, was first planted by the CCC in 1935 and 1936 in order to control soil erosion. It has been a nuisance in the South ever since (Winberry and Jones 1973).

10. The words and pictures in Watkins (1993) convey these images vividly.

11. Emphasis in original. Arithmetic is obviously not one of the farmer's strengths: he could have earned 40 cents per hour ($3.20 per day) for pretending to work on a CWA-financed ditch.

5. The Second New Deal

The facts which will stand out when history is written is that the administration of the WPA has been honest, efficient, and effective. It has achieved the purpose for which it was created. It has provided jobs. It has prevented chaos. It has saved privation and suffering. It has brought men self-respect. It has tided the Nation over an abyss, the depths of which cannot be plumbed.
– Rep. Clarence Cannon (D-MO)

There is no denying that there have been politics in WPA. Whether it has been by members of one party or the other party is not the real issue, for it has occurred in both cases. As long as human nature is what it is, I am sorry to say, any group like WPA will offer a fair opportunity for exploitation.
– Rep. Emmet O'Neal (D-KY)

President Roosevelt announced the Second New Deal in his annual message to Congress on 4 January 1935. Historians routinely point to this speech as marking the beginning of a dramatic leftward shift in administration policy. At the president's urging, Congress produced 'a new body of legislation that, with almost unbelievable speed, launched the American welfare state, a brand-new, large, ungainly infant, destined to survive all the hazards of childhood and a maladjusted adolescence' (Conkin 1975, p. 52).

'Reform' was the Second New Deal's byword. No longer satisfied simply with providing temporary handouts, the more radical New Dealers who wanted to expand the responsibilities of the federal government permanently seized the policy reins. What followed was a new burst of legislative activity that lasted until the 'Roosevelt recession' of 1937, the president's infamous court-packing plan, and his nomination of ultraliberal Alabama senator Hugo Black to the Supreme Court combined to strengthen the hands of the administration's political opponents. With the president's attention being ever more drawn to the gathering war clouds in Europe, political opposition would ultimately bring the New Deal to an end.

The foremost policy fruit of this move to the left was the Works Progress Administration (WPA), perhaps the best known of the Roosevelt administration's emergency relief programs. Indeed, for many, the WPA is synonymous with the entire New Deal. This characterization is understandable in light of the fact that FDR devoted both more energy and more money to the WPA than to any other of the New Deal agencies (Charles 1963, p. 220). In addition, however, the Second New Deal produced the Social Security Act, the crown jewel of the American welfare state. The system of social insurance thereby created may well be the New Deal's most enduring – and most expensive – legacy.

1 THE SOCIAL SECURITY ACT

Hard on the heels of FDR's message to Congress, the administration launched a campaign to provide a system of social security that would protect Americans against the vicissitudes of an unfettered market economy. A Committee on Economic Security was appointed for the purpose of devising such legislation. Headed by Francis Perkins, the Secretary of Labor, the committee sent its proposal to Congress in January of 1935.

The committee's work was given impetus by contentions that the Great Depression had brought particular hardship to the elderly members of the population. By wiping out savings, the economic collapse had left many older workers with little or no funds for retirement. At the same time, widespread joblessness meant that younger workers, who normally would have taken care of their aged parents, were now unable to do so. According to Peter Ferrara (1980, p. 24), 'The Social Security Act was therefore attempting to respond to an acute and unique problem: Great portions of the elderly population had lost their planned means of old-age support.'[1]

The Social Security Act was eventually passed on 14 August 1935 (Ferrara 1980, p. 17). It established ten distinct programs:

> The original Social Security Act provided for a Federal old-age retirement plan and Federal cooperation and financial aid in nine State-initiated and State-administered programs – unemployment compensation, old-age assistance, aid to dependent children, aid to needy blind, maternal and child health services, services for crippled children, child welfare services, public health services and vocational rehabilitation. (Office of Government Reports 1939, p. 61)

The social security tax rate was set initially at 2 percent – half to be paid by the employer and half by the employee – and was assessed against the first $3,000 of earned income (Ferrara 1980, p. 29). Benefits were to be paid monthly in proportion to the wages recipients had earned while working. 'The minimum monthly payment is to be $10, the maximum $85' (Perkins [1935] 1966, p. 276). Of course, large numbers of individuals would soon begin drawing benefits without having made any contributions to the retirement 'fund' themselves.

The macroeconomic impact of the social security program clashed with Keynesian explanations for the depression's cause and with Keynes's prescriptions for recovery. Inadequate demand, according to Maynard Keynes, was chiefly responsible for the protracted downturn and increased spending was therefore in order. The social security system worked against this goal by building up a reservoir of savings. As Herbert Stein (1984, p. 54) explains,

> The intent was to raise a reserve fund by payroll taxes, the income from which would be available to pay retirement benefits in the future when the people being covered by the system when it started would reach retirement age. The accumulation of this fund would be a big addition to national saving, and would compound the problem of excessive saving.

Fortunately for the Keynesians, though, the social security trust fund never became a 'reservoir of savings'. The payment of benefits to individuals who had retired prior to the imposition of the payroll tax forced the system on to a pay-as-you-go basis in 1939 – a method of finance which has continued ever since.

The Social Security Act also provided for federal grants-in-aid to the states to be used for categorical relief to the blind, the aged, and dependent children. In the two former categories, 'the Act limits the Federal aid to not more than $15 per month for the individual, provided the state in which he resides appropriated a like amount' (Perkins [1935] 1966, p. 275). For dependent children, the federal government paid up to one-third of the $18 monthly benefit provided for the first child, and the same portion of the $12 monthly entitlement for each additional child.

Total benefits paid out from the social security program's beginning through 30 June 1939, amounted to $624,871,473. Of this total, $536,305,824 was for old-age assistance and $16,125,435 was for aid to the blind. The remainder ($72,440,214) was for aid to families with dependent children – children in families receiving no support from a father (Office of Government Reports 1939, p. 67).

Ironically, just as the government was building a pool of savings for future retirees, in an effort to encourage consumption spending it enacted an undistributed-profits tax, discouraging corporate savings and making it more likely that earnings would be paid out to stockholders. These two programs were completely at odds with one another. In addition, as Conkin (1975, p. 59) has observed, 'the employee tax represented a significant drain from already low payrolls and thus a further obstacle to recovery.' The payroll tax raised labor costs at a time when millions were desperately looking for work.

John Joseph Wallis (1989, p. 61) has tested the hypothesis that 'states with higher portions of their labor force in covered employment should have sustained larger declines in employment' following the passage of the Social Security Act. He reported evidence supporting the prediction that the legislation raised labor costs, specifically finding that the percentage of covered non-agricultural employees was negatively and significantly related to employment levels across the states. Hence, whatever one's view of its long-run consequences may be, the Social Security Act's contribution to recovery and relief is surely questionable. It tried to encourage saving and did discourage employment at a time when the orthodox economic prescription was for policies that would do exactly the opposite.

2 THE WORKS PROGRESS ADMINISTRATION

Preferring work relief to direct relief and pushed by Harry Hopkins to act on that preference, FDR planned to phase out the Federal Emergency Relief Administration and replace it with a new agency that would provide public employment for some 3.5 million able-bodied persons. Those individuals incapable of work would continue to be the responsibility of state and local relief agencies as they had been before the Great Depression. Work relief was more politically palatable than direct relief, in the administration's view, and while the dole destroyed self-respect, creating make-work jobs for the jobless would restore the human spirit. Dignity came with a price tag, however – an appropriation of almost $5 billion was requested.

President Roosevelt described the new program, albeit somewhat vaguely, in his January 1935 message to Congress. He stated that the work undertaken should be useful, that the projects should employ large numbers of workers, that the funds should be targeted toward areas in distress, and that the projects should not compete with private enterprise (Schlesinger 1960, p. 268). The legislation proposed soon thereafter called for 'the largest appropriation in American history and the largest accretion to the national debt' (Conkin 1975, p. 56).

The bill offered few details about this new federal public works responsibility:

The resolution asked, in effect, for a lump sum to be allocated pretty much at presidential discretion. Its congressional managers had no detailed information about how the funds would be used. And because Roosevelt still had not decided who would be in charge, no administration official was able to take responsibility for future policy in the hearings. (Schlesinger 1960, p. 268)

It nevertheless sailed through the House, passing by a margin of 329 to 78. However, it bogged down in the Senate, where a vocal opposition debated against the measure.

Perhaps the most outspoken critic of the joint resolution was Senator Arthur Vandenburg of Michigan. He sarcastically summed up the legislation in the following terms:

> The whole proposition could be simplified by merely striking out all the text and substituting two brief sections:
> Section 1. Congress hereby appropriates \$4,880,000,000 to the President of the United States to use as he pleases.
> Section 2. Anybody who does not like it is fined \$1,000.
> That is approximately the net result of this proposed legislation (US House of Representatives 1935a, p. 2014).

Stressing the dangers inherent in the vague language of the administration's proposal, Vandenburg went on to say that, 'Responsible representatives of the American people [should] have at least a minimum of information respecting what is to be done with \$4,000,000,000 of their money' (US House of Representatives 1935a, p. 2014).

The senator from Michigan was equally alarmed by the unprecedented spending authority the bill would grant to the president. He calculated that

> This is nearly 70 percent more money than all the Federal funds expended by all the Federal relief agencies from the commencement of their operations in May 1933 up to January 1, 1935. It is probably the largest single appropriation ever made in the history of the world. It far exceeds any previous total normal budget of the whole government of the United States. In other words, it is a grant of power to the Executive to spend more than the equivalent of an entire annual budget (US House of Representatives 1935a, p. 2017).

Despite the opposition of a vocal minority, the measure was ultimately passed by the Senate by a vote of 66 to 13 in early April of 1935. The Emergency Relief Appropriation (ERA) Act of 1935 made \$4,880,000,000 available, of which \$880,000,000 represented the unspent balances of earlier emergency relief appropriations. Some of the funds were allocated to existing agencies engaged in financing heavy construction. Among these were the Bureau of Public Roads, the Public Works Administration, and the Bureau of

Reclamation of the Department of the Interior. The monies were to be used to hire workers from the relief rolls (Office of Government Reports 1939, p. 76).

The newly created Resettlement Administration received $220,000,000 and the Civilian Conservation Corps received some $600,000,000. The old Federal Emergency Relief Administration and the new Works Progress Administration (WPA), which were, in essence, one agency,[2] received $934,000,000 and $1,397,000,000 respectively (Office of Government Reports 1939, p. 77).

The WPA received additional funding from subsequent Emergency Relief Appropriation bills. 'The Act of 1936 made available $1,880,700,000; that of 1937, $1,525,000,000; and that of 1938, $2,329,700,000. The ERA Act of 1939 appropriated $1,477,000,000 for WPA projects' (Office of Government Reports 1939, p. 77). Thus, to state the obvious, throughout the Second New Deal the administration was dependent on Congress for continued appropriations to fund the activities of the Works Progress Administration.

1. Personnel Decisions

In approving the 1935 ERA Act, the Senate did impose one specific requirement on the administration. In particular, the law stipulated that any administrator receiving a salary of $5,000 or more must be appointed with the advice and consent of the Senate. Charles (1963, p. 176) has asserted that the 'inclusion of this statement in the act establishing the work program meant one thing above all else to [Harry] Hopkins and his staff – political patronage.' Hopkins vehemently opposed this condition.

Hopkins's critics claimed that he wished to make all appointments independently so that he could build his own political machine. It is widely acknowledged that Harry Hopkins had presidential aspirations (Charles 1963, p. 106). Whether Hopkins or the Senate let politics systematically influence administrative appointments is less clear. However, there is little doubt that some personnel decisions were based on factors other than merit. In Kansas, for example, a state relief administrator was passed over to head the WPA because of his Republican sympathies. A former mayor was selected instead. But the appointee was quickly overwhelmed by the job and sought refuge in a hotel room for over three weeks, refusing to see anyone (MacMahon, Millet and Ogden 1941, p. 273).

Politics seems to have played a part in the selection of personnel at all levels. Contemporary observers were well aware of the implicit political requirements necessary to be appointed to supervisory and administrative positions within the WPA (MacMahon, Millet and Ogden 1941, p. 275).

2. WPA Organization

Personnel decisions also shaped the organization of the federal work relief program. FDR had to contend with two ambitious administrators who wanted to head the new agency – Harry Hopkins and Harold Ickes. As Charles (1963, p. 108) explains, 'obviously, both wanted to be close to Roosevelt; they wanted the power the position would give. With control of billions of dollars for relief and public works came influence in local, state, and national politics.'

Hoping to bruise as few egos as possible, the president created three divisions within the WPA. A Division of Applications and Information (DAI) was established to serve as a clearinghouse for project proposals. Frank Walker was named as its director. The DAI reviewed applications before forwarding them to the Advisory Committee on Allotments (ACA). Secretary Ickes was named to chair this committee, whose purpose was to advise FDR on decisions concerning the approval of projects and the distribution of WPA dollars (MacMahon, Millet, and Ogden 1941, p. 73). Hopkins headed the WPA's third division, the Works Progress Division.

This unit was given the seemingly insignificant responsibility of checking costs, investigating the availability of workers for projects, and reporting on the implementation of the program (Charles 1963, pp. 111–12). The executive order creating the federal works program did allow Hopkins's division to carry on some small projects of its own, however. This provision proved to be the loophole needed by Hopkins to later dominate the WPA. As Kurzman notes, these 'small projects' eventually accounted for over $10 billion worth of expenditures. Kurzman rejects the charge of desultory planning and suspects that this was the president's intention from the beginning, stating, 'one cannot believe that Roosevelt was entirely naive in his visions for Hopkins' (Kurzman 1974, p. 105).

Indeed, as the program got underway, DAI's clearinghouse function was often bypassed and treated as an unnecessary step in the project approval process. The advisory committee likewise functioned more or less as a rubber stamp (MacMahon, Millet and Ogden 1941, p. 113). Even when the ACA had debated the merits of a proposal and forwarded its recommendation for approval, Roosevelt often scribbled 'disapproved' on a sheet he used to make the actual funding decisions (MacMahon, Millet, and Ogden 1941, p. 110). By October of 1935, both the ACA and the DAI had ceased to exist.

Clearly, FDR personally assumed much of the responsibility for the WPA. The president apparently felt that the successful implementation and administration of the program would prove fruitful in the upcoming 1936 election campaign (Charles 1963, p. 114). Thus, he and Hopkins exercised close control of the WPA's activities. 'With a constant stream of reports, surveys, and observations on projects and personnel, Hopkins was able to obtain a fairly complete picture of the vast activities of WPA' (Charles 1963, pp. 135–36). But Roosevelt was ultimately in charge.

'When Three's a Crowd'
Philadelphia Record, 29 April 1935

The Works Progress Administration was organized along geographic lines, with state boundaries demarcating the agency's principal operating divisions. State administrators supervised the local district offices established within their states. There were 307 districts in all, with a few states, namely Delaware, New Hampshire, Vermont, and Rhode Island, comprising single districts – the states themselves (MacMahon, Millet and Ogden 1941, p. 202).

The state and district offices initially contained five administrative units, but due to the confusion created by overlapping responsibilities, the organizational structure was later simplified. After reorganization, the district offices were divided into four departments: operations, women's and professional projects, employment, and finance and statistics (MacMahon, Millet and Ogden 1941, pp. 206–7).

3. WPA Administration

By most accounts, Hopkins worked hard to keep the WPA's administrative expenses low. Such expenditures accounted for roughly 5 percent of total spending in fiscal year 1936. The average annual salary was $2,251 in the Washington offices of the WPA. In contrast, the average annual salary of state WPA administrators during fiscal year 1937 was $1,633 (Charles 1963, p. 137).

Not everyone agreed with this assessment of the WPA's efficiency, however. For example, the agency's apparently low administrative costs were called into question in 1939 by Senator Holt of West Virginia:

> WPA claims that the administrative expense in my state amounted only to something over $900,000 but the payrolls when checked showed that it amounted to $3,300,000. WPA determined what would be administrative expense and what would not be administrative expense. In one county in our state they said there were only 104 administrative employees but the payroll check shows 160 who earned more than $1,000 as project bosses. (US House of Representatives 1939, p. 7965)

On the basis of his investigation, Senator Holt thought it likely that Hopkins had attempted to mislead the public into thinking that more of the agency's money was going to the needy than was in fact the case by disguising some of the costs of the program.[3] He asked his colleagues rhetorically, 'and if they can hide two and one-half million dollars overhead in the little State of West Virginia, what can they hide throughout the United States?' (US House of Representatives 1939, p. 7965).

The Senator from West Virginia sought to answer his own question by requesting information on the number of WPA employees who received more than $1,000 yearly. He received the following response from Harry Hopkins:

> We have not made it a practice to give out information concerning the individual salaries and addresses of employees except those in a position to formulate policy or direct major portions of the operations. We have felt that the public could have no legitimate interest in such information and that its

release would very possibly result in these persons being subjected to solicitation from salesmen and gossip of neighbors. (US House of Representatives 1939, p. 8078)

Given Harry Hopkins's dual administrative responsibilities, the WPA inevitably took on many of the characteristics of the FERA. However, unlike the FERA, the WPA was a fully federal program. All WPA administrators, whether assigned to Washington or to the agency's state and local district offices, were employees of the federal government and all WPA workers' wages were disbursed directly from the US Treasury (Kurzman 1974, p. 107). While the FERA encouraged and guided the federal relief program and later work relief efforts of the states, the WPA exercised direct control over such activities. It was hoped that this arrangement would reduce some of the tensions that had existed between the FERA and the states regarding the distribution of funds (Patterson 1969, p. 75). For this same reason, the WPA differed from the FERA in its method of distributing money to the states. FERA grants contained explicit matching requirements. The WPA did require states to provide some of their own resources to help finance approved projects, but did not stipulate minimum sponsorship amounts. Neither was a mechanism put in place to force recalcitrant states to cooperate (Patterson 1969, p. 80).

4. Sponsorship

Except for some relatively small-scale work relief activities, state and local governments sponsored WPA projects. This sponsorship requirement offered several advantages. Because state and local governments were responsible for initiating proposals and required to partially fund them, projects were supposedly more likely to be useful. The sponsorship arrangement also helped ensure that projects undertaken had the support of local communities (MacMahon, Millet and Ogden 1941, p. 304).

One study suggests that during the WPA's first two years of operation, municipalities sponsored almost 40 percent of all funded projects. Counties sponsored nearly 27 percent, states almost 16 percent, townships a little less than 15 percent, and the federal government about 4 percent (Charles 1963, p. 143).

The WPA was not a totally disinterested observer, however. The agency often surveyed localities regarding their needs and encouraged local governments to sponsor projects. Because its ultimate goal was to provide employment to some 3.5 million individuals, it helped identify projects that would provide employment to workers and could be sold by potential sponsors as being of use to the citizens in the area.

The agency prepared a 'Guide to Eligibility of WPA Projects' which was made available to the states. Nineteen types of potentially fundable activities were described, including malaria control, recreational and educational programs, and street building and building demolition (MacMahon, Millet and Ogden 1941, p. 308). However, widespread unemployment coupled with the availability of federal dollars for financing public works resulted in the WPA experiencing no shortage of applications and project proposals (MacMahon, Millet and Ogden 1941, p. 310). Moreover, 'to encourage selection of the best projects, WPA headquarters always approved more projects than could be implemented. Thus, state administrators and local authorities had more leeway and could provide more continuity than they could have done otherwise' (Charles 1963, p. 142).

In its first year of operation, total sponsor contributions accounted for roughly 10 percent of total WPA expenditures. The agency later pressured sponsors for greater contributions which climbed to over 18 percent by 1938 (MacMahon, Millet and Ogden 1941, p. 314). As mentioned earlier, the adoption of explicit matching requirements as a method of allocating funds was rejected by the WPA. But some scholars have suggested that Hopkins and Roosevelt based state appropriations largely on the sizes of their contributions (e.g. Wallis 1984).

While the precise relationship between contributions and appropriations is somewhat of a mystery, the fact that sponsors' contributions varied considerably from state to state is well known. This wide variation resulted in accusations of discrimination and calls for reform. The Senate Special Committee to Investigate Unemployment and Relief ('Byrnes Committee') noted in 1938 that

complaint has arisen as to the lack of uniformity in the treatment of the different States by the Federal Government in the matter of sponsors' contributions to the cost of work-relief projects. The appropriation acts have never contained any stipulation on this point, and discretion has been left to the Executive to decide how much of the cost of any project should be contributed by the sponsor. The published reports of the Works Progress Administration show considerable variation in the proportion of the total cost of work-relief projects borne by sponsors in the respective states. (US Senate 1938, p. 1386)

In an effort to eliminate possible bias in the amount of the contribution required of sponsors, a proposal to set a uniform sponsorship share of 25 percent was made. Because Hopkins and Roosevelt wanted to retain control,

Hopkins argued that the requirement would place such a heavy burden on poorer communities that they would get no projects (Charles 1963, p. 162). The proposal was never adopted.

Actual project work was carried out by the state and local district offices. The nature of the WPA's involvement varied from project to project. At times, the WPA hired and paid employees, procured supplies, and provided supervision (Kurzman 1974, p. 108). At other times, the sponsor was responsible for project supervision while the WPA simply supplied the workforce.

5. Wage Policy

The WPA's wage policy was controversial from the beginning. The so-called budgetary deficiency method of pay, by which workers were investigated to determine need and compensated accordingly, was rejected largely because of the administrative complexities inherent in such a system. This method of compensation was also viewed as 'meddlesome and insulting' to recipients (MacMahon, Millet, and Ogden 1941, pp. 38–39). As Kurzman (1974, pp. 108–9) explains, 'the budgetary deficiency method required that the worker be treated like a client: subject to frequent investigation to determine whether he had outside income which should be deducted. . . .'

As an alternative, Hopkins and Roosevelt proposed that WPA compensation be based on a 'security wage', which would be an hourly amount greater than the typical relief payment but less than that offered by private employers. Even so, the administration contended that it was misleading to evaluate the program's effects solely on the basis of the wages it paid. Supposedly more important were earnings through continuous employment over an extended period. Hence, when the security wage was adopted, pay was reported in monthly amounts.

The security wage was opposed by organized labor, which feared that it would have a depressing effect on private-sector wages – wages they were desperately trying to prop up. However, as the proponents of this compensation scheme argued, the steady employment offered would in the long run more than offset the relatively low hourly wage rates paid by the WPA (MacMahon, Millet and Ogden 1941, p. 39). The monthly wage rates of workers employed on WPA projects were determined by 'how long they work, the kind of work they do, and where they do it' (Howard 1943, p. 58). Earnings were $50 per month, on the average (MacMahon, Millet and Ogden 1941, p. 149). Those workers employed in urban areas were treated more favorably, earning considerably more than their rural counterparts (Howard 1943, p. 163).

The original pay schedule included four wage classes, namely unskilled, intermediate, skilled, and professional and technical. The country was also divided into four regions, with the southern states grouped into Regions III and IV, the regions receiving the lowest compensation. Monthly salaries ranged from a high of $94 (for urban professional and technical workers employed in Region I), to a low of $19 – for unskilled rural workers employed in Region IV (MacMahon, Millet and Ogden 1941, p. 150).

Although compensation was reported on a monthly basis, hourly wage rates were important because they determined how many hours an employee would have to work to earn a given monthly income. These hourly rates differed considerably from place to place. Senator Richard Russell of Georgia was less than happy with the WPA's pay schedule:

> For the performance of labor of the same general type . . . a laborer in Tennessee will receive 18 cents per hour compared with 102.5 cents an hour in certain sections of the State of Illinois.
>
> Passing to the intermediate grade, we find in this classification that the rate of hourly compensation varies from 23 cents an hour, the low, also in the State of Tennessee, to a high of $1.57 an hour in the State of New York.
>
> The pay of skilled labor varies from a low of 31 cents per hour in the States of Alabama, Kentucky, Tennessee, and Virginia to a high of $2.25 per hour in the State of New Jersey.
>
> When we come to those who are classified as professional or technical employees we find that the scale of hourly compensation ranges from $3.03 per hour in the State of Pennsylvania to a low of 34 cents per hour paid in the States of Alabama, Kentucky, and Virginia. (US House of Representatives 1938a, p. 911)

Senator Russell went on to complain that wage differentials of ten-fold or more could not be justified on any grounds.

Other senators expressed similar displeasure with WPA wages. Senator Miller of Arkansas, for instance, declared that

> I see no reason why a man working on a road in Arkansas or Georgia should not receive the same amount of pay that the man working on a road in the State of New York or elsewhere receives from Federal funds, especially in view of the legislation which has been enacted by the Congress – for example, the wage and hour law, and other laws of that nature. We are making fish of one and fowl of the other. If the policy of the Congress is to be that we are to have a uniform rate of pay in industry, it appears to me, unless there is some good reason to the contrary unknown to me, that the Government ought to meet the situation. (US House of Representatives 1938a, p. 913)

At least some of the regional variation in the WPA's wage scales could, of course, be explained by geographic differences in the cost of living. But anomalies nevertheless materialized, as Senator Clark of Missouri pointed out in describing one particular public works project:

> The project was a dam across the Mississippi River, one end of the dam being in Illinois and the other end in Missouri. The men were to be engaged in doing precisely the same work, that is, clearing timber on precisely the same project, except that part of them happened to be on the Illinois end of the dam, and the other part on the Missouri end of the dam. A discriminatory ratio was set up of 64 cents an hour on the Illinois side, as against 40 cents an hour on the Missouri side, on the same project, for doing precisely the same work. (US House of Representatives 1938a, pp. 921–22)

Hourly wage rate differentials produced but one source of discrepancy in the compensation of workers in various geographic locations. As Senator Russell pointed out to the Senate, 'In the State of Tennessee the man who is working with a pick and shovel at 18 cents an hour is limited to $26 a month, and he must work 144 hours to earn $26. Whereas the man who is working in Pennsylvania has to work only 30 hours to earn $94, out of funds which are being paid out of the common Treasury of the United States' (US House of Representatives 1938a, p. 913).

Recurring complaints of this sort ultimately resulted in the authorization of up to a 10-percent adjustment in WPA wages whenever such modification seemed necessary. 'Thereafter, piecemeal adjustments in geographic differentiation of the security wage structure were almost continuous' (MacMahon, Millet and Ogden 1941, p. 152). The states assigned to Region IV were subsequently shifted to Region III, and the wage schedule of the former was eliminated.

The Emergency Relief Appropriation Act of 1936 – the legislation funding the WPA that fiscal year – required that the security wage be abandoned. Instead, in language echoing the Davis–Bacon Act of 1931, Congress mandated that workers on WPA projects be paid wages not less than those prevailing in the local area. 'Prevailing' wage rates were to be determined by state WPA officials. The Emergency Relief Appropriation Act of 1939 further stipulated 'that geographic variations in pay should not exceed the differences in cost of living among areas of the country' (MacMahon, Millet and Ogden 1941, p. 157). Ensuing realignments in WPA pay scales narrowed regional differences considerably, producing higher wages for the southern states while wages in the North were reduced. For example, unskilled labor in Region I (the region with the highest wages) received $52 per month after the adjustment; Region III workers in the same category saw their monthly compensation climb to \$46.80 (MacMahon, Millet and Ogden 1941, p. 158).

6. The Allocation of Funds Across the States

The mechanism used to allocate WPA projects, money, and jobs across states and regions has never been fully understood. There is a good reason for this: 'Neither Hopkins nor the Congress of the United States ever implemented a system of appropriations and distribution of funds on a planned basis' (Charles 1963, p. 159). No formal funding formula was adopted; the distribution of WPA largesse was accordingly a matter of administrative discretion.

A number of scholars – and certainly the Roosevelt administration itself – proclaimed that projects were selected for funding on the basis of economic need. The agency's mission was to create jobs for the jobless, and 'Hopkins' primary aim continued to be to provide aid where it was most needed. The correlation between relief received and state need seems to have been fairly close during the lifetime of the WPA' (Patterson 1969, p. 78). Charles (1963, p. 41) emphasizes, however, that 'in the last analysis, need, not facts and figures, determined the amount of aid Hopkins and his staff were willing to give. . . . Hopkins never reconciled himself to letting figures dominate the giving of relief.'

Concerns about the cross-state distribution of WPA funds nevertheless made the agency a 'storm center from the beginning' (Howard 1943, p. 596). The source of many of the concerns – including suspicions that some states were being shortchanged – was the agency's reluctance to divulge any information about how funding decisions were made.

The WPA apparently established employment and funding quotas for each state, but the quotas were kept strictly confidential. Indeed, 'the only sorts of decisions about which the WPA was notably sensitive were the allocation of employment quotas and the issuance of the monthly program budgets to the states' (MacMahon, Millet and Ogden 1941, p. 217). The agency was also eloquently silent about how the money was distributed within the states. Even local officials were sometimes unaware of the quotas established for their districts (Howard 1943, p. 602).

Harry Hopkins was less than forthcoming when testifying before a special committee of the Senate (the so-called Byrnes Committee) created, in part, to investigate the activities of the WPA. A committee member asked Hopkins 'why 2,600,000 jobs were divided among the several states so that areas with smaller populations received more jobs than those with larger populations'. Hopkins responded, 'I have a feeling that we can make a good case for the

way the 2,600,000 are distributed by States.' Senator Henry Cabot Lodge
pressed, 'that is what I am asking you to do.' Hopkins replied, 'I think if we
took the time to go into the details of that we could make a case out of it. A
lot of this is nothing but a matter of opinion. If somebody else were adminis-
trating this and dividing up these 2,600,000 among 48 states he might do it
differently' (US Senate 1938, p. 1396).

Based upon this testimony, the minority report of the committee admon-
ished the administration, stating that 'the allocation of funds to the states for
human relief is not done on a scientific or factual basis, but is merely "a
matter of opinion"' (US Senate 1938, p. 1396). In an editorial published on
29 December 1938, the *New York Times* was likewise strongly critical of
Hopkins's failure to be more forthcoming:

> The allocation of WPA funds cannot indefinitely be permitted to rest upon the
> personal discretion of any one man or small group of men. The relief funds
> belong to the whole country. Their allotment must be placed upon a basis that
> the whole country understands clearly and accepts as fair.

Colonel F. C. Harrington, who took Hopkins's place at the WPA's helm
in December 1939, supplied Congress with the only specific information the
agency ever divulged about the factors that were taken into account when
determining how much aid a particular state would receive:

> In 1940 Colonel Harrington told the House appropriations subcommittee that
> state employment quotas were determined by giving a weight of 40 percent to
> state population, and a weight of 40 percent to the amount of unemployment
> within the state. The remaining weight of 20 percent was attached to various
> factors in the discretion of WPA headquarters, acting upon the advice of its
> regional representatives. (MacMahon, Millet and Ogden 1941, p. 223)

Colonel Harrington was then asked by Representative Wigglesworth of
Massachusetts to furnish for the record the unemployment figures that the
WPA had used in establishing state employment quotas. Although he agreed
to do so, the data were never made available (Howard 1943, p. 597). Colonel
Harrington did, however, eliminate one factor that was thought to have
influenced state appropriations. He said that in the process of distributing
funds, the WPA did not consider the extent to which states financially
supported their own relief loads. (The states, it will be recalled, continued to
be responsible for providing relief to non-able-bodied and other unemployable
persons.)

Observers at the state level suspected that the administration played
favorites. As Patterson (1969, p. 194) has noted, critics of the WPA charged

'that the New Deal was discriminatory – that some states basked in the warmth of presidential friendship while others shivered outside in the cold'. The apparent favoritism, coupled with the administration's unwillingness to be forthcoming about its method of allocating WPA dollars, led to calls for more concrete funding formulas.

> Disturbed by the mysticism that appeared to enshroud the establishment of job quotas for the several states, Congress on a number of occasions has threatened to write into law some mandatory formula to take these matters out of the limbo of inscrutability into which they seemed to have fallen. In each instance, however, administration leaders convinced the lawmakers that although a suitable formula would be an invaluable administrative aid, the necessary statistical raw material (such as reasonably accurate and current estimates of unemployment, by states) was nonexistent. (Howard 1943, pp. 598–99)

One attempt to enact such legislation was made in 1939. Hoping to ensure a more equitable cross-state distribution of WPA dollars, a bill specifying a funding formula was introduced in the House of Representatives. The measure prescribed a formula based on state population and state unemployment rates, thus stripping the administration of its ability to allocate money as it saw fit. Of course, there was considerable opposition to the measure by those who benefited from the status quo. As mentioned earlier, heavily populated cities received disproportionate shares of the monies and hence, not surprisingly, the Conference of Mayors vigorously opposed the House's formula-funding scheme. The legislation was ultimately defeated in the Senate, with most of the opposition coming from western senators (Howard 1943, p. 599), whose constituents, on a per-capita basis, were the recipients of the lion's share of New Deal dollars.

7. Accomplishments of the Works Program

Aside from the jobs created, almost every city and community in the United States possesses some bridge, park, or building that stands as a visible monument to the WPA. The construction and repair of highways and roads accounted for much of the agency's work. Through June of 1938, some 280,000 miles of roads and streets were paved or repaired; 29,000 bridges were built and another 24,000 were reconditioned. Other contributions to the nation's transportation infrastructure included 153 new air fields and 280 miles of runway. Over 150 docks and wharves were constructed to facilitate water transportation (Office of Government Reports 1939, p. 79).

As of 1940, the WPA had erected 4,383 new school buildings and made repairs and additions to over 30,000 others. More than 130 hospitals were built and improvements made to another 1,670 (MacMahon, Millet and Ogden 1941, pp. 4–5). 'WPA workers developed nearly 1,100 new parks and improved some 4,200 others. They completed almost 1,800 new athletic fields, 1,600 playgrounds, over 900 swimming and wading pools, and 4,600 tennis courts . . .' (Office of Government Reports 1939, p. 80).

Nearly 9,000 miles of new storm drains and sanitary sewer lines were laid and some 2,600 miles reconditioned. The agency engaged in conservation work, building fire trails and planting roughly 24 million trees (Office of Government Reports 1939, p. 80). The WPA built or refurbished over 2,500 sports stadiums around the country with a combined seating capacity of 6,000,000 (MacMahon, Millet and Ogden 1941, pp. 6–7). As of 30 June 1938, WPA employees in cutting and sewing rooms had produced over 181,000,000 garments for distribution to families in need (Office of Government Reports 1939, p. 80).

Hopkins is credited with believing that the unemployed should be offered work and, moreover, that the work provided should match the skills of the unemployed as closely as possible. For this reason, the WPA undertook various projects to employ out-of-work artists, actors, and other professionals. Artists painted murals in public buildings while sculptors created works for public display, including park and battlefield monuments.[4] The actress Tallulah Bankhead testified before a starry-eyed Senate Committee on Appropriations regarding the value of these WPA activities. She averred that

> the project has given new life and hope and an opportunity to earn their living in their own profession to thousands of actors, musicians, stage hands, scenic artists, and other theater workers, for whom there was no opportunity for employment in the theater; and brought happiness to millions to whom the theater was a new and thrilling experience. (MacMahon, Millet and Ogden 1941, pp. 8–9)

These so-called white collar projects did not escape criticism, though. The term 'boondoggling' was added to the English language to describe many of the less-than-useful projects carried out by the WPA. Charles (1963, p. 70) provides an example: 'In the spring of 1935, newspapers in New York City carried the account of a project for research scientists investigating the making of safety pins.'

Many other WPA projects drew their share of criticism as well. The program suffered from all the inefficiencies inherent in the government provision of goods and services. The agency was often referred to pejoratively

'Anyway – The Little Fellow's in Line'
Philadelphia Inquirer, 8 April 1935

as 'We Piddle Around'. Indeed, the symbol that came best to represent the organization was a WPA worker leaning on a shovel (Charles 1963, p. 229). With almost 90 percent of the agency's budget devoted to wages, the WPA generally did not employ enough capital to be cost-effective by any standard. Students of the program have estimated that the costs of WPA projects could have been cut by two-thirds if adequate amounts of physical capital had been employed (Charles 1963, p. 57). Charging that the taxpayers were rarely getting their money's worth, Representative Dirksen of Illinois offered the following cost comparisons based on estimates by engineers in the Procurement Division of the Treasury's Public Buildings Branch:

World's Fair Building: Cost estimated at $544,000 by WPA or 43 1/2 cents per cubic foot. The Federal Building, which was built by the Procurement Division, cost only 20 cents per cubic foot.

Queens School in New York: WPA estimate $782,000. Estimated by competent engineers that it could be built for $441,000, or a saving of $341,000 on a single school building.

Laundry and fire station at Great Lakes, Illinois: WPA estimate $375,000. Competent engineers from Procurement Division say it could have been built for $218,000, or a saving of $157,000.

Municipal Building, Allegheny, Pennsylvania: WPA cost $88,200. Procurement Division estimate by private contract $50,000. (US House of Representatives 1939, p. 7269)

Although much of the criticism of the WPA seems justified, defenders of the program emphasize that efficiency was not the program's purpose. The works program was put in place to employ some 3.5 million individuals. Some boondoggles and employee shirking were to be expected in light of the haste demanded by emergency conditions. As such, waste was an unavoidable by-product of the program's noble goal of putting jobless people to work. The WPA had and still has many supporters. According to one of the program's admirers,

federal policy providing work for the jobless . . . has been of inestimable value to millions of workers who otherwise would have been idle and, in many instances, without means of subsistence. Furthermore, the demonstration that a democracy could assure to a substantial fraction of its jobless workers an opportunity to work as well as the actual work that was accomplished represented priceless gains to the American people as a whole. (Howard 1943, p. 841)

8. The National Youth Administration

The National Youth Administration (NYA) was established on 26 June 1935 as a sub-agency of the Works Progress Administration. The NYA enjoyed tremendous popularity because of its involvement with disadvantaged youth. Representative Collins of Mississippi remarked in testimony before his colleagues that, 'In my opinion, the creation of the National Youth Administration is the outstanding accomplishment of the New Deal. Its benefits cannot be measured' (US House of Representatives 1939, p. 7229).

Aubrey Williams, Assistant Administrator of the WPA, served as the NYA's Executive Director. The agency was detached from the WPA on 1 July 1939, obtaining its own funding from the Emergency Relief Appropriation

Act of 1939. During its bureaucratic existence, the NYA spent more than $330 million (Office of Government Reports 1939, p. 55).

The NYA focused its relief efforts in three major areas. Needy young people attending high school or college were assisted through the provision of part-time employment opportunities. Students receiving aid were required to carry three-fourths of a normal course load and obtain satisfactory grades. High school students performed such tasks as repairing school furniture, working in the school's library or maintaining the school's grounds. In return, the student-workers received wages of not more than $6 and not less than $3 per month. During a peak month in 1939 almost 270,000 high schoolers were so employed.

College undergraduate and graduate students were given jobs that matched their chosen majors whenever possible. For example, engineering students enrolled at one university served as research assistants to professors investigating airplane structure. Pay for undergraduate students ranged from $10 to $20 per month, while graduate student compensation ranged from $20 to $30 per month (Office of Government Reports 1939, p. 56).

Investigating college academic records from 20 states, Representative Collins reported evidence that students obtaining NYA aid performed better than average. In particular, 'The University of Wisconsin reports that of 50 who were elected to Phi Beta Kappa, 12 were NYA students, or 25 percent.' Similarly, 'at Washington State University, 8 out of 69 Phi Beta Kappas were NYA or 11.5 percent' (US House of Representatives 1939, p. 7229).

The NYA work program also aided young people who had dropped out of school and were unable to find work. According to government reports, the program not only provided funds to those in need, but in addition allowed youngsters to gain valuable work experience. Young people were allowed to sample several occupations and to select the one they preferred most. After settling on a particular career, on-the-job-training as well as classroom instruction were made available.

It is estimated that 415,000 youngsters were employed on NYA projects during fiscal year 1938–39. A survey of NYA workers revealed the following information: almost two-thirds of the workers were under 21 and the average age was nearly 20. Some 57 percent of the individuals employed were male and nearly 90 percent were white. Only a quarter of the NYA workers had a high school education and two-fifths had not entered the ninth grade (Office of Government Reports 1939, pp. 58–59).

Like the federal government's other work relief programs, the tasks undertaken by the agency were supposed to benefit the public. The work performed by the NYA's participants ranged from assisting in understaffed hospitals to building bus shelters. Necessary equipment, material, and supervision were typically provided by project sponsors.

Finally, the NYA provided career guidance to young people lacking pertinent job market information. The agency published almost 100 occupational studies describing training requirements, wages paid, and duties of various careers. The NYA also set up job-placement services across the country. By September of 1939, these placement centers operated in over 144 cities and 41 states. In total, NYA placement services registered nearly 550,000 youths and placed almost 220,000 of them in private jobs (Office of Government Reports 1939, p. 59).

9. Power and Politics

Of greatest concern to many contemporary critics of the New Deal was the role apparently played by politics in shaping the government's emergency relief efforts. While waste was disturbing, the use of public money to pursue private gains was intolerable. No program was criticized more on these grounds than the WPA. The most noteworthy struggle for personal power was demonstrated in the so-called Battle for Relief (Schlesinger 1960, p. 343).

According to Harold Ickes, who headed the Public Works Administration, the WPA had an unfair advantage in obtaining projects. It was possible for the WPA to contribute up to 100 percent of the funds for a given project while the PWA was limited by law to furnishing only 45 percent of the total. Local governments naturally preferred to have the WPA finance their projects whenever possible. A bargain was eventually struck between Hopkins and Ickes in which projects costing more than $25,000 were to be conducted by the PWA. However, what seemed to be a workable arrangement in theory proved to be far less so in practice. Hopkins would simply break large projects down into components costing less than $25,000 so that the WPA could carry them out (Charles 1963, p. 119). In reality, the agreement did little to settle the two administrators' political differences.

The available evidence indicates that both Hopkins and Ickes were well aware of the personal advantage to be gained through control of the distribution of emergency relief funds. They battled heatedly for primacy. Secretary of the Treasury Henry Morgenthau, for one, voiced his frustration with the bureaucratic infighting between the two powerful New Dealers: 'It seems almost tragic to think that the fate of the unemployed in America could be held up so long by these men both seeking power' (Charles 1963, p. 127).

Harry Hopkins's thirst for political power and his willingness to use the apparatus of public relief for personal gain were revealed in his own words. His most famous statement along these lines was one he later denied ever having made. In an exceptionally candid moment, he boasted that, 'We shall tax and tax, and spend and spend, and elect and elect' (Charles 1963, p. 216). Whether or not Hopkins would ever admit to himself that he allowed political ambitions to influence him, others have not hesitated to draw this conclusion. According to Charles (1963, p. 93), for example, 'a conflict between the altruistic social worker and a shrewd politician in the making shaped much of the rest of Hopkins' career as relief administrator. This conflict had a direct bearing on the work relief activities from 1935 through 1938.'

Evidence from a variety of sources suggests that politics had an important impact on decision-making at the WPA. If the agency's work relief programs represented the acts of a kind and caring government responding to the needs of unfortunate millions, then it appears that the administration's compassion for the poor followed a two-year cycle: 'WPA employment reached peaks in the fall of election years, and the pattern is most pronounced when employment is measured relative to indices of need' (Wright 1974, p. 35).

Further support for the hypothesis of WPA politicking is provided by data showing a more rapid rise in employment levels in one-party states where primary election outcomes were more important to the New Dealers than were the general elections. 'In states like Florida and Kentucky – where the New Deal's big fight was in the primary elections – the rise of WPA employment was hurried along in order to synchronize with the primaries' (High 1939, p. 62). This observation suggests that the New Dealers were not just interested in building a Democratic Party majority, but wanted to elect Democrats sympathetic to their policy agenda.[5]

Instances of financial improprieties and the exploitation of the public works program for personal political gain have been well documented.[6] Minnesota's governor, for example, was forced to resign as head of the relief organization for these very reasons. His replacement was later accused of encouraging social workers to channel aid to certain individuals for partisan purposes. Governor William Langer of North Dakota was charged with the misuse of public funds, found guilty, and served time in prison. Ohio Governor Davey utilized the relief program to build a political machine to the extent that the federal government seized control of relief in the state. In the state of Washington, 'the WPA administrator became involved in politics so deeply that he allowed WPA workers on the job to be assessed for contributions to local Democratic organizations' (Charles 1963, p. 184).

A local WPA administration in Pennsylvania was told in a letter by the Indiana County Democratic Party Committee that she must contribute $27 or jeopardize her reappointment. Also in Pennsylvania, 'evidence was presented that eighteen relief workers on a project in Luverne County were transferred to a project some forty miles from their homes because they wore Republican

'The Sower'
Washington Star, 18 July 1938

buttons and registered as Republicans' (MacMahon, Millet and Ogden 1941, p. 285).

'In Illinois evidence was obtained that some 450 men were added to the WPA rolls in one district in Cook County solely for the period of the primary campaign and that some 70 of these did no WPA work but canvassed their precincts' on behalf of their favored candidate (MacMahon, Millet and Ogden 1941, p. 285). The Barkley–Chandler primary race for the Kentucky Democratic Party nomination to the Senate provides a particularly egregious example of raw politicking. Barkley was pro-New Deal and was the Roosevelt administration's favored candidate. Representative Robison of Kentucky reported that he had seen 'relief funds in action to control the votes of needy people . . . ' (US House of Representatives 1939, p. 7239). The obvious political use of WPA funds prompted Judge Brady M. Stewart, state campaign manager for Governor Chandler, to write angrily to the president. He charged that

> the Works Progress Administration in Kentucky has been converted into an out-and-out political machine, dedicated over and above all other consider-ations to reelecting Senator Barkley. Those with starving mouths to feed are forced to surrender their one remaining privilege of choosing for whom they shall vote, otherwise they and their dependents must go hungry and naked.
>
> Persons are being employed who do no definite work, but are instructed to spend their entire time in political activity. Practically every Federal project is top heavy with foremen, part of whom confine their time and attention to keeping certain men definitely in line for Senator Barkley. . . . (US House of Representatives 1939, p. 7239)

The irregularities in Kentucky led to the appointment of a special committee to investigate the charges of political corruption.

> On the basis of the evidence before it the committee sustained the charges that certain WPA officials and employees in Kentucky had been active in the solicitation of contributions to a campaign fund for Senator Barkley and that a systematic canvass of WPA employees had been made to determine their preference in the senatorial campaign. (MacMahon, Millet and Ogden 1941, p. 284)

The foregoing examples suggest that political considerations influenced the selection of state and local WPA administrators and that at least some WPA workers were used as campaign workers and pressured for political contributions. Other opportunities for political advantage existed in the process of selecting the locations of WPA projects and in distributing the funds appropriated under the New Deal's other relief programs.[7] These opportunities could be exploited to buy votes in the 1936 presidential election campaign and to secure political support from sympathetic senators and representatives. The possibility that politics shaped the distribution of New Deal largesse is explored systematically in Chapters 7 and 8.

The WPA represented the largest program of its kind in American history. It put much-needed dollars into the hands of jobless millions and in the process contributed monumentally to the nation's infrastructure. Despite this record of achievement, serious questions remain concerning whether the program's money, projects, and jobs were distributed with an eye toward serving the public's interest or more narrow private interests. Were the efforts of the WPA and the other relief programs of the New Deal focused primarily on those truly in need? This question is addressed next.

NOTES

1. New Deal reformers asserted that retirement was beyond the means of many workers even before the Great Depression's onset. For evidence showing that industrialization did not adversely affect the economic well-being of older Americans and, hence, supplying arguments contradicting this assertion, see Gratton (1996), who contends that the intrafamily tensions arising from the intergenerational transfers necessary to provide economic security to the elderly better explain the broad popular support social security received.
2. Harry Hopkins headed both the FERA and the WPA's Works Progress Division, a position from which he was soon able to dominate the latter agency. See below.
3. This seems to be a common practice among modern-day charitable organizations. For example, the American Cancer Society routinely includes information on the 'seven warning signs of cancer' in its fund-raising letters so that the cost of the mailings can be counted as an educational expense rather than as an administrative expense. See Bennett and DiLorenzo (1994) for additional examples of such creative accounting.
4. Richard Hofstadter ([1948] 1989, p. 414) describes the origins of the WPA's cultural projects as follows:

    > When relief was being organized in the early stages of the New Deal, someone pointed out to [FDR] that a great many competent painters were poverty-stricken and desperate. Now, Roosevelt had no taste for painting, very little interest in artists and writers as a group, and no preconceived theories about the responsibility of the State for cultural welfare; but his decision to help the artists came immediately and spontaneously. 'Why not?' he said. 'They are human beings. They have to live. I guess the only thing they can do is paint and surely there must be some public place where paintings are wanted.' And so painters were included in the benefits of CWA. Ultimately, under the WPA, relief was extended to musicians, dancers, actors, writers, historians, even to students trying to finance themselves through college. A generation of artists and intellectuals was nursed through a trying period and became welded to the New Deal and devoted to Roosevelt liberalism.

5. This political strategy was even more evident during the primaries leading up to the 1938 midterm elections, when 'Roosevelt hoped to purge several highly critical and increasingly hostile members of his own party and to endorse those who supported the New Deal' (Lowitt [1984] 1993, p. 212).
6. Much of the following material is based on Charles (1963, pp. 174–205). The relevant chapter of his book is entitled 'Politics Galore!'.
7. The WPA did not have a monopoly on charges of political corruption and mismanagement, of course. For instance, 'in the summer of 1934 Ray Bannion, head of the CWA in California, and Pierce Williams, FERA western field representative, along with several other former CWA officials, were indicted "for conspiracy to defraud the Government in allowing certain projects

to have people put on the payroll without materials and equipment with which to work'" (Lowitt [1984] 1993, p. 173). In this case, the charges were subsequently dropped.

6. Did the New Dealers Respond to Economic Need?

It is disappointing to find that the funds have been so administered that the greater proportion has been expended in the States where need, by all reasonable standards, would have been less, and that the tendency is, if followed on through a long period of years in a spending program to make the poor people poorer until they will be more impoverished and more underprivileged than they are at present. . . .

– Senator Richard Russell (D-GA)

That it was heartless, that it caused intense suffering, made no difference to that great humanitarian in the White House, who cares only for the promotion of his own selfish ends. . . .

– Representative John Taber (R-NY)

This chapter begins an empirical examination of the distribution of New Deal emergency relief spending across the states. In particular, the question is here asked whether the money was allocated to those states and regions that had been hit hardest by the Great Depression and where economic need was consequently the greatest. Given the pressure to respond quickly to the crisis, the task of establishing relative need was, to be sure, not an easy one at the time. With the benefit of hindsight, we assess economic conditions in the states and evaluate the administration's efforts to identify needs and to address them.

Much evidence exists suggesting that New Deal expenditures in fact flowed to areas with relatively *less* need. As has been noted previously, on a per-capita basis proportionately more New Deal funds were channeled to states located in the West; the southern states received proportionately smaller allocations. This spending pattern has been censured by some and defended by others. To help resolve this controversy, the most common explanations for the observed distribution of New Deal appropriations are herein summarized and critiqued.

1   GAUGING THE MAGNITUDE OF THE CRISIS

While the Great Depression was a national event of catastrophic proportions, its impact was by no means uniform across regions, states, or even industries. Some sectors of the economy were devastated by the downturn, while others were only moderately affected. Eight states were home to over half the nation's families on relief, and four – Pennsylvania, New York, Ohio, and Illinois – contained one-third of them. Relief rolls across the country comprised from one-fourth of state population to one-twentieth of it (Charles 1963, pp. 26–27). New research (Wallis 1989) sheds light on the less than uniform impact of the Great Depression, yielding annual unemployment estimates that vary significantly across the states during the course of the economic collapse.[1] Surveys of the southern part of the country at the time showed that poverty rates in this region were in some cases unbelievably high – even when considered in light of the Great Depression's overall magnitude. President Roosevelt acknowledged this fact when he called the South the nation's number one economic problem and labeled Birmingham, Alabama, 'the worst hit city in the country' (Biles 1994, p. 20).

The downturn left most of American business paralyzed, but islands of prosperity did exist within the sea of economic despair. Bernstein (1987) provides an interesting and often surprising account of the impact of the Great Depression on particular industries. For example, although most iron and steel producers were hurt badly, tin plate producers enjoyed comparative plenty. Consumers' demands for canned foods, beer, and motor oil grew during the 1930s which increased the derived demand for tin plate. Purchases of household appliances also provided a burgeoning market for iron and steel producers, which helped soften the blow. Surprisingly, refrigerator sales expanded threefold, from around 800,000 in 1930 to 2.3 million in 1937.

The decade of the Great Depression represented a time of tremendous change in the food industry. Thanks to Clarence Birdseye, General Foods Corporation began marketing frozen meat, fish, poultry, and fruits and vegetables. Other new products introduced during the 1930s included prepackaged ice cream, ready-to-eat breakfast cereals, and oleomargarine. Improved food packaging methods stimulated glass and can production and allowed foods to be displayed in a more appealing manner. Distribution channels expanded and became more efficient and the decade witnessed the birth and proliferation of the modern supermarket.

Petroleum producers enjoyed comparative prosperity due in part to increased numbers of automobiles, but primarily because of expanding markets in 'home heating, aviation, and railroading' (Bernstein 1987, p. 66).

Pharmaceutical companies likewise prospered and glass manufacturers benefited from the growing demand for electric lamps.

The manufacturers of tobacco products also weathered the economic storm quite nicely. Cigarette consumption, especially among women, increased substantially during the Great Depression. 'Annual per capita consumption of cigarettes rose from 108 in 1911 to 972 in 1930 and to 1,551 in 1941' (Bernstein 1987, p. 71).

Of course, these isolated business success stories paled in comparison with the weak performance of the remainder of the economy. But even within industries that suffered financial devastation, exceptions did exist. Consider textiles. The downturn almost destroyed the industry, with less than a quarter of the manufacturers reporting positive net incomes in 1930. Nearly a quarter of the firms remained profitable, though. The old and outdated mills of New England, then the center of the nation's textile industry, were the most vulnerable to the economic collapse. Indeed, by 1932, roughly two-thirds of the mills in New Bedford, Massachusetts, had been shut down. Their more technologically advanced competitors in the Southeast fared much better, however, with mills producing stylish women's clothing and material for use in automobiles continuing to operate in the black.[2]

In general, producers of non-durable goods are hit much less hard by recession than are the producers of durables: consumers rationally tend to repair rather than to replace big-ticket items during economic downturns. Building materials and forest products provide a good example. Lumber producers were devastated by the economy's collapse: 'In 1929, over 4000 lumber corporations had reported a positive net income to the Internal Revenue Service. By 1932, only 541 did' (Bernstein 1987, p. 83). Paper producers fared much better. This was especially true of firms that were able to switch to the production of new products to meet consumers' changing demands. The health and beauty aids fields provided a new outlet for paper producers. Paper towels, tissues, and paper plates and cups were becoming increasingly popular with consumers. In addition, cheaper grades of paper were developed which expanded the market for writing paper and books, thereby increasing the derived demand for the product.

In sum, the notion of a moribund national economy during the Great Depression is not a completely accurate one. Bernstein states that many observers have concluded that the 'downturn left all sectors prostrate. In fact, the impact of the crash was not uniform; the variegated response to it of American manufacturing industries demonstrates this clearly' (Bernstein 1987, p. 49).

1. Wallis's Employment Indices

Research by John Joseph Wallis (1989) demonstrates this same point more systematically. While many states saw their economies devastated, others remained reasonably well off. The best available estimates of annual national unemployment rates during the 1930s were produced by Stanley Lebergott (1964). He based his estimates on the Bureau of Labor Statistics establishment sample, using the decennial census as well as the biennial Census of Manufactures as benchmarks. Wallis uses these same data to generate annual state-level estimates of employment. The indices show not only how severe the unemployment situation was within a particular state but also yield state-specific estimates of the duration of the downturn. Wallis's data suggest that the economic collapse was more severe and recovery more protracted in certain areas of the country than others (Wallis 1989, pp. 45–46).

Specifically, the estimates shown in Table 6.1 indicate that the economies of the industrialized East North Central region fell furthest over the 1929–33 period, while less heavily industrialized areas such as the South Atlantic and New England regions suffered less.[3] Wallis reports evidence that the particular types of industries located in a state explain some but not all of the inter-regional differences in economic performance. He constructed a 'composite employment index' designed to help test whether state-level employment differentials were attributable to the industrial characteristics of the states or instead merely reflected national trends. According to Wallis, labor-force composition and national trends explain only part of the cross-state variation in depression-era unemployment (Wallis 1989, pp. 60–61).[4]

Wallis's most surprising result relates to the southern employment situation. While the South was much poorer than the rest of the nation – per-capita income there was half the national average in 1930 – at least some of the region's states came through the storm relatively unscathed. At the depression's trough, for instance, employment in the South Atlantic region stood at 86 percent of its 1929 level. This figure compares quite favorably with the national average employment index, which stood at slightly more than 78 percent the same year. This relatively moderate fall in employment was followed by a strong recovery and, as Wallis shows, by 1940 regional employment was 26 percent higher than it had been in 1929. The East and West South Central regions were not as fortunate, with 1933 employment falling 30 percent below pre-depression levels. But employment in both of these sections also recovered relatively quickly. On the other hand, 'although the New England and Middle Atlantic states had a considerably easier time of it in the Great Crash, they just managed to attain their 1929 levels of employment by 1940' (Wallis 1989, p. 56).

Table 6.1 Regional employment indices (August 1929 = 100)

Region	1931	1933	1935	1937	1939
New England	89.2	81.4	89.5	98.6	94.6
Middle Atlantic	89.8	81.2	87.8	95.1	95.5
East North Central	78.3	69.5	82.1	98.3	93.6
West North Central	88.3	79.1	88.8	98.3	97.3
South Atlantic	92.7	88.3	97.3	112.2	116.5
East South Central	83.7	74.2	82.7	99.0	101.1
West South Central	82.6	71.9	86.3	102.6	106.5
Mountain	74.8	61.6	72.6	88.1	90.7
Pacific	84.0	74.5	88.1	102.1	103.4

Notes:
The indices are based on total employment. See appendix Table 6A.1 for census region definitions.

Source:
Wallis (1989, pp. 65–66).

Wallis (1989, p. 64) did not overstate things very much when he said that 'the availability of the annual, disaggregated employment series provided by [this] paper should help in answering a wide range of questions about the course and consequences of the Great Depression.' His indices will be utilized in a later chapter to help construct a more accurate picture of state economic well-being and to analyze the extent to which economic need influenced the distribution of New Deal dollars. However, it is worth pausing here briefly to assess the reliability of Wallis's employment indices. If they in fact provide an accurate picture of economic conditions in a particular state they should be highly correlated with other measures of that state's economic well-being. A number of variables were selected for this purpose, including personal and corporate income, new vehicle registrations, and bank deposits. (All of the variable names, definitions, and sources are given in appendix Table 6A.2, and their means, standard deviations, maximums, and minimums are shown in appendix Table 6A.3.)

The results (see appendix Table 6A.4) indicate that for the most part, Wallis's indices are positively correlated with other measures of economic well-being, although the estimated partial correlation coefficients themselves are generally quite small. The state-specific employment indices evidently capture some, but not all, of the factors relevant to assessing state and regional variations in economic performance during the Great Depression. Clearly, a wide variety of variables must be taken into account to gain an adequate picture of a state's economic health.

One obvious weakness of the employment indices is that while they are useful for examining how far state employment and, hence, earned income, fell from pre-crash levels, they do not indicate the extent to which wealth varied from region to region and state to state. This defect is important for any analysis of the geographical distribution of New Deal funds because the Roosevelt administration's stated goal was not only to encourage recovery but to address reform, an objective 'defined to mean allocations designed to improve the social and economic status of the "backward" states' (Reading 1972, p. 8). The employment indices do a particularly poor job of measuring need in the agricultural South. With little manufacturing industry, residents of this region were, for the most part, self-employed on farms and in small businesses.

2. Southern Poverty

The story of southern rural poverty, both before and after the crash, is one of much suffering and despair. A survey of the region conducted by the Works Progress Administration (Holley, Winston and Woofter 1940) describes the abject poverty there in painful detail. Inadequate nutrition was a constant problem and hunger was widespread. The lack of proper diets was compounded by deplorable housing conditions. 'On the average the Southern farm house is old and unpainted, without bathroom or basement, and one storey in height. It lacks running water and in one of three cases the roof, doors, and windows, and interior walls and ceilings are in poor condition' (Holley, Winston and Woofter 1940, p. 11).

Poor diets and rudimentary sanitary facilities had the predicted effects on the health of the region's citizens. 'Provisions for prevention of contagion are frequently inadequate, and death rates from such diseases as typhoid and paratyphoid fever and malaria continue to be high as compared with other areas' (Holley, Winston and Woofter 1940, p. 11). Limited access to health care providers only exacerbated the problem.

Farm operators and laborers, the survey said, were in particular need during the winter months because their meager earnings from crops did not tide them over until spring and few between-season employment opportunities existed. Unemployment rates among these groups were the highest in the nation according to the WPA's survey – joblessness on southern farms was 'even more frequent than in the Great Plains drought section' (Holley, Winston and Woofter 1940, p. 50).

As Charles (1963, p. 27) observes, 'an inherent problem faced by the administrator of any relief program is to judge need accurately.' And once need is determined, it becomes the task of the administrator to target those regions where suffering is the greatest. On the basis of anecdotal and survey evidence at least, one would have expected the South to have received a goodly portion of New Deal aid. Indeed, as mentioned earlier, even the president spoke of this region's desperate need for emergency relief.

3. Was Need Addressed? A First Glimpse

As earlier chapters have suggested, New Deal funds were distributed across the nation in a highly uneven manner. Figure 6.1 shows the per-capita allocation of federal emergency relief expenditures, loans, and insurance, by state, aggregated over the 1933–39 period. Wide state-to-state variation in per-capita aid is evident. Not only did the Mountain, Pacific, and Upper Midwestern states benefit disproportionately, their per-capita allocations sometimes exceeded those of the nation's eastern half by factors of three or more. This same information is displayed in chart form in Figure 6.2. The data shown there indicate that over one-third of total New Deal spending was directed to the Mountain and Pacific regions.

The same data used to create the previous map and chart – 48 documents prepared by the Statistical Section of the Office of Government Reports – can be disaggregated into some basic spending categories. Figures 6.3 and 6.4 show the regional distributions of per-capita agricultural and non-agricultural expenditures, respectively. While the West North Central states dominate the former category, the Mountain Region comes in a close second. The Mountain states likewise received the lion's share of the funds allocated under the New Deal's non-agricultural programs. Similar patterns emerge when one examines the per-capita distributions of New Deal loans, insurance, and non-repayable grants (see appendix Figures 6A.1 through 6A.3).[5]

These diagrams indicate that the West, in general, benefited most from the New Deal while, somewhat surprisingly, the site of the 'nation's number one economic problem' (the South) benefitted least. The remainder of this chapter examines some of the attempts to explain why the allocation followed this seemingly perverse pattern.

The process for determining the distribution of New Deal dollars proved to be quite controversial. As might be expected, the competition between regions was heated. Politicians fought energetically to see that federal emergency relief funds were channeled to their constituents. Those who felt

Figure 6.1 New Deal expenditures, loans and insurance by state, per-capita allocations, 1933–39 (1930 population)

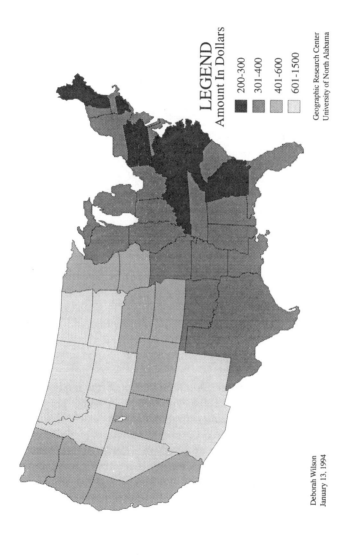

LEGEND
Amount In Dollars

200-300
301-400
401-600
601-1500

Geographic Research Center
University of North Alabama

Deborah Wilson
January 13, 1994

Figure 6.2   Percentage distribution of total New Deal funds per capita, by region, 1933–39

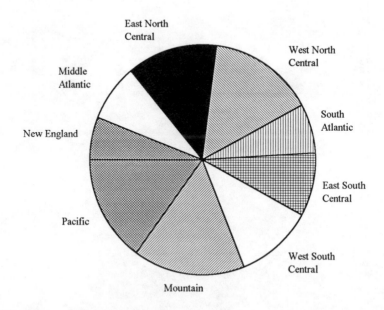

shortchanged complained loudly. Noting the apparent regional disparity and, in particular, his own state's meager share, Senator Reynolds of North Carolina addressed his colleagues and demanded,

> I want the Senator to tell me why the people of North Carolina are not entitled to the same remuneration as are those who reside in the State of New York. Can it be that the people of North Carolina are not just as patriotic as are the people of New York? What can it be, I should like to be advised, what causes this situation, in order that I may tell the people of North Carolina. . . . (US House of Representatives 1939, p. 912)

Expressing similar sentiments, Georgia Senator Richard Russell added that he had

Figure 6.3 Percentage distribution of agricultural funds per capita, by region, 1933–39

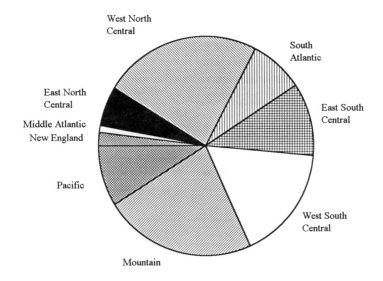

made a study of the administration of the various relief and recovery agencies which has led me to the conclusion that I could no longer justify the confidence which the people of my State have shown in me by sending me to this body did I not protest against the many very evident discriminations against the South in the administration of these various funds. . . . (US House of Representatives 1939, p. 916)

2 THE ADMINISTRATION'S EFFORTS

Harry Hopkins and his staff at the Federal Emergency Relief Administration set up a system for determining where to send the agency's dollars. The governor of a state seeking FERA funds was required to sign a statement detailing the state's need; the request was to be backed by statistical information and other supporting materials. In addition, the agency sent field representatives and administrators to investigate economic conditions in the requesting state. 'They talked with bankers, lawyers, businessmen, financiers,

*Figure 6.4   Percentage distribution of non-agricultural funds per capita, by
          region, 1933–39*

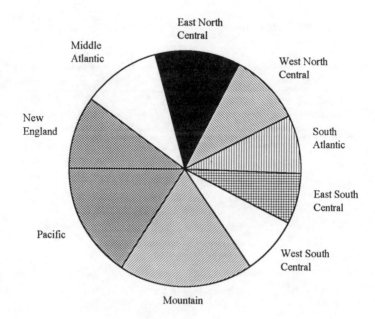

agricultural leaders, farmers, and staffs in the state relief offices' to verify
applications for relief (Charles 1963, p. 36).

Hopkins's most trusted field representative (and most voluminous
correspondent) was newspaperwoman Lorena Hickok, who in July 1933 he
asked to 'go out around the country and look this thing over' (Lowitt [1984]
1993, p. 8). Over the course of the next 18 months, Hickok 'traveled the
length and breadth of the United States', reporting frequently by mail and
occasionally in person, heeding Hopkins's admonition that, 'I don't want
statistics from you. I don't want the social worker angle. I just want your own
reaction as an ordinary citizen' (Lowitt [1984] 1993, p. 8). She ultimately
supplied Hopkins with a wealth of information about the plight of the people
and the FERA's successes and failures.

In the fall of 1934, Hopkins set out to obtain better and more systematic
information. The Municipal Finance Section of FERA supervised 'the most

thorough study ever conducted prior to 1934 of the economic resources of the states in an effort to determine where federal money should go' (Charles 1963, p. 39). Four 'quotas' were established for the purpose of assessing 'need'. Quota one included data on mining, manufacturing, and agricultural production. The second quota consisted of population figures. Federal tax collection statistics made up the third quota, and quota four included property values and other information on economic activity in the state (Charles 1963, pp. 40–41).

According to Charles (1963), balanced by other relevant considerations, FERA used this information to determine grants to the states. Damage resulting from flood, drought, or similar natural disasters, for example, might influence FERA expenditures in a particular state. But 'in the last analysis', perhaps owing to the influence of Lorena Hickok's reactions as an ordinary citizen, 'need, not facts and figures, determined the amount of aid Hopkins and his staff were willing to give except as limited by the total amount available to FERA from federal funds. Hopkins never reconciled himself to letting figures dominate the giving of relief' (Charles 1963, p. 41).

Corrington Gill, Assistant to WPA administrator Harry Hopkins, made this same point in testimony before the Senate Special Committee to Investigate Unemployment and Relief (the Byrnes Committee) in 1938. Asked by Senator Byrnes, who served as the committee's chairman, to tell the committee how employment quotas were determined across the states, Gill responded:

> Our regional representatives, Senator, have been out in these States for over four years now. They are intimately in touch with the States and the conditions in the States. The allotment was determined after several conferences, first with the State administrators and the field representatives, and then the field representatives and Mr Hopkins. (US Senate 1938, p. 51)

In short, according to administration sources, the New Dealers took great pains to determine, and were therefore well aware of, the states and regions where suffering was most acute.

3 THE ADMINISTRATION'S CRITICS

Despite its avowedly painstaking efforts to establish need, and perhaps because the administration's responses to that need relied more on gut feelings than on dry economic statistics, the resulting distribution of emergency relief funds soon became a center of controversy. As one critic later put it, 'the New Deal was discriminatory – some states basked in the warmth of presidential friendship while others shivered outside in the cold' (Patterson 1969, p. 194).

FERA came under fire first. Some states seemed to be treated more favorably than others by the administration: 'In later years disgruntled state officials advanced all kinds of statistical evidence of FERA discrimination. The average monthly relief payment per family varied considerably over the nation: Kentucky families received only $6.78 while the New Yorker received $45.12 in May of 1934' (Patterson 1969, pp. 54–55). Consistent with the data reported above, Tindall (1967, p. 482) claimed that 'relief in the South was disproportionate even to population. With more than a fourth of the nation's inhabitants, the Southern States received less than a seventh of the FERA expenditures.'

Mertz (1978, p. 52) also points out that the South's relief grants from FERA were somewhat lower than the remainder of the country and adds, 'This was frequently justified, occasionally even by Hopkins, with the claim that southern living costs were lower than those in the rest of the country.' This cost-of-living argument is examined more closely later in this chapter.

The Civil Works Administration was also accused of discriminatory spending. 'Many Congressmen objected to the fact that eleven states received 57 percent of the total spent by CWA' (Charles 1963, p. 50). Charles responds that, rather than favoring some states at the expense of others, CWA spending is instead better explained by need. Because depression-era unemployment tended to be concentrated in large cities, it was natural for urban states to receive the most funds. This explanation is likewise explored more fully below.

The WPA was also on the receiving end of criticism. As discussed in the previous chapter, the wages paid to workers doing the same job in different regions of the country came under intense scrutiny as a result of the wide geographical variation in WPA compensation schedules. Once again, the southern region of the nation appeared to be disadvantaged insofar as workers there received the lowest remuneration. Responding to this criticism in the pages of the *New York Times*, Corrington Gill defended the agency's practices, stating that

> It is probable that a good deal of the criticism of the . . . wage policy was the result of snap judgement without having the time or opportunity to ascertain the facts. An examination of the President's regulation indicates that the wails cannot be justified.
>
> The variations between regions and between size of city groups and between occupational classes were based on an exceedingly careful study of the existing differences in the prevailing wage rate structure for the various classes and groups. (*New York Times*, 26 May 1935, section 4, p. 3)

In congressional hearings on the agency, Senator Henry Cabot Lodge (D-MA) noted that the entire Southeast, with a quarter of the nation's population, received the same amount of WPA funds as eight western states with only 8 percent of the population. Testifying on his agency's behalf, Harry Hopkins said that he could present a good case for this disparity but was not pressed to do so (MacMahon, Millet and Ogden 1941, p. 223).

Senator Russell of Georgia was not sympathetic:

> If charts and tables prepared by the Works Progress Administration are to be believed, that instead of equalizing the income of the people of the United States, the manner in which these funds have been distributed to date has a tendency to make the rich States richer, and to make the poor States and the poor people of those States poorer. (US House of Representatives 1939, p. 916)

He went on to charge that

> it is discrimination against the merchant in the Southern States, because he cannot sell as much of his products as the merchants in the States where these funds have been poured out with such a lavish hand. It is a discrimination against every line of business and against every individual citizen of the States that are thus penalized and imposed upon, because every line of business and every individual of these States has been compelled to pay his fair share of the taxes collected, and assume his equal proportion of the debt incurred to raise these enormous relief funds. (US House of Representatives 1939, p. 917)[6]

In sum, then, as now, critics of the New Deal were convinced that the Roosevelt administration distributed emergency relief funds unfairly. States in the western half of the nation seem to have been favored, while those in the South seem to have been shortchanged. Logical explanations for the apparently discriminatory pattern of spending, including some that were offered by the administration itself, are of course conceivable. The possibilities are scrutinized next.

4 ALTERNATIVE EXPLANATIONS FOR THE DISTRIBUTION OF NEW DEAL FUNDS

Explanations abound for the manner in which New Deal dollars were actually distributed across states and regions. Some of these seem plausible and therefore deserve further investigation, while others can be dismissed outright. The most common explanations involve differences in cost of living from region to region, the shortage of accurate data on which to base funding decisions, the political clout of certain states and regions, regional differences in standards of living, and the matching requirements stipulated by some of the New Deal programs.

Some observers simply deny that any bias existed. Charles (1963, p. 41), for example, has stated that 'there was actually a high correlation between the amount states were allocated and their population.' Patterson (1969, p. 78) likewise defends the Roosevelt administration and the WPA, asserting that 'the correlation between relief received and state need seems to have been fairly close during the lifetime of the WPA.'

He then summarizes the dominant explanations for the observed pattern of New Deal spending. Noting that the cost of living varies greatly from region to region and was especially low in the South, Patterson argues that smaller New Deal expenditures in this region simply reflected the fact that every relief dollar would purchase more there. He argues further that the spending pattern could be explained in part by the 'wide differences in amounts contributed for matching money'. Patterson continues, 'lack of sound data on unemployment also confused matters. Hopkins' avowed purpose was to send money where it was most needed. But given the unreliable figures on unemployment available to him, how was he to judge precisely that one state or area was more desperate than another?' (Patterson 1969, p. 55).

Lastly, Patterson (1969, pp. 55–56) explains the New Dealers' apparent favoritism toward the western United States as a compassionate response to need. Although they contributed little from their own resources, the states in the Rocky Mountain region received higher per-capita grants because they were poorer than the New England states. Patterson in effect suggests that a different explanation is relevant for each region – the West got more because it had less (need), the North got more because it had more (matching), and the South got less because it needed less (cost of living). Such special-case stories about the regional variations in New Deal spending leave much to be desired. The development of a more general model is clearly in order.

1. Data Limitations

A lack of adequate data is an unlikely explanation for the manner in which New Deal funds were allocated. By all accounts, the Roosevelt administration was acutely aware of the plight of citizens in the rural South and the weather-ravaged 'Dust Bowl'. Lorena Hickok's copious eyewitness reports and detailed economic statistics collected by the Municipal Finance Section of FERA were readily available to the New Dealers. Claims of inadequate data are also at odds with the testimony offered by Assistant Administrator Corrington Gill to the Byrnes Committee, during which he more or less bragged that the administration was fully informed about economic conditions in the states. It is also noteworthy that while Patterson (1969) explains New Deal spending patterns partly on the basis of insufficient information, Charles (1963) contends that the administration's knowledge of state unemployment rates determined how the money was distributed.

2. Cost of Living

The cost-of-living explanation is superficially plausible and has from time to time been advanced in the administration's defense. In his response to charges of inequity, Corrinton Gill (1935, p. 3) wrote: 'Nineteen dollars a month for unskilled work in the rural South in cash means just as much, if not more than, $55 in New York City.' Tindall (1967, p. 482) later remarked that 'the pattern of regional differences was repeatedly explained by the folklore of lower living costs in the South.'

But angry at the injustices he perceived as having been visited on poor people by the Roosevelt administration, Georgia Senator Russell retorted that

> when some poor devil of a sharecropper or tenant farmer in Texas, with a cash income perhaps of $200 per year, steps up to the post office window to buy a postage stamp, they do not tell him, 'You can get your postage stamp for 2 cents, because your State's per capita WPA expenditures are only $15.40, a low average when compared to the higher national average.' The same man would receive no special consideration in the payment of all the other special taxes – taxes on gasoline, on automobiles, and all other special taxes from which the major portion of our revenue is derived. (US House of Representatives 1939, pp. 920–21)

He went on to present some regional cost-of-living estimates which cast considerable doubt on this explanation. The data, which Senator Russell placed on the record, had been prepared by the US government's Labor Bureau. The figures purported to represent the 'estimated cost of living for a 4-person manual worker's family at maintenance level . . . as of Sept. 15, 1938' (US House of Representatives 1939, p. 922). Annual cost-of-living estimates for selected cities are presented in Table 6.2.

While living costs were indeed lower in the South, the regional differences do not seem to be anywhere large enough to justify the allocation of New Deal funds.[7] For example, the annual cost-of-living estimate presented for the city of Jacksonville, Florida, was $1,260.44, while the corresponding estimate for Buffalo, New York, was $1,283.81. Differentials of this magnitude hardly called for major cross-regional differences in New Deal grants, loans, and wage rates.

Table 6.2   Annual cost-of-living estimates for selected cities as of September 1938

Southern Cities		Rest of Nation	
Richmond	$1,278.94	Boston	$1,350.50
Jacksonville	1,260.44	Buffalo	1,283.81
New Orleans	1,255.96	Denver	1,273.94
Memphis	1,252.77	Kansas City	1,267.21
Birmingham	1,235.50	Indianapolis	1,244.72

Source:
US House of Representatives (1939, p. 922).

In fact, mounting pressure forced the New Dealers to adjust their work relief pay schedules in 1939 more accurately to reflect actual geographical differences in the cost of living. The result was an increase in the amount of relief appropriations going to the South and a reduction in the amount going to other regions. Specifically, 'the Southern minimum rose to $31.20 and the Northern dropped to $39 in most states, and maximums reached $81.90 in most Southern and $94.90 in most Northern states' (Tindall 1967, p. 484).

3. Standards of Living

Perhaps the most detailed source of information on the distribution of New Deal funds available at the time was *The Plantation South*, a comprehensive report prepared by the WPA's Division of Research. The authors of the study examined the amount of funds distributed by four federal bureaus – the FERA, the CWA, the WPA, and the Farm Security Administration (including its predecessor agency, the Resettlement Administration) – from the beginning of the New Deal through March of 1938. The results demonstrated clearly that the impoverished South, whose plight was described so vividly in other parts of the same survey, received the smallest grants from the federal government. North Carolina, for instance, received $23.68 per capita while South Dakota received $115.92 (Holley, Winston and Woofter 1940, pp. 51–52).

The report offered two explanations for the regional disparity. According to *The Plantation South*, the residents of that region received lower benefits because of their lack of political clout as well as their lower standard of living. More specifically, the authors contended that fewer dollars went south

> partly because it is dominantly rural and rural groups have been less articulate than urban groups about their needs, partly because living standards are so low that standards of acceptance for relief have been lower than in other sections, and partly because, for the same reason, amounts of relief granted per case have been relatively lower than in other sections. (Holley, Winston and Woofter 1940, p. 51)

In essence, southerners merited less aid because their standards of living were so low that it simply did not take much to satisfy them. This explanation is clearly at odds with New Deal rhetoric. *The Plantation South* is also surprisingly frank about the role played by politics in shaping the distribution of emergency relief funds. It suggests that political pressure had an important influence on New Deal decision-making, perhaps more important than need.

While not everyone accepts the idea that the South received less aid because southerners' lobbying efforts were not particularly effective, a number of observers have argued that meager benefits proved acceptable to recipients in that region because standards of living there were so low. Tindall (1967, p. 483), among others, believes this to have been the case: 'the conclusion is unavoidable that the differential, like so many other things, reflected differences not in the cost but in the standard of living.'

Corrington Gill hinted at the same justification in his *New York Times* piece, where he stated that 'in most instances the people in this region [the South] have economical places in which to live and the opportunity to grow their own food. In other words, the earnings shown in this [relief] schedule are in recognition of existing conditions in these areas' (*New York Times*, 26 May 1935, section 4, p. 3).

Lorena Hickok's reports to her boss in Washington, Harry Hopkins, provide additional support for this explanation. In her view, a policy of dispensing the same relief payments to all recipients produced

> 'the same old story' involving 'two classes of people': whites 'with white standards of living, for whom relief . . . is anything but adequate.' . . . And then there were the Spanish Americans, or Hispanics. For these people, as well as for blacks east of the Mississippi River, relief was both adequate and attractive. Though some were able to get work, the wages were so low that they were better off on relief. (Lowitt [1984] 1993, p. 19)

According to Hickok, the upshot was that because blacks and Hispanics dominated the relief rolls, 'we are compelled to force the white man's standard of living down to that of the Mexicans and Negroes' (Lowitt [1984] 1993, p. 19), for whom relief 'made possible in many, many cases, a BETTER standard of living' (Lowitt [1984] 1993, p. 17; emphasis in original). As a result, she apparently

> became half convinced that the government should force destitute Negroes and Mexican-Americans off the rolls and into agricultural labor. . . . Then limited FERA money could provide work relief for the middle class without lowering their accustomed living conditions so drastically. While Hickok admitted that a federal double standard of access to relief was hardly defensible, she had heard that such discrimination was quietly practiced in many areas anyway. (Mertz 1978, pp. 56–57)

While tinged with racism, regional and ethnic variations in living standards could possibly justify 'two standards of relief', though, as Hickok realized, 'the idea will sound horrible in Washington' (Lowitt [1984] 1993, p. 19). Accustomed to poverty, individuals at the lower end of the income distribution – and the regions in which they tended to be over-represented – might well have been satisfied with less. Extended family living arrangements, the growing of subsistence crops, and non-market employment opportunities were options available to the residents of the rural South which helped to insulate them somewhat from the depression's full impact. If this reasoning is valid, however, why did the relief going to the rural upper Midwest exceed by nearly five times, on a per-capita basis, that received by the typical southerner? Moreover, were standards of living so much lower in Virginia, North Carolina, and Georgia, that less aid was needed in these states than in the rest of the South (see Figure 6.1)?

In short, the three explanations discussed thus far do not withstand even cursory examination. Given the wide state-to-state variation in per-capita relief, Charles's contention that New Deal dollars were, for the most part, distributed on the basis of population is clearly wrong. The cost-of-living basis for the perverse allocation of New Deal dollars is likewise tenuous. To be sure, cost-of-living differences existed across regions, but their magnitude can in no way account for the wide disparities in funding levels. Moreover, while the standard-of-living explanation is plausible on its face, it fails to rationalize the differences in treatment accorded to states with similarly low living standards.

4. Matching Requirements

One of the more comprehensive attempts to explain the disparities in relief spending involves the matching requirements adopted by some New Deal programs to encourage state and local participation. Half of the initial grants distributed by the Federal Emergency Relief Administration (FERA) were made on this basis, with the remainder being allocated at the discretion of administrator Harry Hopkins and President Roosevelt. According to this explanation, programmatic matching requirements made it possible for a few relatively wealthy states to obtain disproportionate shares of the federal government's emergency relief budget. Because such requirements placed them at a disadvantage, less populous and less wealthy states pushed for more discretion in the allocation of New Deal funds.

In the fall of 1933, FDR approved a proposal to increase the amount of FERA dollars allocated on a discretionary basis. This change 'assured a fairer distribution of relief funds by providing more support for the poor states. Of equal importance were the enlarged discretionary powers of the administrator' (Charles 1963, p. 35).

If some states were in fact favored simply because they had more resources to match federal grants and, thus, were able to obtain larger appropriations, such an observation would go a long way toward explaining the relatively small amounts of aid allocated to the South. But it would also raise questions about why such funding formulas were adopted in the first place. Matching is a commonplace tool of public finance, to be sure. If the New Dealers' chief goal was to provide relief, though, surely they would not have imposed a requirement that systematically channeled more aid to better-off states. In any case, the matching hypothesis is one of the key empirical issues to be explored in the next two chapters.

5. Politics

As noted previously, the idea that politics influenced the allocation of New Deal relief spending was raised by the authors of *The Plantation South*. Charges that the public's money was being used for personal political gain were leveled at the Roosevelt administration on numerous occasions. Harry Hopkins more or less confessed that this was so when he (allegedly) boasted, 'We shall tax and tax, and spend and spend, and elect and elect.'

Suspicions that ordinary political forces were at work at the highest levels of New Deal decision-making erupted in Senator Russell's January 1939 speech to the Senate. The senator had compared the appropriations allocated to his home state of Georgia with those received by Wisconsin – a state with similar land area and population but with many more resources. He found that Wisconsin had obtained over twice as much aid. Senator Ellison Smith of South Carolina interrupted and this colloquy followed:

'And Everywhere That Harry Went the Ram was Sure to Go'
Columbus [Ohio] *Dispatch*, 6 September 1936

Mr. Smith: I have been interested in the analysis the Senator has made of the wealth and population which showed that Wisconsin and Georgia were so nearly equal in those features. I wondered if the Senator had any way of ascertaining the political aspect in those two States.

Mr. Russell: Mr. President, I had not intended to touch upon any political aspects of this question.

Mr. Smith: Why not? The Senator knows that is all there is to it. (US House of Representatives 1939, p. 926)

Indeed, there are at least two reasons for believing that politics is a critical factor in explaining the New Deal's evident western bias. The support of these states was instrumental in securing Franklin Roosevelt's nomination as the Democratic Party's standard-bearer in 1932. History might have played out very differently had 'favorite-son' candidates William Gibbs McAdoo of California and Speaker of the House (and soon-to-be vice presidential nominee) John Nance Garner of Texas not released the delegates pledged to them and thrown their support behind FDR on the convention's fourth ballot (Lowitt [1984] 1993, p. 4). Two years later, the West was again of the highest political importance to the New Dealers 'because of crucial senatorial races involving Democratic incumbents in Utah, Arizona, Montana, and in other states where they hoped to gain a seat: Nebraska, Wyoming, New Mexico, Washington, and California' (Lowitt [1984] 1993, p. 204).

As will be seen in the next chapter, scholars have begun producing evidence that supports the conclusion that politics played a central role in shaping the New Deal. Whether 'that is all there is to it' remains a matter of controversy.

6. National Emergency Council Data

Leonard Arrington's discovery in 1969 of detailed data showing exactly how much money each state received made systematic empirical analysis of New Deal spending possible. The competing hypotheses advanced to explain the observed distribution of funds have subsequently been modeled and tested econometrically. The existing studies are summarized in Chapter 7 and extended in Chapter 8.

The data which form the basis for all modern empirical work on the New Deal were produced by the National Emergency Council (NEC), an agency conceived to coordinate the federal government's emergency relief programs. While the NEC never fulfilled this role, it did 'compile reports on state and federal activities' (Patterson 1969, p. 111).[8] The agency also gathered information to gauge public opinion about the New Deal. The NEC was transferred to the Bureau of the Budget in 1937, and was replaced by the Office of Government Reports in 1939 (Patterson 1969, p. 111). The latter agency prepared the documents – one report for each of the 48 states – which, thanks to Leonard Arrington, supplied a new opportunity for investigating the Roosevelt administration's spending priorities.

Chapter 7 reviews the recent empirical literature that exploits Arrington's data set. The economic factors that influenced the allocation of New Deal funds will be examined and evidence that political motivations underlay the regional pattern of spending will be discussed. The econometric models of Gavin Wright and others who have uncovered electoral effects in the data are summarized. These models are extended and the matching hypothesis is tested explicitly in Chapter 8.

It is important to emphasize here that the political hypothesis of the New Deal is not novel. Historians have often remarked that FDR's reelection prospects in 1936 hinged on the political support he would garner from urban voters and from voters located in a few key 'swing' states. Senator Russell made this same point when he asked why the South seemed to have been shortchanged by the New Dealers. He observed that

> it is very difficult in examining these figures to avoid wondering whether the fact that the States which have received the lowest percent of these expenditures have voted the Democratic ticket in both fair weather and foul so consistently that in many cases their needs are overlooked. (US House of Representatives 1939, p. 926)

NOTES

1. Wallis's estimates are discussed in the following section and summarized in Table 6.1.
2. It is noteworthy in this regard that the 'code of fair competition' written by the textile manufacturers was the first to be approved under the National Industrial Recovery Act.
3. The states included in each of the official US census regions are listed in Table 6A.1.
4. Wallis's regression of his state-level employment index on the composite employment index explains roughly 40 percent of the variation in the dependent variable between 1930 and 1940. While the composite index's coefficient is statistically significant, industrial composition apparently explains only a portion of the Great Depression's impact across the nation. Adding regional dummies 'increases the explanatory power of the estimates by three-fourths, indicating substantial unexplained differences in the employment experience of different regions' (Wallis 1989, p. 59).
5. The main programs included in the loan category are the Reconstruction Finance Corporation, the Farm Credit Administration, the Commodity Credit Corporation, the Farm Security Administration, the Home Owners' Loan Corporation, and the loans made by the Public Works Administration. Federal Housing Administration expenditures to guarantee home mortgages are included in insurance. The final category, non-repayable grants, includes, among other programs, the Agricultural Adjustment Administration, the Soil Conservation Service, the Civilian Conservation Corps, the Federal Emergency Relief Administration, the Civil Works Administration, the Works Progress Administration, and the Social Security Act. A complete list of the programs within the major spending categories is found in Table 8.1.
6. Although much of what Senator Russell had to say seems to have merit, he did engage in some hyperbole. Correlating the percentage of total US taxes paid by each state from 1936 through 1939 with WPA expenditures in each state during the same period reveals that these two variables are positively and significantly related at the 5 percent level of confidence ($r = .8931$, 192 observations).
7. Owing to the South's more rapid economic recovery (see Table 6.1), these 1938 estimates may understate the true cost-of-living differences somewhat.
8. The agency has frequently been referred to as one that looked good on paper but never lived up to its potential. Lacking direction and unsure of their exact responsibilities, NEC officials at the state level were dominated by the field agents of other New Deal programs. After 1935, following

the resignation of its first administrator, the organization's coordinating function was ignored (Patterson 1969, p. 111).

Table 6A.1 Official US census regions

NEW ENGLAND
Maine
New Hampshire
Vermont
Massachusetts
Rhode Island
Connecticut

MIDDLE ATLANTIC
New York
New Jersey
Pennsylvania

EAST NORTH CENTRAL
Ohio
Indiana
Illinois
Michigan
Wisconsin

WEST NORTH CENTRAL
Minnesota
Iowa
Missouri
North Dakota
South Dakota
Nebraska
Kansas

SOUTH ATLANTIC
Delaware
Maryland
Virginia

West Virginia
North Carolina
South Carolina
Georgia
Florida

EAST SOUTH CENTRAL
Kentucky
Tennessee
Alabama
Mississippi

WEST SOUTH CENTRAL
Arkansas
Louisiana
Oklahoma
Texas

MOUNTAIN
Montana
Idaho
Wyoming
Colorado
New Mexico
Arizona
Utah
Nevada

PACIFIC
Washington
Colorado
California

Source:
US Department of Commerce, Bureau of the Census, *Statistical Abstract of the United States, 1934.*

Table 6A.2 Variable definitions for correlation analysis

Variable	Definition
FILE	percentage of a state's population filing personal income tax returns
INC1	personal income reported on tax returns per tax return filed
INC2	per-capita personal income
CORP	corporate income reported on tax returns/population
DEPOSIT	per-capita bank deposits
ORDER	per-capita money orders
CAR	ratio of persons to new car registrations
VEHICLE	ratio of persons to new commercial vehicle registrations
EMPLOY	Wallis's employment index

Source:
FILE, INC1 *(Statistical Abstract of the United States* 1934–40); *INC2* (Schwartz and Graham 1956, p. 142); *CORP (Statistical Abstract of the United States* 1935, 1938, and 1940); *DEPOSIT, ORDER, CAR, VEHICLE* (Office of Government Reports 1940); and *EMPLOY* (Wallis 1989, pp. 65–66).

Table 6A.3 Summary statistics

Variable	Mean	Standard Deviation	Minimum	Maximum
FILE	3.66	2.58	0.53	31.50
INC1	3,058.53	539.50	2,010.00	7,038.00
INC2	443.81	171.08	129.00	929.00
CORP	54.84	193.10	1.38	2,058.50
DEPOSIT	273.27	228.41	27.14	1,291.23
ORDER	16.77	7.97	5.45	56.10
CAR	64.63	30.41	20.20	195.00
VEHICLE	283.81	132.78	85.00	760.00
EMPLOY	90.43	12.93	44.20	137.60

Notes:
Variable units are as follows. *FILE* (percent), *INC1* (dollars), *INC2* (per-capita income in dollars), *CORP* (dollars per capita), *DEPOSIT* (dollars per capita), *ORDER* (dollars per capita), *CAR* (persons per car), *VEHICLE* (persons per commercial vehicle), and *EMPLOY* (1929 = 100).

Table 6A.4 Partial correlation coefficients

	FILE	INC1	INC2	CORP	DEPOSIT	ORDER	CAR	VEHICLE	EMPLOY
FILE	1	0.22 (0.0001)	-0.762 (0.0001)	0.21 (0.0001)	0.585 (0.0001)	0.32 (0.0001)	-0.465 (0.0001)	-0.183 (0.0018)	0.069 (0.213)
INC1		1	0.434 (0.0001)	0.70 (0.0001)	0.376 (0.0001)	-0.128 (0.03)	-0.35 (0.0001)	-0.27 (0.0001)	0.35 (0.0001)
INC2			1	0.404 (0.0001)	0.794 (0.0001)	0.36 (0.0001)	-0.664 (0.0001)	-0.28 (0.0001)	0.183 (0.0008)
CORP				1	0.333 (0.0001)	-0.009 (0.882)	-0.186 (0.0015)	-0.109 (0.0646)	0.173 (0.0015)
DEPOSIT					1	0.095 (0.109)	-0.369 (0.0001)	-0.011 (0.85)	0.1148 (0.036)
ORDER						1	-0.383 (0.0001)	-0.392 (0.0001)	-0.072 (0.109)
CAR							1	0.716 (0.0001)	-0.249 (0.0001)
VEHICLE								1	-0.276 (0.0001)
EMPLOY									1

Note:
Significance levels in parentheses.

Figure 6A.1   Percentage distribution of loans per capita, by region,
1933–39

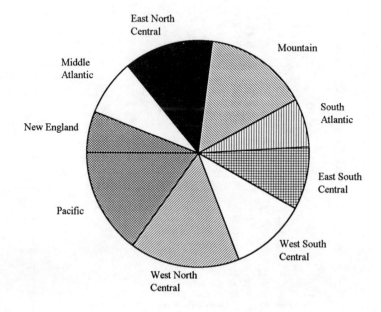

*Figure 6A.2   Percentage distribution of insurance per capita, by region,
              1933–39*

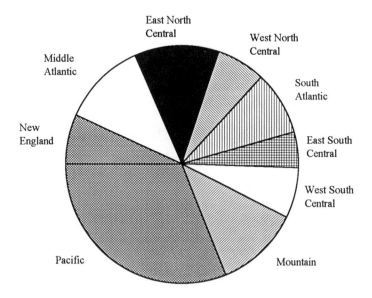

Figure 6A.3   Percentage distribution of non-repayable grants per capita, by region, 1933–39

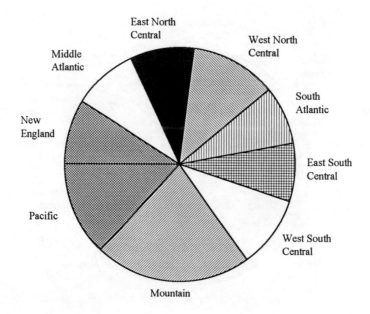

7.   Politics and Patterns of New Deal Spending

Systematic empirical analysis of New Deal spending priorities was made possible by Leonard Arrington's discovery in 1969 of a formerly neglected goldmine of documents produced by an obscure, short-lived federal government agency. 'Prepared late in 1939 by the Office of Government Reports for the use of Franklin Roosevelt during the presidential campaign of 1940, the 50-page reports – one for each state – give precise information on the activities and achievements of the various New Deal economic agencies' (Arrington 1969, p. 311). According to Arrington, these reports were produced to enable the administration to communicate to voters its efforts in combating the depression in each of the 48 states.

As one user of these documents later remarked, 'for statistical and analytical purposes the reports are an invaluable set of compatible data for comparing federal activity in various states during the 1933 to 1939 period' (Reading 1973, p. 792). Arrington's discovery triggered a spate of new empirical analyses of the New Deal. One of the chief purposes of this chapter is to bring the results of these scholarly studies to the attention of a wider audience.

Arrington himself conducted a preliminary analysis of the data, making state-by-state comparisons of total New Deal emergency relief expenditures. Readers of earlier chapters will not be surprised to learn that he found the West to have benefited more than other regions. Listing states in descending order of per-capita benefits received, Arrington underscored the fact that the top 14 entries were all located in the western United States. Despite Franklin Roosevelt's description of the South as the nation's number one economic problem, Arrington's initial calculations showed that 60 percent more was spent on the westerner than the southerner, on a per-capita basis.

In a subsequent paper, Arrington (1970) again highlighted the wide cross-state variation evident in the distribution of New Deal dollars. According to his calculations, 'the average loans and expenditures of all New Deal economic agencies during the period 1933 to 1939 were $291 per capita, but they varied from a high of $1,130 per capita for Nevada to a low of $143 per capita for North Carolina' (Arrington 1970, p. 344). Examining more closely the allocation of New Deal agricultural expenditures across the states, Arrington found that meager benefits were paid to farmers in the four states with the lowest average farm incomes in 1932 (Alabama, Mississippi, Georgia, and South Carolina), while farmers in the four states with the highest average farm incomes that same year (California, Connecticut, New Jersey, and Massachusetts) received the largest payments. Arrington explained this surprising finding by noting that federal government loans and expenditures were primarily aimed at providing relief rather than at redistributing income. That is, existing standards of living were less important to the New Dealers than was the goal of directing aid toward states which had experienced the most precipitous declines in income from 1929 to 1932.

This chapter summarizes the existing empirical evidence on New Deal spending priorities. The econometric models which exploit Arrington's data set and attempt to explain the cross-state distribution of federal emergency relief spending during the 1930s are described and the empirical controversies which they have generated are discussed. A key issue raised by this empirical work – and by the analysis of New Deal spending generally – involves the relative weights that can be attached to politics and to economic need in explaining the allocation of emergency relief funds. Were the Roosevelt administration's actions primarily a public-spirited response to the economic crisis or were they instead shaped by more ordinary political forces?

1 A FIRST CUT AT THE DATA

Don Reading (1973) was the first economist to model the cross-state distribution of New Deal spending econometrically. He, like virtually all of the scholars who subsequently exploited Arrington's data, conducted his analysis at a relatively high level of aggregation, pooling observations on expenditures by state both over time (1933–39) and across programs. While the results of such studies have contributed significantly to our understanding of the Roosevelt administration's spending priorities, potentially important information relating to the idiosyncrasies of individual New Deal agencies and more narrowly defined categories of relief may have thereby been missed.

Reading himself acknowledged an additional problem that plagues all analyses of the documents prepared by the Office of Government Reports, namely that New Deal projects in one state conferred, to varying degrees, spillover benefits on neighboring states. Civilian Conservation Corps camps, for instance, housed workers from many different states and CCC workers were in fact required to send a portion of the money they received home. Hence, to the extent that funds allocated to a New Deal project located in, say

Wyoming, found their way to Colorado (or perhaps New York), the relief benefits received by Wyomians will be overstated. Reading concluded, though, that any ad hoc attempt to account for such interstate effects would contribute more to confusion than to clarity.

The approach Reading took was to test whether the actual pattern of New Deal spending was consistent with the goals FDR articulated in his famous fireside chats. In particular, 'Roosevelt outlined "three related steps" in "efforts toward the saving and safeguarding of our national life." The first step was relief; the second, recovery; and the third, reform' (Reading 1973, p. 796).

Seven independent variables were included by Reading in a regression model designed to explain cross-state variations in New Deal aid over the 1933–39 period. These seven variables fall into three categories corresponding roughly to the objectives FDR claimed to be the administration's top priorities, namely (1) relief and recovery, (2) national assets, and (3) reform. Two variables represent relief and recovery – the percentage decline in real per-capita personal income from 1929 to 1933 (*YDROP33*) and the unemployment rate in 1937 (*UNEMP37*).[1] If the New Dealers in fact followed through on the president's promises, then one would expect more aid to have been directed toward states where per capita incomes fell farthest and where unemployment rates were relatively high. Estimated coefficients that are positive in sign are consistent with the hypothesis that the administration responded to economic need.

Two variables which provide estimates of the value of national assets in each state were also included in Reading's empirical model. One of these was the percentage of land owned by the federal government (*FEDLAND*). This variable takes account of Washington's responsibility for maintaining and improving such lands. Reading also contends that spending was freer in those states with large tracts of federal land because bureaucracies were already in place through which relief funds could be channeled expeditiously.[2] The per-capita number of miles of highways in a state in 1930 (*MILES*) was included on the basis that states large in terms of land area but small in terms of population have difficulty financing road construction and maintenance (Reading 1973).

The so-called reform variables were the level of per-capita personal income in 1933 (*PCY33*), the percentage of tenant farmers in 1930 (*TEN-ANT*), and the percentage of the 1930 population that was black (*BLACK*). *TENANT* captures possible inequities in providing relief to the rural sector and *BLACK* tests whether the New Dealers were responsive to the particular hardships experienced by members of this minority group during the depression – hardships of which the administration was well aware (Reading

1973). All three variables in this category measure the extent to which the administration addressed reform by directing aid to low-income states and states populated by two especially distressed classes of people, tenant farmers and black Americans.

Reading's results are reproduced in Table 7.1. As can be seen there, the percentage of federal land in a state, the per-capita number of highway miles, and the percentage decline in per-capita income between 1929 and 1933 are all positive and significantly related to per-capita total New Deal expenditures. The coefficient on the unemployment rate in 1937 is positive and significant at the 10 percent level. Per-capita income in 1933, the percentage of tenant farmers, and the percentage of the population that was black were all insignificant. Reading's initial specification explained more than 80 percent of the variation in the dependent variable.

A second equation was estimated by Reading in which the same independent variables were used to explain cross-state variations in the sum of New Deal expenditures, loans, and insurance. The results were essentially unchanged, with one major exception – the variable representing unemployment in 1937 lost its statistical significance. These results are also presented in Table 7.1. Reading estimated two other specifications (not shown here) using alternative definitions of the dependent variable, namely per capita loans and per-capita loans plus expenditures. Only *FEDLAND*, *MILES*, and *YDROP33* were significantly correlated with the dependent variable when these regressions were run. In no case were any of the so-called reform variables significant.

As Reading himself observes, his results suggest that, rather than attempting to use the power of the federal government to equalize income differentials between regions of the country, the administration instead was content to pursue policies aimed at returning per-capita incomes to pre-crash levels. Larger amounts of aid went to those states that had experienced the greatest drops in income between 1929 and 1933, while the states that were poor at the depression's outset tended to receive less aid from the New Dealers. Reading's evidence thus indicates that spending was allocated in a manner that addressed relief but neglected reform.

Reading rationalizes these findings by contending that 'people seem to adjust to a given level of income irrespective of size, and reductions in income are met with unrest and discontent. It would be *politically advantageous* to allocate funds to restore income to groups whose incomes have dropped' (Reading 1973, p. 803; emphasis added). Maybe so. But in his conclusion, Reading offers a much more plausible political explanation for the observed allocation of New Deal funds. In particular, he suggests that *states which supported FDR in the 1932 election might have been rewarded with federal*

Table 7.1 Reading's regression results

	Expenditures (per capita)	Expenditures, Loans and Insurance (per capita)
CONSTANT	−151.4	−119.4
FEDLAND	4.04**	5.71**
	(5.18)	(5.10)
MILES	9.99**	11.05**
	(6.13)	(4.78)
YDROP33	5.12**	8.51**
	(2.26)	(2.64)
UNEMP37	16.45*	7.41
	(1.66)	(0.53)
PCY33	0.07	0.12
	(0.88)	(1.09)
TENANT	1.31	2.17
	(1.07)	(1.62)
BLACK	−1.40	−2.48
	(0.90)	(1.12)
R^2	0.84	0.81

Notes:
Student's *t*-statistics in parentheses. Asterisks denote significance at the 5 percent (**) and 10 percent (*) levels.

Source:
Reading (1973, p. 801).

largesse while states that failed to jump on the president's bandwagon were punished by having relief withheld.

This is a testable hypothesis, but not one which Reading himself tackled. Explicit consideration of the role played by presidential politics in the distribution of federal emergency relief funds awaited the work of Gavin Wright, who observed that 'the New Deal years offer a laboratory for testing the hypothesis that political behavior in a democracy can be understood as a rational effort to maximize the prospects of electoral success' (Wright 1974, p. 30).

2 THE PUBLIC CHOICE MODEL

The equi-marginal principle dictates that rational consumers allocate their expenditures in such ways that the marginal utility of the last dollar spent is the same across all goods. If this is not the case, the consumer's total utility can be increased (with no increase in total spending) by cutting back on purchases of goods for which the marginal utility per dollar spent is low in favor of those for which the marginal utility per dollar spent is relatively high. Similar reasoning implies that profit-maximizing firms serving two or more distinct markets should allocate their sales in such ways that the marginal revenue associated with the last unit sold is the same across all markets and that to produce these products at the lowest possible cost, resources should be combined in such ways that the marginal productivity of the last unit hired is the same across all inputs.

The same principle applies to political markets as well. A rational politician seeking election will allocate his campaign budget across constituencies so that the vote-buying power of the last dollar spent is equalized at the margin. To do otherwise would squander scarce campaign resources and jeopardize the office-seeker's political majority. As such, one would not expect politicians to spend much of their contributors' money in areas where the marginal vote-buying power of political advertisements, stump speeches, and photo opportunities is low – a possibility that can arise either because the constituents solidly support the candidate or solidly oppose him. Disbursements from a campaign war chest are more likely to maximize the politician's probability of election if the funds are allocated mainly to jurisdictions where the race is 'close' and a relatively small number of votes can swing the outcome in his favor.

Such rational decision-making rules apply with equal force to the spending choices of incumbent politicians who have the advantage of spending the taxpayers' money as well as their own. Pork barrel affords an opportunity for probability-of-reelection maximizing politicians to buy votes by channeling money and jobs to selected constituents in return for their political support. As in the case of campaign spending, one would expect such largesse to be allocated where the marginal political return is relatively high. 'Safe' constituencies will tend to be ignored in the process.

Economists have long assumed that self-interest motives animate the agents interacting in private markets. Consumers strive to maximize their utility and producers strive to maximize their profits. The public choice model builds on the assumption that similar motivations drive individual actors in the public sector as well: politicians strive to maximize their chances of election or reelection, bureaucrats strive to maximize the sizes of their agencies' budgets, and the special-interest groups that demand political action strive to maximize their utility and profits (Stevens 1993, pp. 173–74).

Traditionally, government intervention has been justified whenever private market institutions fail 'to sustain "desirable" activities or to estop "undesirable" activities' (Bator 1958, p. 351). This public-interest 'model' assumes that government can and should intervene to correct perceived sources of private market failure with appropriate fiscal and regulatory tools, thereby increasing society's welfare.[3] Moreover, whenever government intervention fails to bring about the desired outcome, the failures are attributed to error or ignorance. Rather than seeing government action as purposeful, the public-interest model has it that government's apparent failures result from inadequate funding for bureaus, mistakes due to the incompetence of those charged with the responsibility of implementing well-intentioned programs, or from the failure of politicians and bureaucrats to foresee the full consequences of the policies they have adopted.

As George Stigler (1975, p. 140) has observed, however, the notion that governmental shortcomings can be explained away on the basis of error or ignorance on the part of public policy-makers is 'no explanation at all – anything and everything is compatible with that "explanation"'. While errors are of course possible, as a first approximation, the observed outcome should be treated as the desired outcome. This is especially so when the 'mistaken' policy has persisted over time. Hence, actions taken by the government that are clearly not in the public interest, but rather benefit narrow special-interest groups, cannot be excused as being the result of error. 'Errors' can be corrected. Those left uncorrected must have been committed deliberately. Public choice theory suggests that self-interest-seeking by politicians and bureaucrats makes government outcomes that work against the public's interest likely and, perhaps, even inevitable.

This is not because politicians are generally corrupt, although some are, or that special-interest groups routinely abuse the policy process, although some do. Rather, it is simply because the logic of collective action (Olson 1965) provides higher political returns to the lobbying efforts of small, cohesive groups seeking favors for themselves at taxpayers' expense – and higher political payoffs to the politicians who cater to their demands – than do policies and programs that encompass more global interests. Especially in a geographically based system of representative democracy, the logic of collective action favors policies and programs whose benefits are tailored narrowly to the advantage of politically well-organized groups, but whose costs are spread diffusely over the taxpaying public in general. Concentrated benefits raise the amount the recipients are willing to pay (in the form of votes, campaign contributions, and outright bribes) for the right to receive political largesse; diffuse costs reduce the amount other individuals and groups are willing to pay to avoid having their wealth expropriated for transfer to others (McCormick and Tollison 1981).

'The theory tells us to look, as precisely and carefully as we can, at who gains and who loses, and how much, when we seek to explain. . .' a policy outcome (Stigler 1975, p. 140). For the case at hand, one obvious beneficiary of the New Deal was FDR himself. Elected an unprecedented four times to the presidency, Franklin Roosevelt built in the process a juggernaut electoral coalition of big-city political machines, labor union leaders, and southern Democrats that formed his party's backbone for the next 50 years.

This coalition was not cobbled together overnight. In 1932, for example, Roosevelt was unsure of organized labor's support. By 1936, though, the unions were firmly in the incumbent president's corner. FDR apparently worked hard in the intervening four years to gain their votes. According to Arthur Schlesinger (1958, p. 139), the president soon had Alabama coal miners singing

> In nineteen hundred an' thirty-three
> When Mr. Roosevelt took his seat,
> He said to President John L. Lewis,
> 'In union we must be.'

In the prelude to the 1936 presidential campaign, FDR also saw his reelection hopes depending upon the support of urban voters. As one commentator puts it, Roosevelt would be swept to victory 'if the city machines bring out the vote to an extent which will influence areas surrounding cities in order to carry the more populous states' (Robinson 1970, p. 12). On the other hand, while the president's 1936 reelection strategy required 'leaders within the Democratic party to keep active for the campaign the alliance of South, city machines, and organized labor' (Robinson 1970, p. 16), it was clear that FDR could count on the votes cast by southern electors: 'Democratic managers knew that Southern states do not ordinarily figure in any national strategy planned by the Republican national organization' (Robinson 1970, p. 19). Indeed, 'even if he had not received a single electoral vote from any of the eleven former states of the Confederacy, Roosevelt would have been elected in each of his four presidential campaigns.'[4]

In sum, to the extent that presidential politics motivated New Deal spending, one would predict relatively large expenditures to have been made in states dominated by urban and labor union interests, while the southern states, where FDR's victory was assured, would tend to be bypassed by the federal relief agencies. Certain western 'swing' states were also critical to

Roosevelt's reelection drive and this observation may help explain the New Deal's apparent bias toward that region.[5] Whether or not the New Dealers pursued their own private political interests at the expense of those in economic need will be explored more fully in the remainder of this chapter – and all of the next.

Two caveats are worth emphasizing at this point, however. First, the argument elaborated in the following pages is not that politics shaped the New Deal exclusively. On the contrary, as we have already seen, economic conditions in the states did in fact influence the administration's spending priorities; politics operated at the margin. Second, political explanations are advanced and tested not to produce evidence of corruption or to impugn the motives of the New Dealers personally. New Deal spending patterns are instead seen as rational responses to given political constraints. The public choice model is a positive theory of political behavior, not a normative one.

3 PRESIDENTIAL POLITICKING

American presidents are chosen not by direct popular vote, but on the basis of the votes cast by the presidential electors chosen by the voters of each state. The number of electoral votes at stake in each state is equal to the number of members of that state's congressional delegation, comprising two US senators plus representatives elected to serve in the House of Representatives. House representation is apportioned on the basis of population, with each state being guaranteed at least one representative. Members of the Electoral College are chosen in winner-takes-all contests. The presidential candidate garnering a simple majority of a state's popular vote (or a plurality of the votes in a race involving three or more candidates) wins all of that state's electoral votes. As far as the Electoral College is concerned, 51 percent of the vote is as good as a landslide.

This peculiar institution of American politics means that some states are more important electorally than others. It also means that votes cast in excess of the minimum winning margin in one state are less valuable to a presidential candidate's overall electoral strategy than votes which position the candidate to capture a majority in another. Taking such considerations into account, a political explanation for the allocation of New Deal funds seemed plausible to Gavin Wright (1974), especially so in light of the results of prior national elections. The evidence indicated that the South was solidly in the Democratic Party's fold while the West demonstrated much more variability in voting patterns. Hence, if dollars were distributed to 'buy' votes for FDR, they would be most effective at the margin in the West.

This same regional voting pattern continued throughout the New Deal years. For example, the states comprising the East South Central census region – Kentucky, Tennessee, Alabama, and Mississippi – gave FDR 67.3 percent of the vote in 1932, 68.7 percent in 1936, and 67.7 percent in 1940. On the other hand, FDR garnered 58.4 percent of the vote in 1932 from the Mountain states of Montana, Idaho, Wyoming, Colorado, New Mexico, Arizona, Utah, and Nevada, 64.6 percent of the vote in 1936, and only 55.3 percent in 1940 (Robinson 1970, p. 41).

In order to test the hypothesis that presidential politics influenced the Roosevelt administration's spending priorities, Wright first estimated a regression equation with total New Deal relief funds distributed to each state, summed over the years 1933 through 1939, serving as the dependent variable. The independent variables included the proportion of a state's population living on farms (*FARMS*), the change in state per-capita income from 1929 to 1932 (*YDROP32*), and the number of general relief cases in a state, per capita, in January of 1935 (*RELIEF35*). Only the coefficient on the relief variable was significantly different from zero and the equation explained only 17 percent of the variation in expenditures across the states. These results are reproduced in column 2 of Table 7.2.

Wright next defined a 'political productivity index' based on presidential voting patterns over the years from 1888 to 1928 (*PRODUCTIVITY*). Assuming that, no matter where spent, a federal grant of given size would generate the same vote-responsiveness in FDR's favor, Wright then hypothesized that the closer the historical percentage of the popular vote cast in a state for the Democratic Party's presidential candidate was to .5, the more productive New Deal expenditures would be. Put differently, New Deal dollars would be expected to generate higher political returns in states where presidential races tended to be 'close' than in states where the Democratic Party's vote share was either very high or very low. Wright also included the standard deviation of the Democratic Party's historical vote share to account for the possibility that entrenched voters are more difficult to influence (*VARIABILITY*). New Deal spending, in other words, was more likely to have made a difference in states where presidential voting patterns had been volatile historically than where they had been comparatively stable.

Entering these two variables, along with *FARMS*, the proportion of a state's population living on farms (in order to test the political effectiveness of the farm lobby), Wright ran a 'political model' of New Deal spending whose estimates could be compared with those of the earlier 'need model'. These regression results are presented in column 3 of Table 7.2. While total expenditures were apparently not significantly higher in farm states than elsewhere, both measures of political influence were significant and the equa-

Table 7.2 Wright's regression results

CONSTANT	0.017	–0.115	–0.058
FARMS	0.12	0.151	0.238*
	(0.66)	(1.34)	(1.95)
YDROP32	–0.86		–0.54
	(1.45)		(1.36)
RELIEF35	0.858**		0.093
	(2.07)		(0.34)
PRODUCTIVITY		2.329**	1.36**
		(4.58)	(2.74)
VARIABILITY		0.0285**	0.0109**
		(6.88)	(2.06)
FEDLAND			0.0048**
			(4.79)
UNEMP37			–0.0043
			(0.23)
R^2	0.171	0.587	0.745

Notes:
Student's *t*-statistics in parentheses. Asterisks denote significance at the 5 percent (**) and 10 percent (*) levels.

Source:
Wright (1974, pp. 33–34).

tion explained approximately 59 percent of the variation in the dependent variable.

Estimating another political model (not shown here), which included electoral votes per capita, the standard deviation of the Democratic Party's vote share, and an alternative measure of electoral 'closeness', defined as the difference between FDR's actual winning vote margin and a level of support predicted for him in 1932, Wright found, once again, that all of the political variables were significant and had signs supporting the vote-buying hypothesis. This specification explained approximately 80 percent of the cross-state variation in New Deal expenditures. Hence, as Wright (1974, p. 33) concludes, 'we thus find that a political model explains between 58.7% and 79.6% of the variation in per capita spending over the whole period.'

Next, Wright built a general model that included his political variables, the percentage of land in a state owned by the federal government (*FEDLAND*), and variables designed to capture the administration's relief, recovery, and reform goals – the fall in per-capita income from 1929 to 1932 (*YDROP32*), per-capita relief cases in 1935 (*RELIEF35*), and state unemployment rates in 1937 (*UNEMP37*). These estimates are found in column 4 of Table 7.2. All of the political variables remain significant while the measures of economic distress fail to retain their earlier explanatory power. These results strongly support the hypothesis that New Deal funds were distributed according to a political rather than a need-based formula.[6]

Finally, Wright investigated the allocation of Works Progress Administration (WPA) jobs across the states. Like his previous findings, these results suggested that politics played a key role in explaining the distribution of New Deal spending. The political productivity index and the standard deviation of the Democratic Party's presidential vote share were both positively and significantly related to work relief employment.

To summarize, Wright's empirical evidence points to presidential politics as the chief determinant of New Deal spending. Other things being the same, states where such spending was more likely to make a difference in FDR's margin of victory in the Electoral College – those in which presidential elections had historically been close and where the Democratic Party's vote share tended to be volatile – received significantly more federal assistance than comparable states. Relief was likewise channeled disproportionately to states with relatively large agricultural sectors, a finding that may reflect the political effectiveness of the farm lobby. What is more important is that, while measures of economic conditions in the states have significant explanatory power in isolation from other factors, their statistical significance evaporates when political considerations are taken into account. Politics trumps need.

Wright's analysis suffered from the same limitations as those of Reading, though. Relief spending was aggregated over the entire New Deal period (1933–39) and he modeled the cross-state variation in total expenditures rather than placing them on a more informative per-capita basis. Wright's results nevertheless contributed to a more thorough understanding of the political forces that shaped the New Deal.

4 MATCHING REQUIREMENTS

John Joseph Wallis (1984) built upon the work of Reading and Wright by including an explanatory variable that controls for the matching requirements of some of the New Deal's emergency relief programs. While acknowledging the value of Wright's findings, Wallis asserts that Wright did not consider the possible relationship between the sizes of federal grants to a state and the amount of such aid financed by state and local revenue sources. Wallis contends that federal grants were contingent either explicitly or implicitly on matching state contributions:

> In the cases where explicit matching grants were written into the authorizing legislation (the Social Security categorical relief programs, early FERA grants, and loosely into a large part of the WPA grants), it was clear that national grants to a state were dependent on state and local relief expenditures. In the remaining programs, FERA, CWA, and part of the WPA grants, it was also apparent (although not legally mandated) that the national policies were to reward states with larger expenditures by making larger relief grants. (Wallis 1984, p. 147)

By including a variable controlling for such contributions (*STATE SPEND-ING*), the possibility that matching requirements were the cause of the apparently perverse spending patterns could be tested.

Unfortunately, however, the collection of data on state-level relief expenditures was suspended between 1933 and 1936. The period covered by Wallis's analysis consequently differs from that of the earlier studies. Because of the missing observations, pooled time-series cross-sectional regression analysis is applied by Wallis to state expenditures and federal grants for the years 1937 to 1940.

As described in earlier chapters, matching formulas were used to distribute some federal funds during the Great Depression in order to ensure that state and local governments contributed to the relief effort. The promise of matching federal grants served as a strong incentive for states to increase their own relief spending. One 'problem was that the "neediest" individuals usually lived in states with the lowest levels of state and local government expenditure. To equalize the provision of services meant to give states that spent less larger national grants, which of course, created incentive problems' (Wallis 1984, p. 153). Dual funding may also have caused some states to adopt inappropriate mixes of relief activities, emphasizing programs on which federal matching grants were available at the expense of others better suited to local needs – too much aid for starving artists and too little for starving children, as it were.

Wallis's initial results are presented in Table 7.3. The dependent variable is the total of federal and state emergency relief spending, by state, summed over the years 1937–40. The independent variables are the same as those of Reading and Wright, with two exceptions. In addition to *STATE SPENDING*, Wallis included the percentage of a state's population below age 15 and above age 65 (*DEPENDENT*). The estimated coefficient on the latter variable was

Table 7.3 Wallis's (1984) regression results

STATE SPENDING	–0.35
	(1.00)
FARM	41.8*
	(1.73)
PRODUCTIVITY	95.3*
	(1.7)
VARIABILITY	0.98
	(1.54)
YDROP32	–0.03
	(0.48)
UNEMP37	–2.57
	(1.17)
RELIEF35	81.5**
	(2.37)
DEPENDENT	–192.8*
	(1.67)
FEDLAND	0.66***
	(4.67)

Notes:
Student's *t*-statistics in parentheses. Asterisks denote significance at the 1 percent (***), 5 percent (**) and 10 percent (*) levels.

Source:
Wallis (1984, p. 154).

negative and statistically significant at the 10 percent level of confidence, indicating that, other things being the same, fewer federal dollars were directed to states where people in these two age categories comprised larger percentages of the population. Although Wallis offered no explanation for this result, one plausible line of reasoning is that because a substantial fraction of New Deal aid financed work relief for able-bodied adults, younger and older Americans tended to receive smaller government benefits.

Wallis's key explanatory variable, *STATE SPENDING*, which he defined as 'total expenditures for operation and maintenance, capital outlays, and interest payments' (Wallis 1984, p. 153) net of legal transfers of dollars from the federal to lower levels of government, was not significantly correlated with New Deal spending across the states. When other relevant explanatory factors are controlled for, total relief spending was not higher – and was, in fact, lower (although not significantly so) – in those states which devoted more of their own resources to relief. One of the political variables included in Wright's earlier analysis (*PRODUCTIVITY*) did retain its statistical significance, however. More New Deal funds were channeled to those states where they would be more effective at the margin in producing an electoral vote victory for FDR. As Table 7.3 also shows, New Deal spending tended to be higher in states with larger farm sectors, with more relief cases enrolled as of 1935, and with larger tracts of federal land. Overall, however, Wallis's coefficient estimates are not very precise and the model's explanatory power is weak.

In results not reported here, Wallis does find some limited support for his matching hypothesis in one particular regression specification. *STATE SPENDING*, defined in this case as 'expenditures in all relief programs for operation, maintenance, and capital outlays, net of direct federal grants for relief' (Wallis 1984, p. 155) was positively and significantly correlated with federal spending across states when the dependent variable was redefined to include only selected components of New Deal expenditures, namely federal grants for relief (social security and WPA grants). Given that a matching formula was used explicitly to allocate social security funds, however, this result is not very surprising.

In short, the preponderance of the evidence presented by Wallis suggests that implicit matching requirements explain, at best, only a trifling fraction of the total variation in the cross-state distribution of New Deal funds. As Wallis (1984, p. 155) himself concludes, 'the Wright hypothesis seems to be robust under a variety of specifications. We cannot say much about the effect of total state or local expenditures on total national grants.'

In a subsequent paper, Wallis (1987) identified two serious problems plaguing all previous empirical work on New Deal spending priorities across states, including his own. The first problem had to do with the level of aggregation of the data. As we have seen, Arrington, Reading, and Wright all used total New Deal grants, expenditures, and loans, summed over the seven-year period encompassed by the data source uncovered by the first of these scholars, as the dependent variable in their regression models. This high level of aggregation was forced by the unavailability of yearly observations on key explanatory variables (state income and employment, in particular). Because the researchers were thereby limited to using decennial averages for the values of these regressors, information on possible time-wise variation in the relationships among the variables was lost. Wallis also recognized potential simultaneous-equations bias in the existing models of New Deal spending: 'If national authorities gave larger grants to states with lower (or higher) levels of employment, and grants had a positive (or negative) effect on employment recovery, then it is appropriate, econometrically, to treat the two variables as endogenous' (Wallis 1987, p. 517).

Addressing the first problem, Wallis developed a time series of annual, state-specific employment estimates.[7] The construction of annual employment estimates at the level of the states made it possible to disaggregate New Deal spending into yearly observations and, hence, to take account of both time-wise and cross-sectional relationships in the data. Wallis used similar methods to generate annual, state-specific estimates of per-capita income for the seven-year period covered by the information assembled by the Office of Government Reports.

The initial regression equation estimated by Wallis constituted an attempt to reproduce existing empirical results on this new data set. Total New Deal spending, by state, was the linear model's dependent variable and the independent variables were the same as those used by Reading and Wright. A pooled time-series cross-sectional regression was run on a total of 336 observations (48 states times seven years). The results were consistent with the previous studies. In particular, Wright's political variables continued to be statistically significant determinants of New Deal spending, while economic conditions in the states, at least as measured by unemployment rates in 1937, remained statistically insignificant.

Next, Wallis entered his estimates of annual state-level employment (herein referred to as the *WALLIS INDEX*) and real per-capita income (*PCY*) as explanatory variables. These results are presented in Table 7.4. Both of the political variables, *PRODUCTIVITY* and *VARIABILITY*, were once again positively and significantly correlated with federal relief spending in a state. The estimated coefficient on Wallis's employment index was likewise positive, but not significant. Moreover, and somewhat surprisingly, state per-capita income was also positively associated with federal grants. As Wallis (1987, p. 518) somewhat touchily admits, 'the results are not encouraging for a liberal view of the New Deal. Federal grants appear to have been larger in states with higher incomes and with higher levels of employment, hardly evidence for a policy of encouraging relief, recovery, or reform.'

Attempting to explain why his new empirical results were so similar to those reported in earlier studies that relied on more aggregated data sets, Wallis again contended that matching was the culprit. Apparently forgetting for the moment that the evidence he had published in 1984 supporting such an explanation was fairly weak, Wallis (1987, p. 518) nevertheless argued that 'the positive coefficient on income, and perhaps employment, reflects the fact that high income states spent more on the types of programs for which they could receive national matching grants.'

Table 7.4 Wallis's (1987) regression results

CONSTANT	−0.086***	0.005	0.028***
	(8.2)	(0.56)	(2.6)
WALLIS INDEX	0.0002	−0.0002**	−0.00056***
	(1.6)	(1.9)	(4.6)
PCY (1935 = 100)	0.0001***	0.00001	0.000028**
	(7.8)	(0.87)	(2.3)
PRODUCTIVITY	0.17***	0.095***	0.09***
	(5.3)	(3.8)	(3.5)
VARIABILITY	0.0016***	0.0009***	0.0009***
	(4.8)	(3.5)	(3.4)
FARM	0.11***	0.027**	0.045**
	(8.5)	(2.4)	(3.8)
FEDLAND	0.00061***	0.0003***	0.00019**
	(8.5)	(4.9)	(3.1)
YDROP33	−0.000003	−0.0003	−0.000009
	(0.12)	(1.4)	(0.4)
LAGGED GRANTS		0.55***	0.56**
		(14.1)	(14.0)
R^2	0.63	0.81	−
N	336	288	288

Notes:
Student's *t*-statistics in parentheses. Asterisks denote significance at the 1 percent (***) and 5 percent (**) levels.

Source:
Wallis (1987, pp. 516–20).

He therefore estimated another regression specification in which the one-year lagged value of the dependent variable was included as an explanatory variable. Entering lagged per-capita federal grants on the right-hand side reverses the sign of the estimated coefficient on the Wallis employment index, and it becomes statistically significant at the 5 percent level of confidence. The coefficient on state per-capita income retains its positive sign, but is no longer statistically significant. The political variables perform as usual – their coefficients are positive and significant. Ditto for *FARM* and *FEDLAND*.

In order to take account of possible simultaneity between national grants and state employment levels, Wallis modified his employment index using an instrumental variable approach. New observations on what is here referred to as the *WALLIS INDEX* were generated for each state by regressing national employment trends on that state's employment index, thereby controlling for variations in state-level employment caused by changes in employment at the national level (Wallis 1987, p. 519).

The results from estimating this last equation are presented in Table 7.4's final column. Including the lagged dependent variable reduces the number of observations to 288, but the estimated coefficients on *PRODUCTIVITY* and *VARIABILITY* remain positive and statistically significant nevertheless. Wallis's findings consequently lend support to the political hypothesis of the New Deal. In addition, however, because his state-level employment index is negative and significantly correlated with grants, they also support a need-based model – other things being the same, states that approached their pre-crash employment levels more quickly received less federal aid. On the other hand, and despite holding the previous year's grants constant, high-income states once again seem to have been on the receiving end of substantially more generous emergency relief benefits.

Insofar as his empirical results show that the Roosevelt administration responded to the needs of states where employment fell farther and recovered more slowly, Wallis (1987, p. 519) concludes that they 'restore a measure of substance to the traditional view of the New Deal'. It is also true, though, that his evidence buttresses the idea that political forces were at work. The variables measuring a state's importance to FDR's electoral vote strategy are significant in all of Wallis's empirical models. More federal aid was likewise channeled to high-income states and to states with relatively large farm populations – results which Wallis was unable to explain as being artifacts either of programmatic matching requirements or of simultaneous-equations bias.

5   CONGRESSIONAL INFLUENCE

Gary Anderson and Robert Tollison (1991) conducted the most recent empirical investigation of the cross-state distribution of New Deal funds. Aggregating federal spending over the entire New Deal period, they built an empirical model based on the observation that it is Congress and not the president who appropriates funds: 'The President may have a significant marginal impact on the pattern of activities undertaken by the federal government during his administration, but Congress basically determines the pattern of allocations of funds needed to undertake those activities' (Anderson and Tollison 1991, p. 163).

During the 1930s, as now, appropriations bills originated in the House of Representatives. But an Office of Management and Budget had not yet been created within the executive branch and the president arguably had less of a direct influence on the budget process than he does today.

Anderson and Tollison emphasize that seniority in the legislature was perhaps the chief determinant of political power in the 1930s. They therefore included variables measuring the length of tenure in office, in consecutive months, of the members of each state's congressional delegation as proxies for political influence (*HOUSE TENURE* and *SENATE TENURE*). Membership on key congressional committees is also an important source of political power for legislators. In particular, 'the allocation of federal spending is strongly influenced by the decisions of the Appropriations Committees of both the House and Senate. These committees craft the spending bills which are subsequently put before the full Congress for a vote' (Anderson and Tollison 1991, p. 169). Hence, variables indicating state representation on the two appropriations committees of Congress were included in the model as well. Specifically, the consecutive lengths of service of members of the House and Senate Appropriations Committees was summed for each state to construct observations on *HOUSE COMMITTEE* and *SENATE COMMITTEE*.

Also included were dummy variables denoting states represented by members holding congressional leadership positions: 'The President Pro Tem, Senate Majority leader, the Speaker of the House, and the House Majority Leader are authorized to control the flow of bills and resolutions onto the floor of their respective branches. In other words, they control the "faucet"' (Anderson and Tollison 1991, p. 169). *PROTEM* and *SPEAKER* control for the effect, if any, of a state having a member serving in one of these four agenda-setting posts.

Anderson and Tollison entered two other variables designed to explore the political motivations underlying the New Deal – the percentage of the popular vote cast in each state for Franklin Roosevelt in 1932 (*FDR32*) and state electoral votes per capita (*ELECTORAL VOTES*). While electoral votes per capita had been included as an explanatory variable in previous studies, the results of the 1932 election had not. This latter variable enabled Anderson and Tollison to test Reading's (1973) conjecture that the administration may have set out either to reward political support or to punish political opposition when distributing New Deal funds.

Additional variables from the existing empirical literature were also entered into the Anderson–Tollison regression model. These were the state unemployment rate in 1930 (*UNEMPLOYMENT30*), the percentage of federal land in each state (*FEDLAND*), and the percentage drop in state income between 1929 and 1932 (*YDROP32*). *FARM VALUE*, the per-capita value of farm property in a state in 1929, was also included in the specifications.

The coefficient estimates from three of the regression models run by Anderson and Tollison are displayed in Table 7.5. As can be seen, the drop in income between 1929 and 1932 was not significantly related to New Deal spending in any of the specifications, while the unemployment rate in 1930 was significant in only one of them. The results also suggest that more generous subsidies went to states where farm land tended to be more valuable, a finding indicating that small family farms were not the principal targets of the AAA and other New Deal agriculture programs.

Of chief interest to Anderson and Tollison was the influence exerted by the various political variables on the allocation of New Deal funds. The estimated coefficient on electoral votes per capita was positive and significant in all of the models, while the percentage of the popular vote cast for FDR in 1932 was consistently positive but significant in only one of them. Congressional seniority, as measured by *HOUSE TENURE* and *SENATE TENURE*, was not significantly correlated with New Deal spending in any of the models estimated. The variable denoting a key leadership position in the House (*SPEAKER*) was likewise insignificant, but the states represented by the Senate's majority leader and its president pro tem consistently received more federal aid than their less-well-represented counterparts. Finally, membership on the House Appropriations Committee was positive and significant in two of the specifications and Senate Appropriations Committee membership was positive and significant in all the models estimated by Anderson and Tollison.

Thus, in pointing out a weakness in the prior literature, namely the failure to consider the important role played by Congress in determining the distribution of federal emergency relief spending, Anderson and Tollison add empirical weight to the political hypothesis of the New Deal. Other things, including economic conditions, being the same, states represented on the appropriations committees of Congress as well as those holding leadership positions in the Senate appear to have been favored in the funding process. The evidence also suggests that electorally rich states and states that voted heavily for FDR in 1932 were rewarded by the New Dealers.

These findings, along with the results reported in the other empirical research surveyed in this chapter, indicate that politics had an important influence on New Deal spending priorities. Politics was not the only determinant of how emergency relief funds were allocated across the states, but it seems to have been at least as important as economic need. While New Deal funds tended to go to the states where unemployment was particularly severe, they also tended to go to the states that were particularly important to FDR electorally. At the same time that President Roosevelt spoke of the responsibility of aiding the truly needy, the New Dealers saw to it that, at the margin, funds were allocated in ways that enhanced his reelection prospects.

Table 7.5 Anderson's and Tollison's regression results

CONSTANT	−105.9	27.56	−175.74
	(−0.53)	(0.15)	(−1.01)
YDROP32	−1.61	2.15	2.38
	(−0.43)	(0.64)	(0.76)
UNEMPLOYMENT30	13.2	9.77	16.94**
	(1.27)	(1.03)	(2.00)
FARM VALUE	259.39***	215.4***	212.77***
	(5.55)	(4.81)	(5.41)
FEDLAND	6.09***	5.5***	4.3***
	(7.62)	(7.31)	(5.65)
FDR32	1.22	0.87	2.19*
	(0.76)	(0.62)	(1.64)
PROTEM	288.85***	110.6	139.21*
	(3.38)	(1.11)	(1.81)
SPEAKER	8.95	−6.41	−3.87
	(0.15)	(−0.12)	(−0.08)
SENATE TENURE	−0.09	−0.10	−0.04
	(−0.59)	(−0.71)	(−0.38)
HOUSE TENURE	38.18		−86.06
	(0.27)		(−0.73)
SENATE COMMITTEE	0.46**	0.34*	0.33**
	(2.24)	(1.76)	(1.95)
HOUSE COMMITTEE		842.35***	
		(2.87)	
ELECTORAL VOTES			19,280.11*
			(4.49)
R^2	0.85	0.87	0.90

Notes:
Student's t-statistics in parentheses. Asterisks denote significance at the 1 percent (***), 5 percent (**), and 10 percent (*) levels.

Source:
Anderson and Tollison (1991, p. 172).

Perhaps, after all, 'the New Deal was not big government's Garden of Eden, but rather the more familiar stomping ground of homo economicus' (Anderson and Tollison 1991, p. 175).

Yet all of the conclusions drawn from existing empirical studies of the New Deal are based on models that aggregate New Deal spending over time, across programs, or both. Are the same conclusions justified when one looks at, say, agriculture and work relief efforts independently, or at New Deal agencies that had only brief bureaucratic lives? Were grants and loans distributed on the same basis as expenditures? These and other important empirical questions are taken up in the next chapter.

NOTES

1. Other than the decennial census years of 1930 and 1940, 1937 was the only year during the Great Depression that state-by-state estimates of unemployment were made.
2. One could also argue that, other things being the same, more federal aid was needed by states with large tracts of federal land because federal land is exempt from state and local taxes, thereby shrinking the local tax base and reducing the resources available for financing relief locally. Most of the states with large tracts of federal land also happen to be located in the western United States, a fact which has complicated the interpretation of this variable considerably. See below.
3. The public-interest model is, in fact, not a model that conforms with widely accepted standards of scientific methodology: 'The essential problem with the public interest theory of regulation is that its form is conditionally normative, and not necessarily positive (explanatory and predictive)' (Aranson 1990, p. 290).
4. This point has also been stressed by Brinkley (1984, p. 113).
5. As discussed in the previous chapter, the West may have been favored both as a reward for its role in helping FDR secure his party's nomination in 1932, and to help supporters of the New Deal win reelection in key 1934 Senate races.
6. As noted previously (see note 2), the interpretation of *FEDLAND* is ambiguous. This variable may simply stand as a proxy for the western states. If so, one cannot be sure that spending was higher there because the region was important electorally (on grounds not explained by *PRODUCTIVITY* and *VARIABILITY*) or because there were legitimate economic reasons for these states to have been favored by the New Dealers.
7. Wallis constructed his employment indices from data collected by the Bureau of Labor Statistics (BLS). The BLS establishment survey contained self-reported employment and payroll information from a large sample of firms. From these data, the monthly percentage change in employment (the so-called link relative coefficient) was calculated. The employment series for each state was then generated by applying the link-relative coefficients to starting, or base-period, values. This same method was used by Lebergott (1948) to estimate a national unemployment series for the 1930s. To ensure accuracy, Wallis benchmarked his estimates against both available census data and Lebergott's series.

8. The Political Economy of the New Deal

Government isn't infallible by any means. Government is only beginning to learn a lot of these new tricks. We are all going to school.
                                              – Franklin D. Roosevelt

It is unthinkable that any relief agency of the Federal Government, engaged in a charitable and humanitarian task, would be deliberately prostituted by politicians.
                                              – Judge Brady M. Stewart

It is beyond dispute that the New Dealers spent much more money in some states than they did in others. On a per-capita basis, people living in the western and mountain regions of the United States, in particular, received substantially greater amounts of federal aid than did the visibly poor inhabitants of what President Roosevelt himself called the 'nation's number one economic problem' – the South.

Roused to action by critics such as Georgia Senator Richard Russell, the obvious disparities in the cross-state distribution of emergency relief funds triggered a firestorm of political controversy. Unanswered calls for the administration to explain its spending priorities eventually led to demands that an explicit funding formula be adopted to govern the apportionment of Works Progress Administration (WPA) dollars. In particular, as initially written the Emergency Relief Appropriation Act of 1939 contained the following language:

Employment on work projects . . . shall be apportioned on the following basis: (1) Forty-five percent of the total number employed, in the ratio which the population of each State bears to the total population of all States as shown by the latest available Federal census; (2) Forty-five percent of the total number employed, in the ratio which the number of unemployed persons in each State bears to the total number of unemployed in all States; and (3) Ten percent of the total number employed at the discretion of the Works Projects Board . . . to meet unusual local conditions. (US House of Representatives 1939, p. 7273)

177

The measure's proponents hoped to force the administration more adequately to address need as opposed to other goals, whatever they may have been. If passed, the New Dealers would lose much of the discretion they had exercised previously, thus ending much of the mystery surrounding the distribution of federal aid.

The congressional debate concerning the wisdom of imposing an explicit formula on the WPA predictably followed regional lines. Representative Case of South Dakota based his opposition to the legislation on the grounds that substituting rules for discretion would irresponsibly handcuff the administration's responses to unforeseen economic or meteorologic contingencies. A drought in one region or a hurricane in another could not adequately be dealt with if the president had control of only 10 percent of the funds. Representative Martin of Colorado added, 'what will come out of this only time can tell; that is, except one thing – trouble. Trouble will be certain to come out of it' (US House of Representatives 1939, p. 7313). He went on to insist that congressional micromanagement of spending priorities would create monumental administrative headaches. According to Rep. Martin, 'this is a bill of formulas and intricate formulas. It has lifted [the WPA] from the sphere of simple arithmetic into the realm of higher mathematics. It is so wound up in formulas that it is not any wonder that the Works Progress Administration states it will virtually wreck the works-progress program' (US House of Representatives 1939, p. 7314).

On the other side of the Capitol's rotunda, Senator Schwellenbach of Washington argued that it would be unfair to the West to base funding decisions on 1930 census of population figures. Even though these were the latest population data available, they would not take into account the tremendous in-migration the western states had subsequently experienced.

A majority of the Congress was apparently swayed by arguments such as these – the proposed formula was defeated. But while the victors may have been sincere in their own beliefs, it is plain that their rhetoric was self-serving. As indicated above, 'much of the opposition to this formula came from western senators' whose states were among the leading beneficiaries of the federal government's public works program (Howard 1943, p. 599). The most vocal opponents of the proposed formula represented the states of South Dakota, Colorado, and Washington. On a per-capita basis, South Dakota received the seventh largest allocation of WPA dollars, Colorado received the sixth largest, and Washington the ninth largest of the 48 states. Western politicians were evidently well aware of their advantageous position and worked hard to maintain it. Senator Russell makes this same observation:

I have from time to time discussed with the Administrator of the funds the injustices that were resulting. I have offered amendment after amendment on the floor of the Senate, and all of them have been voted down by the representatives of States that were in most instances more favored. (US House of Representatives 1939, p. 925)

In short, politics cannot be ignored when explaining the federal government's activities during the Great Depression. Evidence presented in earlier chapters suggests that FDR used public funds to his own political advantage by channeling aid toward states rich in electoral votes. In addition, powerful members of key congressional committees apparently were able to influence the allocation of relief funds in favor of their respective constituencies. To be sure, economic need played a part in determining where the money went, but it is far from clear that such considerations were decisive. Indeed, according to Gavin Wright (1974), political variables explain more of the variation in the cross-state distribution of New Deal funds than economic variables do (see Table 7.2).

Important questions about the Roosevelt administration's spending priorities nevertheless remain to be addressed. First, existing empirical studies have been conducted at relatively high levels of aggregation. With the exception of John Joseph Wallis, researchers hitherto have pooled the data over time – and all of them have summed federal emergency relief appropriations across spending categories, lumping together agriculture, housing, public works, direct relief, and other diverse programs into a single number for each state. Does the evidence of political influence on patterns of New Deal spending hold up when the data are examined in finer detail? Second, the contention that the observed regional biases in the distribution of New Deal spending can be explained by programmatic matching requirements has not yet been fully laid to rest. Did some states benefit disproportionately from the New Deal simply because they contributed more of their own resources to the relief effort? And, if so, why were such funding formulas adopted in the first place?

Third, the possibility has been raised that ideological opposition to the New Deal made some states, especially those in the South, reluctant to participate in the federal government's relief efforts. According to the author of a recent American economic history textbook, 'reform attempts may have been thwarted by conservative state governments not wishing to see change. States with higher incomes and less in need of reform were more cooperative with federal officials and received more grants' (Smiley 1994, p. 133). Even Gavin Wright (1986, p. 302) now seems at least partially to accept this explanation:

In 1974 I published an interpretation of New Deal spending in terms of a national political strategy: the South was a low-priority region for the Democrats because it always voted Democratic in national elections, while the West was uncertain. This analysis explains much of the national pattern, but I now see that I was missing an important component: much of the southern political leadership didn't want the money.

Did some states refuse New Deal largesse on ideological grounds?

New empirical evidence is presented in this chapter which sheds light on these crucial questions. Capitalizing on the government reports discovered by Leonard Arrington and utilizing previously unexploited data from the *Congressional Record*, the existing evidence of political influences on patterns of New Deal spending is herein reproduced and extended. This chapter also explores the possibilities that matching requirements and ideological opposition to an expanded role for the federal government in providing relief help explain the observed regional biases in the distribution of federal aid during the 1930s. The results of the empirical analysis of New Deal spending data and of evidence gleaned from congressional testimony suggest that matching and ideology provide little explanatory power. In the end, political considerations remain the key determinants of New Deal spending.

1 REASSESSING POLITICAL INFLUENCE

Because information on economic conditions in the states during the 1930s was not available on an annual basis until quite recently, previous empirical attempts to explain the distribution of federal emergency relief funds have been conducted at a relatively high level of aggregation. Reading (1973), Wright (1974), and Anderson and Tollison (1991) pooled all of the data used in their analyses over the entire New Deal period (1933–39). Such pooling results in a total of 48 observations on the total amount the federal government spent in each state. It also requires that explanatory variables be defined correspondingly by, for example, averaging the data over the seven-year period or choosing a particular year as being representative of the theoretical relationship being tested.

Empirical expedients of this sort obviously suppress time-wise variations in the data. They raise questions of causality as well. Both Reading and Wright, for instance, used the state unemployment rate in 1937 as a measure of economic 'need'. They asked whether, other things being the same, states with more unemployment received more federal aid. Two problems of interpretation are posed by this specification. First, were unemployment rates sufficiently highly correlated over time that one would expect the same relationship to hold between federal spending in 1933 and state unemployment in 1933 as between 1933 spending and 1937 unemployment? Second, what meaning can be given to an estimated coefficient that is negative in sign? Was spending lower in states where unemployment was higher, or was unemployment lower where spending was higher? Similar questions are raised by the cross-sectional relationships between total New Deal spending in a state summed over the years 1933–39 and state per-capita income in 1933, and between total spending and persons on state relief rolls in January 1935.

Thanks to John Joseph Wallis's construction of an annual state-level employment index and to the richness of the information produced by the Office of Government Reports, it is now possible to estimate a disaggregated model of New Deal spending. It is also possible, again as a result of the level of detail contained in the 48 state reports released by the Roosevelt administration in 1939, to break total federal relief spending down into specific spending categories (loans, insurance, and non-repayable grants) as well as to model the distribution of relief by program type (agriculture and work relief, for instance) and by individual New Deal agencies. (The programs contained within each of the major spending categories are listed in Table 8.1.)

The model developed by Anderson and Tollison (1991) serves as the point of departure for the following empirical analysis. In addition to measures of economic need in a state and of that state's importance to President Roosevelt's reelection strategy, Anderson and Tollison incorporated measures of congressional influence into their analysis to control for the fact that seniority in the legislature and membership on the appropriations committees of the House and Senate translated into political power – power that the administration needed on its side in order to assemble a legislative majority that would pass and continue to support its spending programs.

To begin the analysis, we present the results of estimating pooled cross-sectional, time-series regressions for which each of the major New Deal spending categories alternately serves as the dependent variable. Encompassing the seven years and 48 states covered by the documents produced at the Roosevelt administration's behest, the data set contains a total of 336 observations. The independent variables, whose selection was guided by the existing empirical literature, are defined in Table 8.2. (The variables chosen are not always exact matches. For example, Anderson and Tollison included the state unemployment rate in 1930 as an explanatory variable in their spending equation while Wallis's employment index is used here.) Disaggregating the data in this way has the advantage of matching the politi-

Table 8.1 New Deal programs within major spending categories

AGRICULTURAL SPENDING
   Expenditures
      Agriculture Adjustment Administration
      Farm Security Administration
      Soil Conservation Service
      Research, Extension, and Agriculture Education
      Forest Service Funds
   Loans
      Farm Credit Administration
      Commodity Credit Corporation
      Farm Security Administration
      Rural Electrification Administration

INSURANCE
   Federal Housing Administration
      Title I – Notes Insured
      Title II – Mortgages Insured

LOANS
   Reconstruction Finance Corporation
   Farm Credit Administration
   Commodity Credit Corporation
   Farm Security Administration
   Farm Tenant Purchase
   Rural Electrification Administration
   Public Works Administration
   Federal Reserve Banks
   Home Owners' Loan Corporation

NON-REPAYABLE GRANTS AND LOANS
   Agricultural Adjustment Administration
   Farm Security Administration
   Soil Conservation Service
   Agriculture Experiment Stations
   Agriculture Extension Work
   College Agricultural and Mechanical Arts
   Forest Funds
   Forest Service (Roads)

Table 8.1 (continued)

Bureau of Public Roads (Public Roads Administration)
Civilian Conservation Corps
Public Building, Treasury Department
Public Works Administration
Federal Emergency Relief Administration
Civil Works Administration
Works Progress Administration (Works Projects Administration)
Social Security Act
Rivers, Harbors, and Flood Control
Mineral Lease Act Payments
Special Funds
Vocational Education and Rehabilitation
Office of Education – ERA Funds
US Employment Service
Books for the Blind
Federal Water Power Act Payments
Federal Surplus Commodities Corporation
National Guard
Veterans Administration
Balance of Expenditures from ERA Acts of 1935, 1936,
   1937, and 1938
Land Utilization Program
National Youth Administration

Source:
Reading (1972).

cal influence of a state's congressional delegation (in terms of seniority and committee memberships) with the year in which spending actually occurred rather than arbitrarily selecting one year as a base for constructing an aggregate measure of that influence.

Two other extensions of the existing empirical literature are worth noting. First, we explore the role played by the members of specialized congressional committees, such as agriculture, public buildings, and public lands, in determining the distribution of New Deal funds. Second, we include a set of six dummy variables explicitly to control for time-wise variations in federal emergency relief spending. In so doing, the beginning of the New Deal period

Table 8.2 The determinants of New Deal spending: Variable definitions

YDROP	Percentage decline in state real per-capita personal income, 1929–33.
EMPLOY	Wallis's employment indices (1929 = 100).
FARMVALUE	Average value per farm, 1930 dollars.
FARMLAND	Percentage of state land in federal ownership, 1937.
FDR32	Percentage of popular votes cast for Roosevelt, 1932.
ELECTORAL	Number of a state's Electoral College votes, per capita, 1932.
PROTEM	Dummy variable set equal to 1 if one of a state's US senators served as president pro tem of the Senate between 1933 and 1939.
SPEAKER	Dummy variable set equal to 1 if one of a state's US representatives served as either Speaker of the House or House Majority Leader between 1933 and 1939.
SENATE	Length of consecutive tenure of a state's two US senators, by year, 1933–39.
HOUSE	Length of consecutive per-capita tenure of all of a state's US representatives, by year, 1933–39.
SENATEAG	Length of consecutive tenure of a state's US senators serving on the Senate Agriculture Committee, by year, 1933–39.
SENATEPBG	Length of consecutive tenure of a state's US senators serving on the Senate Committee on Public Buildings and Grounds, by year, 1933–39.
SENATEPL	Length of consecutive tenure of a state's US senators serving on the Senate Committee on Public Lands, by year, 1933–39.
SENATEFIN	Length of consecutive tenure of a state's US senators serving on the Senate Finance Committee, by year, 1933–39.
HOUSEAG	Length of consecutive tenure of a state's US representatives serving on the House Agriculture Committee, by year, 1933–39.

Table 8.2 (continued)

HOUSEPB	Length of consecutive tenure of a state's US representatives serving on the House Committee on Public Buildings, by year, 1933–39.
HOUSEPL	Length of consecutive tenure of a state's US representatives serving on the House Committee on Public Lands, by year, 1933–39.
HOUSEWAYS	Length of consecutive tenure of a state's US representatives serving on the House Committee on Ways and Means, by year, 1933–39.

Sources:
YDROP: Hurwitz and Stallings (1957, pp. 195–265); *EMPLOY*: Wallis (1989, pp. 65–66); *FARM VALUE*: US Department of Commerce (1932); *FEDLAND*: US House of Representatives (1939); *FDR32*: Robinson (1970); *ELECTORAL*: US Department of Commerce (1935); *PROTEM, SPEAKER, SENATE, HOUSE, SENATEAG, SENATEPBG, SENATEPL, SENATEFIN, HOUSEAG, HOUSEPB, HOUSEPL,* and *HOUSEWAYS*: US House of Representatives (1932, 1933, 1935, 1938).

was adopted as the reference point. Hence, the estimated coefficients on the included dummies (1934–39) reflect the level of per-capita relief spending in the given year relative to 1933.

Because the empirical results are qualitatively similar across spending categories, the following discussion focuses on the regression specification in which total New Deal spending per capita serves as the dependent variable. The results for loans and grants are reported separately in appendix Tables 8A.1 and 8A.2.

The estimates shown in Table 8.3 suggest that both politics and economics influenced the distribution of emergency relief funds across states. The variables measuring economic need do not tell a consistent story, though. In particular, the estimated coefficients on *YDROP* and *EMPLOY* (lagged one year) are both positive and significant at the 1 percent level.[1] While the first of these results suggests that, other things being the same, more federal aid was channeled to states where incomes had dropped most precipitously between 1929 and 1933, the second indicates that more funds went to states where employment recovered more quickly to pre-crash levels. This somewhat perverse finding, which was also reported by Wallis (1987),[2] has been explained on the basis of programmatic matching requirements, a possibility that is explored more fully below. It is worth noting here, though, that the matching hypothesis is undercut somewhat by observing that, while the esti-

Table 8.3 The determinants of New Deal spending: Total spending per capita

CONSTANT	−59,924	−55,735
	(−3.58)***	(−3.53)***
YDROP	1,004.12	998.84
	(5.21)***	(5.51)***
EMPLOY	−179.98	−201.63
	(−1.30)	(−1.49)
EMPLOY(-1)	463.09	462.35
	(4.32)***	(4.40)***
FARMVALUE	0.91	0.84
	(3.59)***	(3.64)***
FEDLAND	472.34	446.97
	(5.59)***	(5.91)***
FDR32	277.16	230.91
	(2.69)***	(2.48)**
ELECTORAL	2,951,262	2,967,097
	(5.84)***	(6.51)***
PROTEM	29,060	31,590
	(2.56)**	(2.84)***
SPEAKER	−5,363.19	−5,594.90
	(−0.95)	(−1.01)
SENATE	−153.64	−147.50
	(−1.00)	(−1.13)
HOUSE	−392,717	−375,568
	(−3.48)***	(−3.60)***
SENATEAG	707.94	733.21
	(3.77)***	(4.28)***
SENATEPBG	30.36	
	(0.14)	
SENATEPL	4.80	
	(0.02)	
SENATEFIN	−653.08	−654.87
	(−3.49)***	(−3.68)***
HOUSEAG	31.28	
	(0.13)	
HOUSEPB	502.17	584.42
	(1.62)	(2.16)**
HOUSEPL	−387.69	
	(−1.14)	

Table 8.3 (continued)

HOUSEWAYS	70.47	
	(0.66)	
R^2	0.78	0.78
F	43.05	54.26

Notes:
Student's *t*-statistics in parentheses. Asterisks denote significance at the 1 percent (***) and 5 percent (**) levels. The estimated coefficients and associated *t*-statistics for the six included year dummies are as follows. In the first model, they are 1934: 36,514 (8.29); 1935: 36,814 (8.34); 1936: 28,457 (5.69); 1937: 24,046 (4.33); 1938: 16,151 (3.10); and 1939: 30,868 (5.56). In the second model, they are 1934: 37,694 (8.89); 1935: 37,868 (8.84); 1936: 29,751 (6.13); 1937: 25,275 (4.65); 1938: 17,358 (3.41); and 1939: 31,957 (5.87).

mated coefficient on the lagged value of *EMPLOY* is likewise consistently positive and significant in regressions explaining the cross-state distribution of non-repayable grants (see Table 8A.2), it is positive (but not significantly so) when loans per capita is the dependent variable (see Table 8A.1). Hence, measured in terms of employment, states with healthier economies received proportionately more federal aid in the form of grants *they were not expected to repay* while repayable loans were directed in slightly greater amounts to their harder-hit sisters.

Such perversity is evident in the agricultural sector as well. The New Dealers allocated significantly more funds to states where the nation's most valuable (in 1930) farms were located. This finding is consistent with Rexford Tugwell's lament that 'the AAA benefited only about 20 percent of the total farm population, primarily the larger, commercially oriented farmers who were better off than most anyway. Little flowed to sharecroppers and other tenants or to farm laborers and, in some instances, they were worse off' (Barber 1996, p. 74).[3] Insofar as the most valuable farm land tends to be located in the West North Central and Mountain regions of the United States, the positive and significant coefficient on *FARMVALUE* may also help explain the New Dealers' apparent sectional bias – toward the West and against the South – a bias that is likewise reflected in the positive and significant coefficient on *FEDLAND*.

The regression results offer strong support for the hypothesis that presidential politics played a decisive role in shaping the New Deal. Consistent with Wright's (1986) findings, the coefficient on *ELECTORAL* is positive and significant in all of the models in which it is included (see also appendix Tables 8A.1 and 8A.2). The signs and significance of the estimated coefficients on *FDR32* add more weight to the hypothesis of a political motivation for the administration's spending priorities. The states that gave Franklin Roosevelt larger percentages of the popular vote in 1932 were rewarded with significantly more federal aid than less-supportive constituencies. These rewards were nontrivial: a one percentage point increase in support for FDR in the 1932 presidential election translated into nearly $300 in additional per-capita federal aid over the 1933–39 period. Similarly, an additional electoral vote per capita led the New Dealers to spend nearly $3 million more per person at the margin.

By contrast, the variables measuring congressional influence offer, for the most part, little explanatory power. *PROTEM* and *HOUSE* are two of the exceptions, and the estimated coefficient on the latter variable is negative and significant, suggesting that states with more senior congressional delegations received less aid than otherwise. There are two possible (and somewhat related) explanations for the unanticipated behavior of *HOUSE*. One is that support for FDR's programs was overwhelming in that chamber.[4] The other is that the House's political leadership was disproportionately from the South and, because the voters in this region could be counted on to vote the Democratic ticket, New Deal spending was more politically productive elsewhere.[5]

States represented on the Senate Agriculture Committee and the House Committee on Public Buildings received significantly more federal aid during the New Deal than those without such representation. Membership on the Senate Finance Committee unaccountably seems to have worked in the opposite direction, however.

Table 8.4 shows the results from estimating a purely political model of New Deal spending. Insofar as the two regression specifications explain about two-thirds of the variation in per-capita total federal aid across states, it appears that politics ranked high on the Roosevelt administration's list of priorities. In particular, the New Dealers allocated significantly more emergency relief funds to electoral-vote-rich states and to the states in which FDR had garnered greater percentages of the popular vote in 1932. (The estimated coefficient on $FDR32^2$ provides evidence of diminishing returns to such political support.) Congressional influence was likewise crucial in determining a state's share of the New Deal pie. Although the estimated coefficient on *HOUSE* is again negative and significant, other things being the same, more federal aid was channeled to states represented on three key committees of the Congress, namely the Senate Agriculture Committee and the committees of the House and Senate having oversight responsibilities with

Table 8.4 The political determinants of total New Deal spending

CONSTANT	−120,323	−67,110
	(−4.11)***	(−2.23)**
FDR32	4,064.01	3,139.15
	(4.79)***	(3.51)***
FDR32²	−28.85	−23.23
	(−4.80)***	(−3.65)***
ELECTORAL	3,806,179	
	(6.75)***	
PROTEM	24,403	84,465
	(1.85)*	(8.13)***
SPEAKER	−544.37	−2,393.98
	(−0.09)	(−0.34)
SENATE	−123.80	−53.38
	(−0.71)	(−0.29)
HOUSE	−567,860	−493,006
	(−4.40)***	(−3.59)***
SENATEAG	899.42	788.66
	(4.27)***	(3.52)***
SENATEPBG	−274.12	−622.00
	(−1.10)	(−2.39)**
SENATEPL	1,310.59	2,115.06
	(4.97)***	(8.42)***
SENATEFIN	−408.14	−440.79
	(−1.91)*	(−1.93)*
HOUSEAG	443.58	245.22
	(1.53)	(0.80)
HOUSEPB	−230.72	−212.60
	(−0.65)	(−0.56)
HOUSEPL	1,074.02	1,037.91
	(3.00)***	(2.71)***
HOUSEWAYS	−24.87	−280.25
	(−0.20)	(−2.20)**
R^2	0.68	0.64
F	32.32	27.73

Table 8.4 (continued)

Notes:
Student's *t*-statistics in parentheses. Asterisks denote significance at the 1 percent (***), 5 percent (**), and 10 percent (*) levels. The estimated coefficients and associated *t*-statistics for the six included year dummies are as follows. In the first model, they are 1934: 40,216 (8.02); 1935: 41,286 (8.57); 1936: 34,230 (6.92); 1937: 31,469 (6.61); 1938: 21,734 (4.48); and 1939: 37,220 (7.93). In the second model, they are 1934: 41,814 (7.80); 1935: 42,437 (8.25); 1936: 35,345 (6.70); 1937: 32,224 (6.34); 1938: 22,130 (4.27); and 1939: 37,204 (7.42).

respect to the nation's public lands. The president pro tempore of the Senate was also evidently quite effective in influencing the distribution of New Deal funds in his constituents' favor.

In sum, while both economics and politics seem to have influenced the distribution of federal emergency relief funds across the states, the evidence presented here suggests that political considerations were the chief determinant of the Roosevelt administration's spending priorities. To be sure, more federal aid was allocated to states where incomes had dropped the most between 1929 and 1933. It is also true, however, that the distribution of New Deal funds is largely unexplained by economic conditions. Indeed, the political variables alone explain two-thirds of the variation in per-capita federal emergency relief spending across the states. Adding observations on income and employment to the model increases its explanatory power only by about ten percentage points. And, generally speaking, the results suggest that the states with the longest unemployment lines received less help from the New Dealers than other jurisdictions where the numbers of people holding jobs had recovered more quickly to pre-crash levels. The money instead tended to flow to states where farms were more valuable (in 1930) and where more of the land was owned by the federal government. Both of these results are consistent with FDR's political indebtedness to the West.

The weight of the evidence thus points to a political explanation for New Deal spending patterns: other things being the same, more federal aid was allocated to states which had supported FDR most solidly in 1932 and which were crucial to the president's 1936 Electoral College strategy. Whether such influences remain significant when the data are disaggregated by spending program is taken up next.

2 AGRICULTURAL PROGRAMS

The Roosevelt administration's response to the economic crisis precipitated by the 1929 stock market crash was massive in its scope. The New Deal targeted virtually every sector of the economy and offered aid in a variety of forms, including direct cash assistance for the needy, government jobs for the unemployed, and subsidies of various sorts for producers. But not all of these relief programs were implemented at once. Neither were they guided by the same philosophies nor did they focus on the same economic goals. Indeed, as we have seen, the programs of the New Deal sometimes worked at cross-purposes.

Hence, it is possible that relevant information is lost when New Deal expenditures are aggregated across spending categories. The variables that help explain, say, the cross-state distribution of agricultural relief are not necessarily the same as those which explain the distribution of monies appropriated for public works projects or for housing programs. To begin remedying this weakness in the existing literature, in what follows the results of estimating a number of disaggregated spending models are reported and discussed.

Agriculture – the Roosevelt administration's top priority upon taking office in 1933 – is addressed first. The programs included under this heading are the ones shown in Table 8.1 and include both the spending and lending activities of the Agriculture Adjustment Administration, the Farm Security Administration, the Soil Conservation Service, Farm Credit Administration, the Commodity Credit Corporation, and the Rural Electrification Administration), among others. The new variables utilized in this analysis, their definitions, and their sources are presented in Table 8.5; the definitions of *FARMVALUE, SPEAKER, PROTEM, FDR32, ELECTORAL, SENATEAG* and *HOUSEAG* are the same as before (see Table 8.2).

Two dependent variables are used alternately in the regression analysis. They are *AGFARMER*, which is defined as the ratio of New Deal agricultural spending in a state to that state's 1935 farm population, and *AGFARM*, the ratio of agricultural spending in a state to the number of farms in that state as of 1930. The amount of agricultural relief is hypothesized to depend on various characteristics of a state's farming sector – the average value per farm in 1930 (*FARMVALUE*), the percentage of a state's land area devoted to farming in 1930 (*FARMLAND*), the percentage of farms operated by tenants in 1930 (*TENANT*), and the percentage of a state's 1935 farm population that was black (*BLACKFARMER*) – as well as on variables measuring the possible impact of presidential politics and congressional influence on the distribution of federal funds. In these models, a state's ability to affect congressional decision-making with respect to agricultural relief is proxied by representation on the agricultural committees of the House and Senate. As before, these variables measure the length of continuous committee service of the states so represented.

Table 8.5 Variable definitions: Agricultural model

AGFARM	Ratio of total agricultural spending in a state to the number of farms within that state, 1930.
AGFARMER	Ratio of total agricultural spending in a state to that state's farm population, 1935.
BLACKFARMER	Percentage of a state's farm population that is black, 1935.
FARMLAND	Percentage of a state's land area in farms, 1930.
TENANT	Percentage of a state's farms operated by tenants, 1930.

Sources:
The observations on *AGFARM, AGFARMER, FARMVALUE, BLACKFARMER, FARMLAND*, and *TENANT* are from US Department of Commerce (various years).

The results are presented in Table 8.6. Confirming earlier empirical findings (and lending additional support to Rex Tugwell's criticisms of the New Deal's agricultural programs), the coefficient estimates suggest that states in which the average farm was more valuable received significantly more federal aid. The estimates also indicate that states where blacks accounted for larger percentages of the farm population received fewer New Deal dollars. The percentage of farms operated by tenants is insignificant in both models. *TENANT* and *BLACKFARMER* are highly correlated, though (r = .668 with a p-value of .0001), and so the marginal contributions of race and tenancy status to the determination of the amount of agricultural aid allocated to a state cannot be disentangled.[6] The Roosevelt administration's rhetoric to the contrary, the plight of the tenant farmer seems to have been largely overlooked. Moreover, the New Dealers' claims of sensitivity to the hardships visited on blacks by the agricultural sector's collapse appear to be unfounded.

As far as politics is concerned, there is evidence that representation on the Senate Agricultural Committee was a significant determinant of the amount of federal aid that flowed to a state's farmers. Farmers in states that supported FDR in the 1932 election were likewise rewarded with significantly larger expenditures. The estimated coefficient on *ELECTORAL* is also positive and significant, suggesting that the president's 1936 Electoral College strategy had an important impact on the distribution of agricultural relief. None of the other variables measuring congressional influence, including representation on the House Agriculture Committee, are statistically significant.

Table 8.6 The determinants of New Deal agricultural spending

	AGFARMER	AGFARM
CONSTANT	−92.55	−452.67
	(−3.75)***	(−3.68)***
FARMVALUE	0.004	0.017
	(8.54)***	(8.24)***
FARMLAND	−0.402	−1.61
	(−2.69)***	(−2.16)**
BLACKFARMER	−0.956	−2.77
	(−3.10)***	(−1.80)*
TENANT	0.464	0.145
	(1.60)	(0.10)
FDR32	0.990	5.64
	(2.31)**	(2.65)***
ELECTORAL	2,004.61	7,642.84
	(2.30)**	(1.76)*
SPEAKER	1.636	20.85
	(0.15)	(0.39)
PROTEM	20.112	35.39
	(0.89)	(0.31)
SENATEAG	0.886	3.56
	(2.72)***	(2.20)**
HOUSEAG	−0.386	−2.33
	(−0.83)	(−1.00)
R^2	0.54	0.50
F	23.35	19.68

Notes:
Student's *t*-statistics in parentheses. Asterisks denote significance at the 1 percent (***), 5 percent (**), and 10 percent (*) levels. The estimated coefficients and associated *t*-statistics for the six included year dummies are as follows. In the first model, they are 1934: 38.69 (5.02); 1935: 68.18 (8.88); 1936: 44.73 (5.83); 1937: 53.18 (6.94); 1938: 47.87 (6.26); and 1939: 64.81 (8.47). In the second model, they are 1934: 187.91 (4.90); 1935: 334.19 (8.75); 1936: 220.88 (5.79); 1937: 264.70 (6.95); 1938: 241.80 (6.35); and 1939: 324.10.

To the extent that New Deal agricultural expenditures targeted 'need', the empirical results suggest that the administration's spending priorities were perverse. More federal aid was distributed to states where *less* of the land was under cultivation and where the average farm was more valuable. One possible explanation for these results is that, at least initially, FDR's brain trust backed agricultural relief programs whose goal was to raise farm incomes by reducing farm output. An important component of this strategy was to limit the nation's farm acreage by buying 'marginal' farm land and taking it out of production. Indeed, 'enough funding was pieced together from various "emergency" programs to purchase nearly 10 million substandard acres by 1936' (Barber 1996, p. 77). Hence, while the administration's acreage-reduction goals were apparently never met,[7] the negative sign on *FARMLAND* may be picking up the reverse-causality effect of the greater expenditures made in states with disproportionate numbers of 'marginal' farms; such expenditures would of course tend to raise the average value of the remaining farms.[8]

In any case, the evidence presented here suggests that politics motivated the New Deal's agricultural programs as it did other facets of the federal government's emergency relief efforts during the 1930s. Agricultural appropriations were distributed in ways that provided more help for states supporting FDR's presidential aspirations than for those whose economies had been devastated by the farm crisis. The evidence also suggests that when New Deal spending programs are broken down into more finely defined categories, congressional influence on the distribution of emergency relief funds – in this case representation on the Senate Agricultural Committee – becomes more apparent.

3   THE CIVIL WORKS ADMINISTRATION

The activities of the Civil Works Administration (CWA) provide a nearly ideal laboratory for testing hypotheses about the New Dealers' underlying motivations. Several characteristics of the program make it exemplary for this purpose. First, the agency was in existence for less than six months. Empirical problems associated with aggregating data and performing time-series analysis can therefore be avoided. Second, the program was by design a federal one. There were no matching requirements and allocations consequently were independent of state governments' willingnesses and abilities to contribute resources of their own to the relief effort. Finally, the expenditures came during the worst point of the Great Depression, the winter of 1933–34, when need was arguably the greatest and individuals the most desperate.

Hence, if compassion was the impetus for the New Deal, it should be apparent from the activities of this agency.

The definitions and sources of the variables included in our analysis of the distribution of CWA funds are shown in Table 8.7. The dependent variable in all equations is CWA expenditures per thousand persons in a state. Included among the independent variables is *EMPLOY33*, which is the state-level employment indexes compiled by John Joseph Wallis for the year 1933, the year that CWA expenditures were initiated. This variable measures employment in each state relative to its 1929 level. Harry Hopkins served as the CWA's administrator. It was Hopkins, it should be recalled, who asked the Municipal Finance Section of the Federal Emergency Relief Administration to gather information that could be used to assess need across the states. If Hopkins took account of unemployment when distributing emergency relief funds, a negative sign is expected.

Table 8.7 Variable definitions: CWA model

ORDER	Per-capita domestic money orders issued, 1933.
EMPLOY33	Wallis's employment index, 1933.
PCY33	State income per capita, 1933.
BLACK	Percentage of the population that is black, 1930.
ESTABLISHMENT	Percentage change in the number of business establishments, 1931–33.
URBAN	Percentage of a state's population living in urban areas, 1930.
ELECTORAL33	Electoral votes per capita, 1933.
SENATE33	Consecutive years of service of a state's US senators, 1933.
HOUSE33	Consecutive years of service of a state's US representatives, per capita, 1933.
FERA	FERA expenditures per 10,000 persons.

Sources:
BLACK and *ELECTORAL33*: US Department of Commerce (1932, 1938); *ORDER*: Office of Government Reports, Vol. II (1939); *PCY33*: US Department of Commerce, *Personal Income by States* (1956, p. 140); *ESTABLISHMENT*: US Department of Commerce, *Biennial Census of Manufacturers* (1931, 1933); *URBAN*: US Department of Commerce, *Census of Population*, Vol. I: *Population Number and Distribution of Inhabitants* (1931); *EMPLOY33*: Wallis (1989, pp. 65–66); and *SENATE33* and *HOUSE33*: US House of Representatives (1933).

The variable *URBAN* is included to test Charles's (1963) assertion that states with greater percentages of urban dwellers would have received more aid from the CWA. He justified such a spending pattern on the basis of greater economic need in the cities. A positive coefficient on *URBAN* would provide support for this contention. The racial composition of a state's population is included to test the validity of the standard-of-living rationale for the distribution of New Deal funds (see Chapter 6). As some scholars have hypothesized, restoring individuals to their accustomed standard of living was perhaps all the New Dealers set out to do. If this is so, then those who had less would have received less; a negative sign would therefore be expected on *BLACK*. Of course, outright racial discrimination would lead to this same result.

Two other variables, *ORDER* and *ESTABLISHMENT*, are included in the first set of models to control for the amount of business activity within a state. All else equal, states experiencing disproportionate numbers of business failures between 1931 and 1933 would be expected to receive greater appropriations, so that the estimated coefficient on *ESTABLISHMENT* is expected to be positive. *ORDER* is per-capita money orders purchased in a state and, interpreted as a measure of economic well-being, its coefficient should be negative if rhetoric and reality match. Per-capita income in 1933 serves as an alternate measure of economic conditions in a state; its coefficient should likewise be negative if the New Dealers were solicitous of the welfare of those experiencing hard times.

The results of estimating a basic 'need' model of CWA expenditures are presented in Table 8.8. In the first equation, the estimated coefficient on *EMPLOY33* is negative and statistically significant, suggesting that the administration took the unemployment rate into account when distributing CWA funds. And, moreover, the New Dealers provided more aid to those states where the problem of unemployment was more serious. Income was evidently not a significant determinant of CWA relief, however: the estimated coefficient on *PCY33* is negative, as expected, but not significant.[9] The negative and significant coefficient on *BLACK* is consistent with an administration effort to restore standards of living (relief), but not with the stated objective of at least some New Dealers to achieve fundamental reform. This model explains roughly 33 percent of the variation in per-capita CWA expenditures.

The second equation includes *ORDER*, whose estimated coefficient is positive and significant. This result suggests that more of the CWA's projects were allocated to states with relatively more economic activity. *EMPLOY33* is once again negative and statistically significant, but *BLACK* is not.[10] Almost 60 percent of the variation in the dependent variable is explained by

Table 8.8 A need-based model of the CWA

CONSTANT	16,975	10,684	12,385
	(4.99)***	(3.87)***	(3.97)***
PCY33	−1.27		−0.55
	(−0.28)		(−0.14)
ORDER		184.9	
		(5.15)***	
ESTABLISHMENT	−1,409.84	−37.0	−1,004.42
	(−0.79)	(−0.53)	(−0.66)
BLACK	−635.07	−14.04	−577.09
	(−2.52)**	(−0.62)	(−2.68)***
URBAN	−304.85	−0.26	201.34
	(−0.23)	(−0.02)	(0.17)
EMPLOY33	−96.70	−74.5	−80.06
	(−3.09)***	(−3.03)***	(−2.96)***
FERA			0.33
			(4.07)***
R^2	33.44	58.92	52.57
F	4.22	12.05	7.57
N	48	48	48

Notes:
Student's *t*-statistics in parentheses. Asterisks denote significance at the 1 percent (***) and 5 percent (**) levels.

this specification. The estimated coefficients on *ESTABLISHMENT* and *URBAN* are not statistically different from zero in either specification. The plight of the unemployed thus seems to have been the CWA's top priority and, once this factor is controlled for, urban states and states with greater numbers of business failures received no more aid, on the average, than those where these two indicators of economic conditions were less pressing.

The impact of Harry Hopkins's dual administrative responsibilities is examined in the last column of Table 8.8. FERA and CWA grants are positively and significantly correlated, reflecting the fact that half of the latter agency's case load consisted of individuals transferred from FERA's relief rolls. (Members of the unemployed population who were not receiving aid accounted for the other half of the CWA's cases.) The most important result here, though, is that the signs and statistical significance of the other explanatory variables are unaffected when the simultaneous determination of CWA and FERA spending is taken into account.

The next set of models examines the role of politics in the distribution of CWA funds. These results are presented in Table 8.9. As can be seen, the estimated coefficients on the three broadly defined political variables included in the regression model (*SENATE33*, *HOUSE33*, and *ELECTORAL33*) are consistently positive and significant, suggesting that congressional seniority and electoral-vote richness were important determinants of a state's share of CWA appropriations. (Indeed, by themselves, these three variables explain nearly 29 percent of the variation in CWA expenditures.) Somewhat surprisingly, however, representation on specialized congressional committees (other than the Senate Committee on Public Lands) does not seem to have increased a state's ability to attract CWA projects.

The measures of 'need' are largely unaffected when political considerations are taken into account. (In fact, the negative sign on *PCY33* becomes significant in one of the specifications.) As such, these estimates provide evidence that, at least as far as the CWA is concerned, both politics and economics determined the distribution of emergency relief funds during the Great Depression. It is worth noting, though, that *ELECTORAL33* and *HOUSE33* exert by far the largest marginal impacts on CWA spending. The latter finding can be interpreted to mean either that the Roosevelt administration used CWA funds to gain the support of key members of the House or that these members used their political influence to funnel disproportionate shares of the relief agency's budget to their constituents. The magnitude of the estimated coefficient on *ELECTORAL33* suggests that presidential politics weighed heavily when decisions about spending the CWA's budget were being made. Politics may also help explain the positive coefficient on *URBAN*, possibly indicating an attempt on the administration's part to build electoral support from big-city machines. Alternatively, this result is also consistent with Charles's contention that cities were where need was the greatest.

In sum, evidence from the Civil Works Administration provides the first solid support for a need-based model of New Deal spending. More of that agency's appropriations were directed to states where, by John Joseph Wallis's measures, the number of people with jobs had declined most precipitously between 1929 and 1933. It is also true, however, that economic need was not the administration's only priority: for better or worse, politics also seems to have played a significant role in determining which states benefited from the CWA's attempts to prime the economic pump.

Table 8.9 *The determinants of CWA spending*

CONSTANT	9,745.62	10,169.5	8,478.43
	(3.42)***	(3.53)**	(2.92)***
PCY33	−0.21	−11.05	−5.26
	(−0.06)	(−2.35)**	(−1.33)
ESTABLISHMENT	−1,572.17	−1,258.03	−2,949.68
	(−1.16)	(−0.92)	(−1.92)*
BLACK	−602.72	−539.32	−511.20
	(−3.17)***	(−2.78)***	(−2.54)**
URBAN	352.19	3,264.54	2,109.38
	(0.34)	(2.34)**	(1.65)
EMPLOY33	−62.15	−59.22	−27.68
	(−2.54)**	(−2.36)**	(−0.99)
FERA	0.33	0.29	0.25
	(4.53)***	(3.87)***	(3.10)***
SENATE33	75.29		66.67
	(3.18)***		(1.91)*
HOUSE33	45,052.4		60,148.1
	(2.21)**		(2.86)***
ELECTORAL33		260,206	
		(3.30)***	
SENATEPL			120.06
			(2.22)**
SENATEPBG			−55.85
			(−1.26)
HOUSEPL			32.28
			(0.70)
HOUSEPB			3.29
			(0.08)
R^2	64.89	62.72	70.56
F	9.01	9.61	6.99
N	48	48	48

Notes:
Student's *t*-statistics in parentheses. Asterisks denote significance at the 1 percent (***), 5 percent (**), and 10 percent (*) levels.

4 THE FEDERAL EMERGENCY RELIEF ADMINIS-
   TRATION

Similar conclusions can be drawn from empirical analyses of spending by the Federal Emergency Relief Administration (FERA). Although the agency was longer-lived than the CWA, it seems to have been subject to much the same political and economic influences. Because Harry Hopkins was in charge of both agencies, perhaps one should not be too surprised by the similarities.[11]

The results of estimating two regression equations which model the per-capita distribution of FERA expenditures across states are reported in Table 8.10. One of the explanatory variables controlling for geographic variations in economic conditions (*YDROP*) is statistically significant and of the 'right' algebraic sign: other things being the same, more of FERA's resources were allocated to states where incomes had dropped the most between 1929 and 1933. On the other hand, more FERA dollars were distributed to states with large tracts of land in federal ownership, and less was spent in states where greater fractions of the population were black. Wallis's employment index is not a significant determinant of FERA spending when time-wise variations in the dependent variable are taken into account.

The statistical significance of *YDROP*, *FEDLAND* and *BLACK* is in general unaffected when political variables are added to the model. Only one of these new variables is statistically significant, though. All else equal, popular support for FDR in the 1932 election is a positive and significant determinant of FERA spending, suggesting that Harry Hopkins allocated some of the agency's resources with an eye toward rewarding states for their past contributions to Roosevelt's national vote total.[12] Electoral-vote-rich states did not receive disproportionate shares of FERA largesse, however, and congressional influence on the distribution of New Deal funds is not evident in these results.

Overall, the evidence from FERA suggests that the New Dealers responded both to economic need and to the exigencies of presidential politics. In contrast to the CWA, though, political considerations do add as much explanatory power as do other explanatory variables. It is nevertheless true that the marginal effect of popular political support for FDR in 1932 is of about the same magnitude as the depression's impact on personal incomes.

5 THE MATCHING HYPOTHESIS REVISITED

The evidence presented thus far paints a picture of the New Deal in two sharply contrasting colors. While the Roosevelt administration spoke in elo-

Table 8.10 The determinants of FERA spending

CONSTANT	1,039.53	−2,763.97
	(0.31)	(−0.70)
YDROP	82.25	68.95
	(2.09)**	(1.67)*
PCY	−1.08	−0.05
	(−0.60)	(−0.02)
EMPLOY	32.48	32.28
	(1.11)	(1.07)
FEDLAND	65.17	46.13
	(5.17)***	(2.69)***
BLACK	−41.89	−95.81
	(−1.85)*	(−2.58)**
ELECTORAL		80,626
		(1.02)
FDR32		67.15
		(1.78)*
HOUSE		−6,392.02
		(−0.23)
SENATE		0.77
		(0.03)
R^2	66.32	66.89
F	54.54	39.40

Notes:
Student's *t*-statistics in parentheses. Asterisks denote significance at the 1 percent (***), 5 percent (**), and 10 percent (*) levels. The estimated coefficients and associated *t*-statistics for the six included year dummies are as follows. In the first model, they are 1935: 9,098 (11.21); 1936: -2,232 (-2.54); 1937: -5,245 (-5.33); 1938: -5,608 (-6.16); and 1939: -5,625 (-5.70). In the second model, they are 1935: 9,068 (11.08); 1936: -2,329 (-2.63); 1937: -5,350 (-5.30); 1938: -5,686 (-6.16); and 1939:-5,707 (-5.61).

quent terms about alleviating suffering and promoting recovery – noble goals indeed – politics had a significant impact on the New Dealers' spending priorities. To be sure, economic conditions in the states help explain the allocation of emergency relief funds. But the administration's responses to these conditions did not always follow the pattern predicted by its stated goals. While more CWA projects were in fact distributed to those states where employment recovery lagged the most (and more FERA funds were distributed to states where incomes had fallen most precipitously from pre-crash levels), for instance, more agricultural relief went to states where the average farm was more valuable. On the other hand, the impact of presidential politics – the fraction of a state's voters casting their ballots for FDR in 1932 and the number of electoral votes at stake in 1936 – is consistently significant. Moreover, these political variables by themselves generally explain more of the cross-state variation in New Deal spending than do variables measuring a state's economic 'need'.

FDR's hagiographers are quick to offer a possible explanation for the absence of clear evidence that need was the primary determinant of New Deal spending. As stated previously, a number of scholars have pointed to programmatic matching requirements as a plausible reason why the spending pattern that emerged was consistent with the administration's compassionate motives. In particular, the federal government's purpose was noble but intransigent states blocked its relief efforts. States with more progressive leaders were willing to raise the funds for matching purposes while other states – especially those in the South – were not.

John Joseph Wallis (1984) has most fully developed this hypothesis. He states that 'from the very beginning Congress and national relief officials were concerned that state and local governments should bear their share of the relief burden, and they therefore utilized matching grants' (Wallis 1984, p. 147). Some of the programs had explicit matching formulas written into the authorizing legislation; others did not. According to Wallis, even the programs that did not have matching requirements explicitly in place nevertheless based national grants on state and local contributions to the federal government's relief efforts. Wallis observes that 'in the remaining programs . . . it was also apparent (although not legally mandated) that the national policies were to reward states with larger expenditures by making larger relief grants' (Wallis 1984, p. 147).

Wallis uses this matching hypothesis to explain the seemingly perverse allocation of funds across the states. In a subsequent paper he explains:

> The New Deal would find its most cooperative partners in financing relief and recovery programs in those states least in need of reform, i.e., those states with higher incomes. Not only might congressmen from those low income, southern and agricultural states resist reform, so might the states themselves be able to frustrate reform by refusing to carry their share of the programs' costs. An individual state could effectively block a relief program within its boundaries simply by refusing to participate financially. Such a program would be politically palatable to the extent that it gave states that wanted more

liberal relief and reform a high option, financed in part by state funds, and allowed states with little desire for reform to do little. (Wallis 1987, p. 514)

Wallis tested this hypothesis in his 1984 paper by estimating the following equation:

$$NG = A_n + c_1 SE_i + c_i Z + e_n,$$

where NG is national grants, SE represents relief expenditures by state i, and Z is a vector of economic and demographic control variables. Wallis's data source, *Financial Statistics of the States*, provides annual observations on state expenditures, but the series was suspended between 1933 and 1936. Thus, he was limited to estimating a pooled cross-sectional time-series regression of federal grants to the states over the years 1937 to 1940.

Wallis expected the sign of the coefficient c_1 to be positive a priori because 'state and local governments had considerable influence over the administration of federal programs during the New Deal' (Wallis 1984, p. 151). If so, states that made larger expenditures of their own would be rewarded with more federal aid. The independent variable measuring these state contributions, SE, included 'total expenditures for operation and maintenance, capital outlays, and interest payments net of intergovernmental grants' (Wallis 1984, p.153).

In the first specification, Wallis gauges the influence of state spending levels on total federal grants. While the control variables behaved as they had in previous research, state spending was not significantly correlated with federal spending: other things being the same, states that contributed more of their own resources to the relief effort received no more federal aid than their less generous neighbors. Thus, Wallis's initial results suggest that programmatic matching requirements – both explicit and implicit – did not contribute to explaining the allocation of total New Deal grants across the states.

Next, Wallis redefines the dependent variable so that it includes only those grants made by the Social Security Board and the Works Progress Administration (WPA). But grants made by the Social Security Board were explicitly matched with state funds. Hence, a positive relationship between national grants and state expenditures in this case would show only that the mandated formula was followed. Wallis acknowledges this uncomfortable fact, explaining that the estimates are qualitatively the same if social security is excluded. He nevertheless includes such grants because 'the WPA reportedly took all relief programs into consideration when making grants' (Wallis 1984, p. 153).

In this second specification, the estimated coefficient on state expenditures is positive and statistically significant. Specifically, 'a dollar increase in per-capita state expenditures led, at the margin, to an increase of $1.73 in per capita federal grants' (Wallis 1984, p. 154). Hence, the matching hypothesis is buttressed by this result.

In sum, Wallis finds limited evidence supporting the matching hypothesis of New Deal spending. While the distribution of total federal grants cannot be explained by an implicit requirement that states contribute resources of their own to the relief effort, such considerations do seem to have helped determine the allocation of social security and WPA grants. But because the Social Security Board adhered to an explicit matching formula, in effect Wallis's results merely imply that (implicit) matching may have been an important factor in the distribution of WPA dollars. This possibility is explored more fully in the remainder of the chapter.

1. Sponsor Contributions and the WPA

If one factor can be eliminated as an explanation for the WPA's spending priorities, that factor is the relief effort supplied by state and local governments. This conclusion is clear from the testimony of Colonel Harrington, WPA Administrator after Harry Hopkins's resignation. Recall that while the WPA assumed responsibility for work relief, it was left to state and local governments to provide funds for the so-called unemployables. According to Harrington, 'in determining state employment quotas the WPA took no account of a state's attitude toward assuming what was termed its reasonable share of its own relief load' (Howard 1943, p. 597). He provided a hypothetical example of two cities with the same level of unemployment and population. One of the cities gives adequate local relief while the other does not. Both cities would, so testified Harrington, get the same amount of help from the WPA.

John Joseph Wallis asserts that while the WPA did not formally adopt strict matching requirements for allocating funds, the states were expected to shoulder a portion of the cost burden nonetheless. However, proposals to standardize such responsibilities by mandating that the agency employ explicit matching formulas were consistently defeated by Congress.

An effort was in fact made by Senator James Byrnes of South Carolina to force sponsoring agencies to contribute 25 percent of the total cost associated with WPA projects. This proposal was vigorously opposed by Harry Hopkins. He argued that many states and localities simply could not afford to take on this responsibility and would therefore be unable to obtain WPA grants.[13] Representative Martin of Colorado agreed, stating that if sponsors were held to such a high contribution standard, those areas in the direst straits would be forced to forego worthwhile WPA projects: 'If it is rigidly carried out it will wipe states, counties, cities, towns, and districts from the WPA map' (US House of Representatives 1939, p. 7314). In short, explicit matching requirements were evidently rejected by Congress because their burden would have fallen disproportionately on the poorest states and localities.

It is now possible to put speculation about matching's role in the distribution of WPA grants to rest. The actual amount of money contributed by sponsors to WPA projects was in fact recorded in the *Congressional Record* (US House of Representatives 1939, p. 921) and, to the best of our knowledge, exploited here for the first time.

The percentage of total WPA expenditures contributed by the individual states is presented in Table 8.11. The Roosevelt administration seems to have turned the Biblical admonition, 'every one to whom much is given, of him will much be required' (Luke 12:48), on its head. Contrary to Wallis's assertion, those states that received the largest grants tended to be those states that made the smallest contributions. (Indeed, WPA expenditures by state and sponsor contributions by state are negatively and significantly correlated at the 5 percent level of confidence with a correlation coefficient of −.455.) For example, Tennessee, a relatively poor state, contributed 33.2 percent of total WPA expenditures while the relatively rich state of Pennsylvania contributed only 10.1 percent. The 12 southern states (Alabama, Kentucky, Tennessee, Mississippi, Louisiana, Arkansas, Texas, Virginia, North Carolina, South Carolina, Georgia, and Florida) contributed 22.04 percent, on the average, while the average contribution for the nation as a whole was 18.82 percent. The regional breakdown of sponsors' contributions is shown in Figure 8.1.

Georgia Senator Richard Russell, who entered the percentages contributed by the individual states into the record, saw the apparent disparity in sponsor contributions as supplying further evidence of the administration's favoritism. He complained that

> the poorer states – discriminated against as they are in the matter of per capita expenditure, in monthly wage, and in hourly wage – are, in addition, required to contribute more from their poverty toward sponsored projects than the wealthier States are. Not only is the per capita expenditure shown to be high where per capita income is high, but the requirements of sponsors for contributions to projects is lower in the rich States and is higher in the poor States, and has been throughout the administration of this program. (US House of Representatives 1939, p. 921)

Russell went on to say that

> it is not only a discrimination in favor of the wealthier communities, but it has taken funds from the poorer communities that were sadly needed to provide

Table 8.11 Percentage of total WPA expenditures contributed by sponsors

NEW ENGLAND		18.7	SOUTH ATLANTIC		18.6
Maine	20.1		Delaware	13.1	
New Hampshire	19.0		Maryland	25.4	
Vermont	24.2		Virginia	21.7	
Massachusetts	13.2		West Virginia	15.3	
Rhode Island	17.2		North Carolina	23.5	
Connecticut	18.2		South Carolina	20.8	
			Georgia	19.2	
MIDDLE ATLANTIC		12.7	Florida	19.4	
New York	11.6				
New Jersey	16.4		EAST SOUTH CENTRAL		24.9
Pennsylvania	10.1		Kentucky	20.6	
			Tennessee	33.2	
EAST NORTH CENTRAL		15.7	Alabama	20.9	
Ohio	12.9		Mississippi	24.8	
Indiana	15.1				
Illinois	16.9		WEST SOUTH CENTRAL		20.5
Michigan	16.6		Arkansas	17.4	
Wisconsin	17.2		Louisiana	18.1	
			Oklahoma	21.8	
WEST NORTH CENTRAL		20.0	Texas	24.8	
Minnesota	17.6				
Iowa	24.7		MOUNTAIN		24.0
Missouri	13.9		Montana	16.6	
North Dakota	19.7		Idaho	28.3	
South Dakota	16.9		Wyoming	29.3	
Nebraska	22.5		Colorado	18.4	
Kansas	24.7		New Mexico	17.4	
			Arizona	26.0	
PACIFIC		17.1	Utah	25.5	
Washington	16.5		Nevada	30.3	
Oregon	18.9				
California	16.0				

Source:
US House of Representatives (1939, p. 921).

Figure 8.1 Percentage of total WPA spending contributed by sponsors, by census region

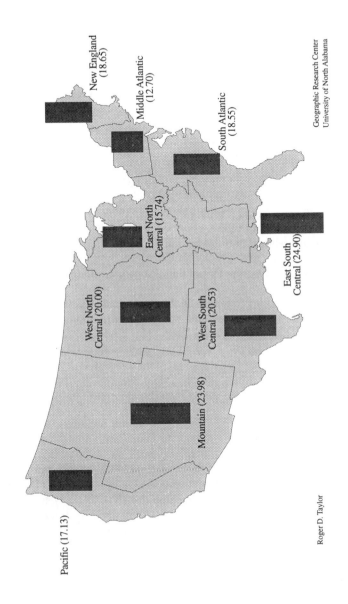

New England
(18.65)

Middle Atlantic
(12.70)

South Atlantic
(18.55)

East North
Central (15.74)

East South
Central (24.90)

West North
Central (20.00)

West South
Central (20.53)

Mountain (23.98)

Pacific (17.13)

Geographic Research Center
University of North Alabama

Roger D. Taylor

207

direct relief for unemployables, and which were needed to match Federal contributions for old-age assistance, for health purposes, and for crippled and dependent children. (US House of Representatives 1939, p. 921)

Rather than using WPA expenditures to equalize incomes around the nation, the Roosevelt administration seemed to have systematically penalized the very states and regions where economic needs were arguably the most pressing. Poorer states were required to contribute proportionately larger, not smaller, amounts of money and materials in return for getting their projects approved. And, again, the region that was most unfavorably treated was the South.

Senator Russell, representing a relatively poor state and objecting to the unfairness of the status quo, nevertheless was one of the proponents of the adoption of a uniform 25 percent matching requirement. 'Some of us endeavored to equalize it at 25 percent all over the United States, fixing the same scale for rich States and poor States alike' (US House of Representatives 1939, p. 921). Although such a requirement would have been more difficult for the poorer states to meet, everyone would at least have had to contribute the same percentage of the total cost.

2. Empirical Evidence Regarding Sponsor Contributions

In what follows, we attempt to shed empirical light on the relationship between WPA expenditures and sponsor contributions. Two sets of linear regression equations are estimated. The first equation models sponsor contributions as a function of economic conditions in the states. In the second model, WPA spending is regressed on a number of explanatory variables, including sponsor contributions. Taken together, the results of estimating these two sets of equations weaken explanations based on the matching hypothesis considerably.

In the first model, the percentage of the total cost of WPA projects contributed by the states serves as the dependent variable; it is expressed as the deviation from the mean in standardized units so that ordinary least squares regression analysis can be utilized. This specification includes as independent variables 1935 per capita income by state (*PCY35*), the values of Wallis's employment index in the same year (*EMPLOY35*), the average value of an acre of land in a state as of 1930 (*VALUEACRE*), and the percentage of the state's land owned by the federal government in 1937 (*FEDLAND*). Nineteen thirty-five serves as the benchmark year for the analysis because the WPA was authorized by that year's Emergency Relief Appropriation Act.

The measures of economic well-being within a state – *PCY35* and *EMPLOY35* – are expected to be positively correlated with sponsor contributions. That is, states with more vibrant economies (as measured by the extent to which employment had recovered to pre-crash levels) and with higher per-capita incomes could have afforded to bear more of the burden of financing WPA projects. States with higher land values per acre are expected to contribute larger percentages as well. Because states cannot tax federal land, those states where more of the land was owned by the federal government might be expected to make smaller contributions, all else equal.

The results of estimating this regression specification are presented in Table 8.12. Contrary to a priori expectations, states with larger per-capita incomes, as Senator Russell complained, contributed significantly smaller amounts. On the other hand, states with greater federal ownership of land were required to contribute more of their own resources toward the sponsorship of WPA projects. The most important result, though, is that greater economic well-being within a state – at least as measured by income per capita – did not translate into larger contributions. Just the reverse seems to have been true.

Table 8.12 The determinants of sponsor contributions

CONSTANT	−0.339	1.06	−3.48
	(−0.25)	(0.58)	(−1.71)
PCY35	−0.0034		
	(−3.41)***		
YDROP		−0.0001	0.009
		(−0.06)	(0.46)
EMPLOY35	0.015	0.002	0.018
	(1.00)	(0.10)	(0.99)
VALUEACRE	0.0033		
	(0.48)		
FEDLAND	0.027	0.021	0.023
	(3.89)***	(3.28)***	(3.25)***
UNION		−0.03	
		(−2.10)**	
URBAN		−0.02	
		(−3.16)***	
FDR32			0.021
			(2.29)**
R^2	38.4	46.0	27.34
F	6.7	7.16	4.05

Notes:
Student's *t*-statistics in parentheses. Asterisks denote significance at the 1 percent (***) and 5 percent (**) levels.

The results of estimating two slightly different versions of the sponsor contribution model are also reported in Table 8.12.[14] *YDROP*, the percentage decline in income per capita between 1929 and 1933, is entered as an alternative measure of economic conditions in the states. In addition, however, three new explanatory variables explore the political determinants of sponsor contributions. As before, *FDR32* is the percentage of the popular vote cast for Franklin Roosevelt in the 1932 presidential election. *UNION* is the fraction of a state's labor force belonging to organized labor unions,[15] and *URBAN* is the percentage of a state's population living in urban areas. The latter two variables test Robinson's (1970) observation that FDR's 1936 reelection strategy hinged in part on the support of the big-city political machines and organized labor.

The coefficient estimates support a vote-buying model of sponsor contributions. Both *URBAN* and *UNION* enter negatively and significantly, suggesting that, other things being the same, states with greater percentages of urban voters and labor union members were allowed to contribute smaller shares of the cost of WPA projects. On the other hand, the purchase price of WPA projects was significantly higher in states that were deemed 'safe' because they had supported FDR heavily in 1932. By varying required sponsor contributions in these ways, wealth was transferred from Democratic Party strongholds – chiefly located in the South – to buy votes from urban and labor constituencies.

The next step in investigating the matching hypothesis is to construct a model of WPA expenditures across the states. The ratio of total WPA grants to 1930 population serves as the dependent variable in the analysis. Sponsor contributions serves as the key explanatory variable. If the willingness and ability of states to contribute their own resources to the relief effort was an implicit requirement for obtaining federal funds, then the estimated coefficient on this variable should be positive. Such a result would indicate that states which contributed more toward the cost of financing WPA projects received larger grants, holding other factors constant.

In addition to sponsor contributions, two other variables are introduced that have not been utilized in any of the previous literature. Charles (1963) provides much of the logic for including these variables. He notes that

Hopkins devoted considerable attention to his relations with Congress, particularly from 1935 on. While he continually ignored several congressmen because of their obnoxious ways of opposing the New Deal . . . , he gave special attention to senators and congressmen who supported the work relief program. (Charles 1963, p. 162)

One way the New Dealers could gauge congressional support was by observing the voting records of senators and representatives. Hence, if Charles's assessment of the attention Hopkins paid to congressional relations

'The Big-Check Suit That Was Hung on Harry'
Kansas City Star, 28 November 1938

is correct, the members who voted for the public works program may have been rewarded by the administration when funds were distributed. Although the WPA's continued existence depended on yearly appropriations and, thus, yearly congressional reauthorization, the most important of these votes was the initial one – the vote on the Emergency Relief Appropriation Act of 1935 that created the agency.

The measure sailed through the House of Representatives, but encountered resistance in the Senate. The opposition there was organized and the debate acrimonious. Most of the controversy centered on the unprecedented power the proposed legislation granted to the executive branch. Senator Vandenberg of Michigan warned that 'one day we are all called to account. Adequate explanation is impossible. All subsequent calamity traces back to the hour when we surrender to this bill.' He went on to say that, 'and if these be not the seeds of fascism, then I miss my guess' (US House of Representatives 1935a, p. 2019).

In light of these considerations, the percentages of each state's representatives and senators voting in favor of the Emergency Relief Appropriation Act of 1935 serve as independent variables in the next set of equations to be estimated (*HOUSEYES* and *SENATEYES*). These votes are recorded in the US House of Representatives (1935a, pp. 942, 5135) and presented in Table 8.13.

These voting records belie claims that ideological support for the New Deal was weakest in the South and, moreover, that the political leaders from that region maneuvered in the halls of Congress to thwart the administration's relief efforts. At least as far as the WPA is concerned, southern politicians were no enemies of the New Deal.[16] Far from it. With the exception of Virginia, the South's congressional delegations voted nearly unanimously for the Emergency Relief Appropriation Act of 1935. Even Georgia's Senator Russell seems to have voted for the measure. Contrary to the conventional wisdom, the bulk of the opposition to the WPA seems to have come from New England, the Middle Atlantic states, and the Midwest.

The hypothesis that anti-New Deal ideology explains the South's relative lack of success in attracting federal dollars is further undercut by the observation that serious opposition to the administration did not arise in the region until fairly late in the game: 'The rift with southern Democrats began with Roosevelt's daring plan to pack the Supreme Court in 1937' (Biles 1994, p. 141). These strained relations deteriorated further later that year following FDR's nomination of the 'highly unpopular' and ultraliberal senator from Alabama, Hugo Black, to the US Supreme Court (Biles 1994, p. 144), and the president's southern support ended for good during the 1938 congressional elections when he campaigned in the region personally in an effort to purge 'three particularly bitter southern antagonists, senators Walter George of Georgia, Cotton Ed Smith of South Carolina, and Millard Tydings of Maryland' (Biles 1994, p. 146). All three incumbents ultimately were reelected, but Roosevelt's interference in state politics – going so far as to cut the flow of patronage to the three New Deal opponents and dispensing campaign funds to their challengers – left a bitter taste that sealed southern opposition to the administration's programs until events in Europe allowed

Table 8.13　　*Percentage of state congressional delegations voting for the Emergency Relief Appropriation Act of 1935*

	Senate (%)	House (%)		Senate (%)	House (%)
Alabama	100	100	Nebraska	100	100
Arizona	100	100	Nevada	100	100
Arkansas	100	100	New Hampshire	50	100
California	–	95	New Jersey	50	54
Colorado	100	100	New Mexico	100	100
Connecticut	100	100	New York	100	70
Delaware	0	0	North Carolina	100	100
Florida	100	100	North Dakota	100	100
Georgia	100	50	Ohio	50	74
Idaho	100	100	Oklahoma	50	100
Illinois	100	73	Oregon	50	100
Indiana	100	82	Pennsylvania	100	68
Iowa	100	75	Rhode Island	50	100
Kansas	100	100	South Carolina	100	100
Kentucky	100	88	South Dakota	100	100
Louisiana	–	100	Tennessee	100	100
Maine	0	100	Texas	100	100
Maryland	50	100	Utah	100	100
Massachusetts	–	62	Vermont	100	0
Michigan	50	50	Virginia	50	57
Minnesota	0	44	Washington	100	100
Mississippi	100	100	West Virginia	100	100
Missouri	100	91	Wisconsin	100	100
Montana	100	100	Wyoming	100	100

Note:
'–' indicates no vote recorded.

Source:
US House of Representatives (1935a, pp. 942, 5135).

him to begin mending fences by replacing 'Dr. New Deal' with 'Dr. Win-the-War' (Biles 1994, p. 148).

In any case, the results of OLS estimation of the relationship between WPA expenditures per capita and sponsor contributions are presented in

Table 8.14. Slightly more than 63 percent of the variation in the dependent variable is explained by the first specification, while the second accounts for nearly 44 percent. The results indicate that the distribution of WPA grants, like most of the New Deal programs examined thus far, had little to do with economic hardship. The variable controlling for state economic well-being, 1935 per-capita income, is statistically insignificant in the first model and significantly positive in the second. Hence, at least in the second equation, WPA grants tended to flow into those states with higher per capita incomes. Consistent with earlier results, the estimated coefficient on *BLACK* is negative and significant. This result contrasts sharply with some of the historical accounts of the New Deal which emphasize its color-blindness. For example, Carl Degler (1959, p. 398) asserts that, 'Evenhandedly distributed federal relief funds were a gift from heaven to the black man, who was traditionally hired last and fired first.' Rather than providing evidence of racial discrimination on the New Dealers' part, though, the fact that *BLACK* is negatively correlated with WPA spending can also be interpreted to support contentions that the New Deal was not about reform, but was instead designed to return individuals to their pre-crash standards of living.

Table 8.14 WPA expenditures and sponsor contributions

CONSTANT	51.6	22.92
	(3.46)***	(1.39)
SPONSOR	−1.68	−1.51
	(−4.3)***	(−3.18)***
PCY35	0.020	0.0606
	(1.21)	(3.5)***
SENATE	0.502	0.251
	(2.22)**	(0.94)
HOUSEYES	0.0452	0.127
	(0.55)	(1.3)
SENATEYES	0.20	0.188
	(3.00)***	(2.29)**
BLACK	−0.733	
	(−4.52)***	
R^2	63.36	43.7

Notes:
Student's *t*-statistics in parentheses. Asterisks denote significance at the 1 percent (***), and 5 percent (**) levels.

The empirical results in Table 8.14 also add weight to political models of New Deal spending. Other things being the same, states enjoying greater seniority in the US Senate were the recipients of larger appropriations from the Works Progress Administration. *SENATE* loses its significance in the second model, however. What is more important is that congressional support for the original legislation funding the WPA also yields explanatory power. As expected, the coefficient on *SENATEYES* is positive and significant in both specifications, suggesting that votes cast in support of the Emergency Relief Appropriation Act of 1935 translated into larger grants from the agency. On the other hand, *HOUSEYES*, while positive, is not significant in either equation. The significance of the Senate variable and the lack of significance of the House variable is consistent with the overwhelming support enjoyed by the administration in the latter chamber. In the Senate, where the opposition was more vocal and majority support for the bill less certain, favorable votes were rewarded with larger federal appropriations.

The variable of chief interest in both models, of course, is the share of WPA expenditures from state sources (*SPONSOR*). This variable is consistently negative and significant at the 1 percent level of confidence. The results suggest that, other things being the same, states making larger contributions to WPA projects received smaller, not larger, appropriations. This finding casts substantial doubt on the matching explanation espoused by Wallis. More specifically, a 1 percent increase in sponsor contributions from a state led, at the margin, to a $1.68 reduction in per-capita WPA grants.

Arguments to the contrary, the WPA does not seem to have implicitly based its funding decisions and employment quotas on the willingness of the state to contribute its own resources to the relief effort. Rather, those states that contributed the greatest amounts received the smallest grants. And, consistent with the charges of Senator Russell and other critics of the New Deal, the evidence presented herein suggests that the poorer states were required to contribute larger amounts of treasure and materials in order to 'purchase' WPA projects. At the very least, the results suggest that the matching explanation for the observed cross-state allocation of funds is of dubious merit.

6 CONCLUSION

Government is widely viewed as a benevolent entity with the responsibility of protecting vulnerable individuals from the vicissitudes of powerful market forces that lie beyond their control. The actions taken by Washington during the Great Depression are frequently cited as the leading example of all the good that can be done by a vigorous and compassionate state and routinely offered as a role model for the governments of today to strive to emulate. The conventional wisdom about the period of the New Deal is that government directed all of its efforts toward rescuing ordinary people from the economic crisis visited on them by Wall Street and that in the process of responding to the emergency, the New Dealers were incapable of considering their own personal interests. Self-interest was the motivation only of the greedy businessmen and speculators who were responsible for triggering the crash in the first place. To those who have adopted this point of view, the decade of the 1930s demonstrates the humanitarian heights to which an activist, public-spirited federal government can climb.

The New Dealers and their supporters do not deny that mistakes were made, but the errors that inevitably occurred are attributed, not to design, but to the normal failings expected of imperfect human beings forced to respond quickly to an unprecedented crisis and to take action while sailing in 'uncharted waters'. Franklin Roosevelt himself offered such an explanation when he said in a 1936 speech that, 'Governments can err, presidents do make mistakes, but the immortal Dante tells us that divine justice weighs the sins of the cold-blooded and the sins of the warm-hearted in different scales. Better the occasional faults of a government that lives in a spirit of charity than the consistent omissions of a government frozen in the ice of its own indifference' (Williams 1994, pp. 189–90). Thus, whatever sins the New Dealers may have committed deserve forgiveness because their sins were motivated by compassion for the 'forgotten man'.

But the rhetoric of the New Dealers simply does not match reality. Emphasizing the seductive powers of the billions of dollars worth of federal funds made available for distribution, Senator Vandenberg of Michigan pointed to a public choice explanation for New Deal spending when he remarked that, 'the human urge will be upon all States to get all they can, and the inevitable fallibility of human – and especially political – judgements will curse the net result' (US House of Representatives 1935a, p. 2019). And, indeed, the evidence presented in this chapter suggests that political self-interest was perhaps the most important motive underlying the administration's spending decisions. A state's popular vote support for FDR in the 1932 presidential election and its importance to the president's Electoral College strategy are consistently significant determinants of the amount of federal aid it received.

The political competition for New Deal dollars became too much even for some of the administration's strongest supporters. Senator Richard Russell of Georgia began the decade as 'a liberal and progressive Democrat. In times past in my own State I have been charged with being a radical because I have never hesitated to espouse principles and legislation to change the existing order when the general welfare demands it.' Russell went on to explain that he had supported every bill brought forth by the New Dealers to appropriate money to provide relief. The apparent injustices that followed, especially those that worked against the interests of the poor and the powerless, caused him to rethink his position, however. His faith in the federal government damaged, the Senator continued his apostasy:

> I have never until recently been able to see the slightest merit in the contention which is ofttimes advanced that each State should care for its own unemployed; that each State should seek to relieve the needs of those within its borders who are in distress. But I must regretfully conclude that . . . the poorer States would have been better off if they had gone along with their own poverty-stricken people and endeavored to take care of them. (US House of Representatives 1939, p. 924)

In short, rather than representing the zenith of government involvement in the economy, the New Deal may instead represent the nadir.

NOTES

1. *EMPLOY* is entered with a one-year lag to avoid a possible problem of reverse causality. However, if the contemporaneous value of *EMPLOY* is entered by itself, the estimated coefficient on it is also positive and significant at the 1 percent level. Taken together, these results suggest that the perverse relationship with the dependent variable is not the result of simultaneous-equations bias.
2. See Table 7.4 and the surrounding discussion.
3. It is also consistent with evidence summarized in Hofstadter (1955, p. 123) that, during the Progressive Era, 'in all farm organizations, including the more "radical" Farmers' Union, membership is dominated by farmers of high economic status (and to a lesser degree of medium status) and that low-status farmers are a negligible part of the membership of all such organizations.' Hofstadter (1955, p. 124), in fact, charges that 'implacable opposition' by Farm Bureau Federation lobbyists killed the Resettlement Administration and the Farm Security Administration, the Roosevelt administration's 'most significant organized effort to do something about' the problems of marginal farmers.
4. Indeed, the partial correlation coefficient between *HOUSE* and *FDR32* is .288 with a p-value of .0001.
5. With a few notable exceptions, House leadership positions were indeed dominated by members from the South during the 1930s. On the other hand, Nevada Senator Key Pittman was President Pro Tem of the Senate throughout the New Deal period. At the beginning of the 2nd session of the 72nd Congress (5 December 1932), George H. Moses (NH) was President Pro Tem of the Senate, John Nance Garner (TX) was Speaker of the House, and Henry T. Rainey (IL) was House majority leader. The leadership roster for the remainder of the decade was as follows. Seventy-third Congress: President Pro Tem – Key Pittman (NV); Speaker – Henry T. Rainey (IL); majority leader – Joseph W. Byrnes (TN). Seventy-fourth Congress: President Pro Tem – Key Pittman (NV); Speaker – Joseph W. Byrnes (TN); majority leader – William B. Bankhead (AL). Seventy-fifth Congress: President Pro Tem – Key Pittman (NV); Speaker – William B. Bankhead (AL); majority leader – Sam Rayburn (TX). Source: US House of Representatives (1932, 1933, 1935, 1938).
6. In results not reported here, an interaction term, *BLACKFARMER*TENANT*, was included to gauge the joint impact of the two variables. The estimated coefficient was negative and significant at the 5 percent level in both specifications.
7. 'The goal established in 1934 had called for the purchase of 5 million acres *per year* over a 15-year span' (Barber 1996, p. 127, emphasis added). Most of the land purchased under these 'emergency' programs (6.4 million acres, to be precise), 'equivalent of two-thirds of the combined area of the states of Massachusetts, Connecticut, and Rhode Island', was located in the

Great Plains and Intermountain regions of the United States (Barber 1996, p. 127). This observation may help explain why *FEDLAND*, a variable measuring the percentage of a state's land under federal ownership, is consistently positive in empirical models of New Deal spending.

8. Evidence that the administration's land-use strategy did not work as expected is given by the fact that there were still some 900,000 farmers on relief in 1935 (Barber 1996, p. 76).

9. Similar results are obtained when *YDROP*, the percentage decline in state income between 1929 and 1933, is substituted for *PCY33*.

10. This is apparently due to negative and significant partial correlation between *BLACK* and *ORDER* (r = −.45 with a p-value of .001).

11. In results not reported here, though, CWA spending is an insignificant determinant of FERA spending.

12. Examining voting data from 1,067 southern counties, Fleck (1996) reports evidence supporting this conclusion. In particular, he finds a positive and significant relationship between FERA expenditures over the 1933–35 period and voter turnout rates in the 1932 presidential election. At the margin, a 1 percent increase in the percentage of a county's eligible voters who cast ballots in November 1932 led to a 2 percent increase in the amount of money spent by FERA in that county. In other words, 'reelection-seeking politicians' (Fleck 1996, p. 1) rationally rewarded politically active voters with greater shares of FERA largesse.

13. As noted earlier, because such requirements would also have limited Hopkins's discretion in distributing federal funds, his opposition to this proposal was not entirely selfless.

14. For more details, see Couch and Smith (1997).

15. The observations on union membership were taken from Lumsden and Peterson (1975).

16. For anecdotal evidence that leading Texas politicians, such as Sam Rayburn and Lyndon Johnson, saw the New Deal as a way of purchasing political support for themselves with northern tax dollars, see Caro (1990). Also see Brinkley (1984, p. 104), who suggests that in any case the South may not have been penalized for whatever ideological opposition it expressed:

> One of the shining lights of depression liberalism in the South was the so-called 'Little New Deal' that Dave Sholtz constricted as governor of Florida. And yet what qualified Sholtz for admission to the liberal pantheon was little more than his willingness to permit the federal government to spend money in his state. Harry Hopkins complained frequently to the White House that Florida was embracing New Deal relief agencies largely to avoid having to shoulder any responsibility itself for the indigent; that Sholtz consistently failed to contribute the state's expected share to welfare programs. Hopkins refrained from cutting off relief funding to the uncooperative Florida government only because he was reluctant to punish the state's unemployed for the failings of their political leaders.

Table 8A.1 The determinants of New Deal spending: Loans per capita

CONSTANT	−26,367	−30,511
	(−2.66)***	(−3.29)***
YDROP	455.93	499.06
	(4.02)***	(4.63)***
EMPLOY	29.38	68.96
	(0.36)	(0.88)
EMPLOY(-1)	88.10	85.72
	(1.39)	(1.39)
FARMVALUE	0.63	0.59
	(4.20)***	(4.41)***
FEDLAND	19.74	35.89
	(0.39)	(0.80)
FDR32	109.53	100.65
	(1.79)*	(1.83)*
ELECTORAL	648,702	754,999
	(2.17)**	(2.81)***
PROTEM	−10,891	−10,453
	(−1.62)	(−1.58)
SPEAKER	1,298.40	2,998.11
	(0.39)	(0.97)
SENATE	68.38	28.12
	(0.75)	(0.38)
HOUSE	18,827	22,620
	(0.28)	(0.37)
SENATEAG	234.86	243.38
	(2.10)**	(2.52)**
SENATEPBG	−134.02	
	(−1.02)	
SENATEPL	96.22	
	(0.64)	
SENATEFIN	−71.53	
	(−0.65)	
HOUSEAG	−160.87	
	(−1.09)	
HOUSEPB	267.92	
	(1.46)	
HOUSEPL	−97.25	
	(−0.48)	

Table 8A.1 (continued)

HOUSEWAYS	−20.39	
	(−0.32)	
R^2	0.58	0.57
F	16.91	23.27

Notes:
Student's *t*-statistics in parentheses. Asterisks denote significance at the 1 percent (***), 5 percent (**), and 10 percent (*) levels. The estimated coefficients and associated *t*-statistics for the six included year dummies are as follows. In the first model, they are 1934: 21,907 (8.39); 1935: 9,888 (3.78); 1936: -2,274 (-0.77); 1937: -8,215 (-2.49); 1938: -6,516 (-2.11); and 1939: -3,647 (-1.11). In the second model, they are 1934: 21,869 (8.69); 1935: 9,707 (3.82); 1936: -2,778 (-0.97); 1937: -8,976 (-2.80); 1938: -7,140 (-2.37); and 1939: -4,442 (-1.38).

Table 8A.2 *The determinants of New Deal spending: Non-repayable grants*
            per capita

CONSTANT	−31,540	−33,763
	(−2.75)***	(−3.00)***
YDROP	598.89	546.84
	(4.57)***	(4.26)***
EMPLOY	−234.24	−190.81
	(−2.47)**	(−2.00)**
EMPLOY(-1)	375.37	332.76
	(5.10)***	(4.50)***
FARMVALUE	0.15	0.37
	(0.85)	(2.17)**
FEDLAND	408.96	412.28
	(7.06)***	(7.47)***
FDR32	173.50	196.00
	(2.45)**	(2.85)***
ELECTORAL	2,425,510	2,267,260
	(7.00)***	(6.92)***
PROTEM	37,785	37,149
	(4.85)***	(4.66)***
SPEAKER	−6,714.23	−6,550.22
	(−1.74)*	(−1.68)*
SENATE	−263.66	−288.80
	(−2.51)**	(−3.23)***
HOUSE	−425,348	−419,972
	(−5.49)***	(−5.68)***
SENATEAG	564.51	608.92
	(4.38)***	(5.00)***
SENATEPBG	202.20	
	(1.34)	
SENATEPL	−36.93	
	(−0.21)	
SENATEFIN	−547.79	
	(−4.27)***	
HOUSEAG	178.58	
	(1.05)	
HOUSEPB	317.84	503.48
	(1.50)	(2.64)***
HOUSEPL	−388.12	−415.61
	(−1.66)*	(−1.76)*

Table 8A.2 (continued)

HOUSEWAYS	80.83	
	(1.10)	
R^2	0.82	0.80
F	54.59	63.50

Notes:
Student's t-statistics in parentheses. Asterisks denote significance at the 1 percent (***), 5 percent (**), and 10 percent (*) levels. The estimated coefficients and associated t-statistics for the six included year dummies are as follows. In the first model, they are 1934: 14,446 (4.78); 1935: 26,943 (8.90); 1936: 25,581 (7.46); 1937: 27,751 (7.28); 1938: 19,571 (5.48); and 1939: 28,654 (7.52). In the second model, they are 1934: 14,585 (4.78); 1935: 26,964 (8.77); 1936: 25,309 (7.25); 1937: 27,371 (7.04); 1938: 19,329 (5.30); and 1939: 28,304 (7.28).

9. Summary and Conclusions

No one knew whom it would hit next; the jobless were everywhere – in the cities, in the towns, on the farms. Their helplessness, their bewilderment, were often written in their faces, reflected in their discouraged gaits, and mirrored in their run-down dwellings.

– Carl Degler

Crisis is the rallying cry of the tyrant.

– James Madison

The Great Depression was a time of unprecedented economic hardship. At the economy's lowest point, a quarter of the workforce was unemployed and many individuals remained jobless for years. With business all but paralyzed, a hungry and desperate nation turned to the federal government for succor. Campaigning for the presidency with promises of relief, reform, and recovery, Franklin Delano Roosevelt was swept into office in November 1932.

Hopes were certainly high on Inauguration Day the following March. With the only thing to fear being fear itself, 'the state could hasten the glorious era of abundance. It had to discipline the sinful, aid the righteous, provide the mechanisms of a fair and stable market, and broaden the opportunities for all' (Conkin 1975, p. 26). *Laissez-faire* attitudes had precipitated the economic collapse, or so it was widely thought. With older ways of economic thinking apparently discredited and the callous indifference of the previous administration no longer tolerable, it was time for action. A benevolent government guided by the compassion of the New Dealers would restore hope and prosperity.

Government's response to the economic crisis was swift – and massive. Through a myriad new programs – the Works Progress Administration, the Civilian Conservation Corps, the Public Works Administration, the Federal Emergency Relief Administration, the Civil Works Administration, the Farm Credit Administration, the Resettlement Administration, and the Reconstruction Finance Corporation, to name a few – the New Dealers endeavored to jumpstart the economy. Policies to reduce agricultural output and to raise farm prices were put in place. Schemes for propping up wages and for eliminating destructive 'cutthroat competition' were embraced. Public works projects were launched on a monumental scale. Billions of dollars in federal funds were distributed across the nation, presumably targeted toward those most in need.

However, needs were not uniform across the country. Some states and regions had been devastated by the economy's collapse while others were only moderately affected. Apparently aware of the variability of the depression's impact, the administration undertook 'the most thorough study ever conducted prior to 1934 of the economic resources of the states in an effort to determine where federal money should go' (Charles 1963, p. 39). Testifying before the US Senate's Byrnes Committee in 1938, Corrington Gill, Assistant Administrator of the WPA, stated that the New Deal's policy-makers were 'intimately in touch with the States and conditions in the States'.

Despite avowals of care in determining need, contemporary observers criticized the administration sharply for the manner in which federal aid was distributed. Southern politicians, in particular, thought that their constituents had been shortchanged, supporting their charges with evidence that the New Dealers had allocated emergency relief funds in ways that worked disproportionately to the benefit of other states and regions. These allegations, which have been confirmed by later studies showing that, on a per-capita basis, the Midwestern, Mountain, and Pacific states garnered the lion's share of New Deal treasure, contradict the administration's rhetorical sensitivity to the needs of the region that President Roosevelt himself called the nation's number one economic problem. Hence, while the New Dealers claimed to be targeting need, many remained skeptical of their underlying motives.

Numerous explanations for the observed geographical distribution of funds have been offered. The most common of these involve differences in the cost of living from region to region, regional differences in standards of living, programmatic matching requirements stipulating that states and localities contribute resources of their own to the relief effort, and last, but not least, politics. Senator Richard Russell of Georgia, one of the New Deal's harshest contemporary critics, charged that political considerations largely determined which states basked in the warmth of the administration's favor and which suffered in the cold of neglect. His accusations are certainly consistent with modern public choice theories of political action which suggest that government programs and policies are shaped, not by the public interest, but by the self-interests of the politicians and bureaucrats who control the levers of civil authority. These self-interests provide powerful incentives for the individuals placed in positions of public responsibility to take actions whose outcomes are more closely aligned with their own personal goals of ensuring reelection, expanding agency budgets, or maximizing their post-government employment opportunities than they are with the global interests of the taxpaying public.

The discovery by Leonard Arrington in 1969 of a set of government publications detailing New Deal expenditures by state made it possible to investigate each of these competing explanations empirically. 'Prepared late in 1939 by the Office of Government Reports for the use of Franklin Roosevelt during the presidential campaign of 1940, the fifty page reports – one for each state – give precise information on the activities and achievements of the various New Deal economic agencies' (Arrington 1969, p. 311). The documents, produced for the purpose of showcasing the administration's efforts in combating the depression and released on the eve of the 1940 presidential election, afforded students of the New Deal the opportunity to gain fresh insights into this critically important decade in America's (indeed, the world's) economic history.

The scholarly research utilizing this data source suggests that the economic conditions in a particular state played only a minor role in determining that state's share of the available federal aid. As a matter of fact, those states in greater economic distress often received smaller grants than their better-off neighbors. But while the econometric evidence supporting a need-based model of New Deal expenditures is generally weak, and the direction of the observed relationships frequently perverse, political variables consistently have been found to explain a significant fraction of the cross-state variation in federal emergency relief spending. In accord with the predictions of a public choice model of the New Deal, the empirical evidence suggests that, in formulating its responses to the unprecedented economic crisis, the Roosevelt administration was not immune to the influence of politics.

Recent contributions to the literature have advanced a pork barrel hypothesis of the New Deal in which certain characteristics of a state's congressional delegation – seniority in the legislature, membership on key committees of Congress, and so on – as well as the state's importance to FDR's reelection strategy are critical to understanding how the federal government responded to the massive economic dislocations of 1929–41. But while the evidence adduced hitherto does not refute the idea that goals other than a desire to alleviate the human suffering caused by the Great Depression motivated the allocation of New Deal dollars, the existing studies are subject to a number of criticisms. In particular, the empirical results reported thus far have almost uniformly been based on analyses of spending data aggregated over the entire period of the New Deal and across all of its programs.

Our purpose has been to revisit the depression era and, more specifically, to investigate in finer detail the causes and consequences of the actions taken by the federal government during this historic economic collapse. Disaggregating New Deal expenditures over time, and including explanatory variables designed to capture the importance of individual states to the Roosevelt administration's political goals, yields additional empirical support for the pork barrel hypothesis. In particular, states that supported FDR in the 1932 presidential election were consistently rewarded with larger amounts of federal aid. In addition, measured on a per-capita basis, those states rich in Electoral College votes received significantly more funds from the New Dealers. In fact, a model including only political factors as explanatory variables explains nearly half of the state-to-state variation in federal emergency relief expenditures during the New Deal. Just as importantly, when time-wise variations in New Deal spending are taken into account, economic conditions in the states (as measured by the extent to which employment had recovered to pre-crash levels) do not contribute significantly to explaining how much aid was received.

Similar results are obtained when total New Deal expenditures are broken down by major program category. For example, agricultural relief also tended to flow disproportionately into those states that were rich in electoral votes and that supported the administration in the 1932 presidential election cycle. Those states with representation on the Senate's Agriculture and Forestry Committee likewise received larger appropriations. And, while the empirical evidence suggests that the Civil Works Administration did indeed allocate more funds where the number of people holding jobs had declined most precipitously between 1929 and 1933, it also seems to be true that CWA dollars were more generously directed to those states whose congressmen and senators had greater seniority in the legislature and, hence, greater political clout. Like the administrators of the government's agricultural relief programs, the CWA also rewarded those states with more electoral votes per capita, suggesting once again that FDR's reelection goals helped shape the New Deal's spending priorities.

Overall, we find more empirical support for a model of the New Deal based on presidential politics than we do for one based on congressional influence. In fact, seniority in the House of Representatives often seems to have worked against a state's interests, although this result is confounded by the fact that many of the chamber's senior members represented the South, a region solidly in the Democratic Party's camp and, hence, not critical to the president's reelection strategy. It is noteworthy, though, that the more closely congressional representation is tied to a specific spending category – agricultural programs being the leading example – the stronger the evidence seems to be that the legislative branch played a significant role in the distribution of New Deal funds.

Some New Deal scholars, while acknowledging the explanatory power of political variables, have offered one plausible alternative explanation for the apparently perverse pattern of New Deal spending. The argument is that programmatic matching requirements enabled wealthier states to garner the lion's share of the available funds. John Joseph Wallis has most fully developed this hypothesis. He contends that, 'The New Deal would find its most cooperative partners in financing relief and recovery programs in those states least in need of reform, i.e., those states with higher incomes.' He goes on to say that, 'an individual state could effectively block a relief program within its boundaries simply by refusing to participate financially' (Wallis 1987, p. 514). In short, states that were for ideological reasons unwilling, or for financial reasons unable, to raise the necessary matching funds simply lost out.

If matching requirements, whether explicit or implicit, were in fact routinely imposed on states as conditions for receiving federal aid, one would have to ask why the New Dealers would have adopted a funding formula that directed more money where it was needed less. And, if the answer was to punish the administration's ideological foes, the people standing in soup-kitchen lines could be forgiven for failing to appreciate the consequences fully.

At the end of the day, however, Wallis was able to produce only limited evidence in support of the matching hypothesis. Total New Deal expenditures in a state were not significantly correlated with that state's own contribution to the relief effort, but WPA appropriations were. Thus, according to Wallis, the matching explanation holds up for WPA spending.

Data on sponsors' contributions to WPA projects were located by us in the *Congressional Record* and used to test the matching hypothesis directly. Contrary to Wallis's evidence, those states that received the largest WPA grants made the smallest contributions to the relief effort. Moreover, those states in the greatest economic distress were required to contribute the most. The relatively poor state of Tennessee contributed 33.2 percent of the total cost of the WPA projects located within its borders, for example, while the relatively rich state of Pennsylvania contributed 10.1 percent. When we analyze the determinants of WPA expenditures per-capita in a multiple regression framework, we find that states with higher per capita incomes received larger appropriations and that states contributing greater amounts for matching purposes received smaller appropriations – results which render the matching hypothesis untenable. Those states with more seniority in the US Senate and whose members helped pass the Emergency Relief Appropriation Act of 1935 also received more WPA funds, suggesting that, once again, politics mattered. Senator Russell seems to have gotten it right when he charged that the agency's implicit matching requirements redistributed 'funds from the poorer communities that were sadly needed to provide direct relief for unemployables, and which were needed to match Federal contributions for old-age assistance, for health purposes, and for crippled and dependent children' (US House of Representatives 1939, p. 921).

Beginning in March of 1933, Franklin Roosevelt embarked boldly (some might say recklessly) on a course leading to an unprecedented expansion in the size and scope of the federal government. As Robert Higgs (1987) has documented so well, it was the sheer magnitude of the economic crisis that made the New Deal possible. Extraordinary times seemed to call for extraordinary measures. Yet, whatever else might be said about the New Deal (and much has been said), the fact of the matter is that it did not work. Despite massive expenditures of American treasure, economic recovery would ultimately have to be purchased with effusions of American blood. To reiterate, 'recovery occurred in 1932 for New Zealand; 1933 for Japan, Greece, and Romania; 1934 for Chile, Denmark, Finland, and Sweden; 1935 for Estonia, Hungary, Norway, and the United Kingdom; 1936 for Germany; and 1937 for Canada, Austria, and Italy. The United States . . . did not recover before the end of the sample in 1937' (Romer 1993, pp. 23–24).

There are a number of reasons why American economic policy failed. One is the First New Deal's wrong-headed strategy of responding to the colossal decline in real output by implementing programs designed to reduce production even further. Another is a series of disastrous monetary policy initiatives, beginning with a sharp contraction in the money supply at the depression's outset and ending with a doubling of required reserve ratios at a time (1936–37) when recovery seemed to be underway. Yet another is the uncertainty created by the brain trust's anti-market rhetoric, especially so during the Second New Deal, which seemed to put private property rights in jeopardy (Higgs 1997).

To this list must now be added the administration's political goals. As the evidence presented herein suggests, the distribution of the billions of dollars appropriated by Congress to prime the economic pump was guided less by considerations of economic need than by the forces of ordinary politics. Perhaps the New Deal failed as a matter of economic policy because it was so successful in building a winning political coalition: FDR was reelected overwhelmingly in 1936 and again in 1940 in part due to the support of the big-city machines, organized labor, and other constituencies which benefited disproportionately from New Deal largesse. Insofar as the region was 'safe' for the Democrats, the administration's comparative neglect of the nation's number one economic problem – the South – can likewise be explained by politics.

While much more research remains to be done before the political forces that shaped the New Deal are fully understood, it seems safe to conclude at this point that explanations of public policy during the Great Depression that do not take account of the political self-interests of the New Dealers themselves are seriously incomplete. As it has illuminated the study of the purposes and effects of more recent policy regimes, so the public choice model sheds light on the origins of big government in the United States. If the modern welfare state is riddled by special-interest-group politics, can one plausibly assume that these same pressures were absent at the creation?

Bibliography

Alston, Lee J. (1983), 'Farm foreclosures in the United States during the interwar period', *Journal of Economic History* **43** (December), 885–902.

Amberson, William R. (1935), 'The New Deal for sharecroppers', in Howard Zinn (ed.) (1966), *New Deal Thought*, Indianapolis, IN: Bobbs-Merrill, pp. 239–43.

Anderson, Gary M., William F. Shughart II and Robert D. Tollison (1988), 'A public choice theory of the Great Contraction', *Public Choice* **59** (October), 3–23.

Anderson, Gary M. and Robert D. Tollison (1991), 'Congressional influence and patterns of New Deal spending, 1933–1939', *Journal of Law and Economics* **34** (April), 161–75.

Aranson, Peter H. (1990), 'Theories of economic regulation: From clarity to confusion', *Journal of Law and Politics* **6** (Winter), 247–86.

Arrington, Leonard J. (1969), 'The New Deal in the West: A preliminary statistical inquiry', *Pacific Historical Review* **38** (August), 311–16.

Arrington, Leonard J. (1970), 'Western agriculture and the New Deal', *Agricultural History* **44** (October), 337–53.

Barber, William J. (1996), *Designs within Disorder: Franklin D. Roosevelt, the Economists, and the Shaping of American Economic Policy, 1933–1945*, Cambridge: Cambridge University Press.

Bator, Francis M. (1958), 'The anatomy of market failure', *Quarterly Journal of Economics* **72** (August), 351–79.

Bennett, James T. and Thomas J. DiLorenzo (1994), *Unhealthy Charities: Dangerous to your Health and Wealth*, New York: Basic Books.

Bernstein, Barton J. (1968), *Towards a New Past: Dissenting Essays in American History*, New York: Pantheon Books.

Bernstein, Michael A. (1987), *The Great Depression*, Cambridge: Cambridge University Press.

Biles, Roger (1994), *The South and the New Deal*, Lexington: University Press of Kentucky.

Bittlingmayer, George (1995), 'Output and stock prices when antitrust is suspended: The effects of the NIRA', in Fred S. McChesney and William

F. Shughart II (eds), *The Causes and Consequences of Antitrust: The Public Choice Perspective*, Chicago: University of Chicago Press, pp. 287–318.

Brinkley, Alan (1984), 'The New Deal and southern politics', in James C. Cobb and Michael V. Namorato (eds), *The New Deal and the South*, Jackson: University Press of Mississippi, pp. 97–115.

Carlton, Dennis W. (1983), 'A reexamination of delivered pricing systems', *Journal of Law and Economics* **26** (April), 51–70.

Caro, Robert A. (1990), *The Years of Lyndon Johnson: Means of Ascent*, New York: Knopf.

Charles, Searle F. (1963), *Minister of Relief*, Syracuse, NY: Syracuse University Press.

Conkin, Paul K. (1975), *The New Deal*, New York: Thomas Y. Crowell Co.

Couch, Jim F. (1995), 'New Deal, old pork: The politics and economics of federal emergency relief spending during the Great Depression', unpublished dissertation, University of Mississippi.

Couch, Jim F. and Lewis Smith (1997), 'New Deal programs and state matching funds: Reconstruction or re-election?', unpublished manuscript, University of North Alabama.

Degler, Carl N. (1959), *Out of Our Past: The Forces that Shaped Modern America*, New York: Harper and Brothers.

Degler, Carl N. (ed.) (1970), *The New Deal*, Chicago: Quadrangle Books.

Ferrara, Peter J. (1980), *Social Security: The Inherent Contradiction*, San Francisco: Cato Institute.

Fleck, Robert K. (1996), 'Reelection incentives and the value of the vote: A model of the effects of turnout on distributive policy and a test using FERA spending in the South', unpublished manuscript, Montana State University.

Friedman, Milton and Anna J. Schwartz (1963), *A Monetary History of the United States, 1867–1960*, Princeton, NJ: Princeton University Press.

Galbraith, John K. (1988), *The Great Crash*, Boston: Houghton Mifflin.

Gill, Corrington (1935), 'The relief wage scale: Its critics answered', *New York Times* (26 May), 3.

Gratton, Brian (1996), 'The poverty of impoverishment theory: The economic well-being of the elderly, 1890–1950', *Journal of Economic History* **56** (March), 39–61.

Graves, John Temple II (1937), 'The big world at last reaches Gee's Bend', in Carl N. Degler (ed.) (1970), *The New Deal*, Chicago: Quadrangle Books, pp. 136–49.

Haddock, David D. (1982), 'Basing-point pricing: Competitive vs. collusive theories', *American Economic Review* **72** (June), 289–306.

Higgs, Robert (1987), *Crisis and Leviathan: Critical Episodes in the Growth of American Government*, New York: Oxford University Press.

Higgs, Robert (1997), 'Regime uncertainty: Why the Great Depression lasted so long and why prosperity resumed after the war', *The Independent Review* **1** (Spring), 561–90.

High, Stanley (1939), 'The WPA: Politicians' playground', *Current History* **50** (May), 23–25, 62.

Hill, Frank E. (1937), 'The CCC marches toward a new destiny', in Carl N. Degler (ed.) (1970), *The New Deal*, Chicago: Quadrangle Books, pp. 120–27.

Hofstadter, Richard (1955), *The Age of Reform: From Bryan to F.D.R.*, New York: Vintage Books.

Hofstadter, Richard ([1948] 1984), *The American Political Tradition and the Men who Made It*, New York: Vintage Books.

Holley, William C., Ellen Winston and T. J. Woofter, Jr (1940), *The Plantation South*, Washington, DC: US Government Printing Office.

Hosen, Frederick E. (1992), *The Great Depression and the New Deal*, Jefferson, NC: McFarland and Co.

Howard, Donald S. (1943), *The WPA and Federal Relief Policy*, New York: Russell Sage.

Hughes, Jonathan and Louis P. Cain (1994), *American Economic History*, New York: Harper Collins.

Hurwitz, Abner and Carlyle P. Stallings (1957), 'Interregional differences in per capita real income changes', in Conference on Research in Income and Wealth, *Regional Income*, Studies in Income and Wealth, Vol. 21, Princeton, NJ: Princeton University Press, pp. 195–265.

Irons, Peter H. (1982), *The New Deal Lawyers*, Princeton, NJ: Princeton University Press.

Kealey, Terence (1996), *The Economic Laws of Scientific Research*, Houndmills, Hampshire, UK: Macmillan Publishing Ltd and New York: St. Martin's Press.

Kurzman, Paul A. (1974), *Harry Hopkins and the New Deal*, Fairlawn, NJ: R. E. Burdick, Inc.

Kuznets, Simon (1950), 'Shares of upper income groups in income and savings', Occasional Paper No. 35, New York: National Bureau of Economic Research.

Lebergott, Stanley (1948), 'Labor force, employment, and unemployment, 1929–1939', *Monthly Labor Review* **67** (July), 50–53.

Lebergott, Stanley (1964), *Manpower and Economic Growth*, New York: McGraw-Hill.

Lloyd, Robert E. (1994), 'The political economy of the FHA', *Critical Review*

8 (Winter), 61–72.

Lowitt, Richard ([1984] 1993), *The New Deal and the West*, Norman: University of Oklahoma Press.

Lumsden, Keith and Craig Peterson (1975), 'The effect of right-to-work laws on unionization in the United States', *Journal of Political Economy* **83** (December), 1237–48.

MacMahon, Arthur, John Millet and Gladys Ogden (1941), *The Administration of Federal Work Relief*, Chicago: Public Administration Service.

Margo, Robert A. (1993), 'Employment and unemployment in the 1930's', *Journal of Economic Perspectives* 7 (Spring), 41–59.

McCormick, Robert E. and Robert D. Tollison (1981), *Politicians, Legislation, and the Economy: An Inquiry into the Interest-Group Theory of Government*, Boston: Martinus Nijhoff.

McElvaine, Robert S. (1984), *The Great Depression*, New York: Times Books.

McKenzie, Richard B. (1985), *Competing Visions*, Washington, DC: Cato Institute.

Mertz, Paul E. (1978), *New Deal Policy and Southern Rural Poverty*, Baton Rouge: Louisiana State University Press.

Mishkin, Frederic S. (1989), *The Economics of Money, Banking, and Financial Markets*, Glenview, IL: Scott Foresman.

Namorato, Michael V. (1988), *Rexford G. Tugwell: A Biography*, New York: Praeger.

Office of Government Reports (1939), *Activities of Selected Federal Agencies*, Report No. 7, Washington, DC: Office of Government Reports.

Office of Government Reports (1940), *Report No. 10*, vol. II (48 reports).

Olson, Mancur (1965), *The Logic of Collective Action: Public Goods and the Theory of Groups*, Cambridge, MA: Harvard University Press.

Patterson, James T. (1969), *The New Deal and the States*, Princeton, NJ: Princeton University Press.

Perkins, Frances (1935), 'The principles of social security', in Howard Zinn (ed.) (1966), *New Deal Thought*, Indianapolis, IN: Bobbs-Merrill, pp. 274–81.

Rauch, Jonathan (1994), *Demosclerosis: The Silent Killer of American Government*, New York: Times Books.

Reading, Don C. (1972), 'A statistical analysis of New Deal economic programs in the forty-eight states', unpublished dissertation, Utah State University.

Reading, Don C. (1973), 'New Deal activity and the states, 1933–1939', *Journal of Economic History* **33** (December), 792–810.

Robinson, Edgar E. (1970), *They Voted for Roosevelt*, New York: Octagon

Books.

Romer, Christina D. (1993), 'The nation in depression', *Journal of Economic Perspectives* **7** (Spring), 19–39.

Schlesinger, Arthur M. (1958), *The Coming of the New Deal*, Boston: Houghton Mifflin.

Schlesinger, Arthur M. (1960), *The Politics of Upheaval*, Boston: Houghton Mifflin.

Schwartz, Charles F. and Robert E. Graham (1956), *Personal Income by States Since 1929*, Washington, DC: US Government Printing Office.

Sherwood, Robert E. (1950), *Roosevelt and Hopkins: An Intimate History*, New York: Harper and Brothers.

Smiley, Gene (1994), *The American Economy in the Twentieth Century*, Cincinnati, OH: South-Western Publishing Co.

Stein, Herbert (1984), *Presidential Economics: The Making of Economic Policy from Roosevelt to Reagan and Beyond*, New York: Simon and Schuster.

Stevens, Joe B. (1993), *The Economics of Collective Choice*, Boulder, CO: Westview Press.

Stigler, George J. (1971), 'The theory of economic regulation', *Bell Journal of Economics and Management Science* **2** (Spring), 3–21.

Stigler, George J. (ed.) (1975), 'Supplementary note on economic theories of regulation (1975)', in *The Citizen and the State: Essays on Regulation*, Chicago: University of Chicago Press, pp. 137–41.

Temin, Peter (1976), *Did Monetary Forces Cause the Great Depression?*, New York: Norton.

Tindall, George B. (1967), *A History of the South*, vol. 10, Baton Rouge: Louisiana State University Press.

Todd, Walker F. (1992), 'History of and rationales for the Reconstruction Finance Corporation', *Economic Review* (Federal Reserve Bank of Cleveland) **28**, 22–33.

Trend, M. G. and W. L. Lett (1985), 'Government capital and minority enterprise: An evaluation of a depression-era social program', unpublished manuscript, Auburn University.

Tugwell, Rexford G. (1932), 'The principle of planning and the institution of laissez faire', *American Economic Review* **22** (March), 75–92.

Tugwell, Rexford G. (1937), 'Behind the farm program: Rural poverty', in Carl N. Degler (ed.) (1970), *The New Deal*, Chicago: Quadrangle Books, pp. 171–79.

US Department of Commerce (1932–1940), *Statistical Abstract of the United States*, Washington, DC: US Government Printing Office.

US House of Representatives (1932), *Congressional Directory*, Washington,

DC: US Government Printing Office.

US House of Representatives (1933), *Congressional Directory*, Washington, DC: US Government Printing Office.

US House of Representatives (1935), *Congressional Directory*, Washington, DC: US Government Printing Office.

US House of Representatives (1935a), *Congressional Record*, Washington, DC: US Government Printing Office.

US House of Representatives (1938), *Congressional Directory*, Washington, DC: US Government Printing Office.

US House of Representatives (1938a), *Congressional Record*, Washington, DC: US Government Printing Office.

US House of Representatives (1939), *Congressional Record*, Washington, DC: US Government Printing Office.

US House of Representatives (1939a), *Federal Ownership of Real Estate and its Bearing on State and Local Taxation*, House Miscellaneous Document No. III, Washington, DC: US Government Printing Office.

US Senate (1938), Special Committee to Investigate Unemployment and Relief ('Byrnes Committee'), *Unemployment and Relief: Hearings Before a Special Committee to Investigate Unemployment and Relief*, Washington, DC: US Government Printing Office.

Vedder, Richard K. and Lowell E. Gallaway (1993), *Out of Work: Unemployment and Government in Twentieth-Century America*, An Independent Institute Book, New York: Holmes and Meier.

Wager, Paul W. (1945), *One Foot on the Soil*, Tuscaloosa, AL: Weatherford Printing Co.

Wallace, Henry A. (1939), 'The new farm act: Balanced abundance for farm and city', in Howard Zinn (ed.) (1966), *New Deal Thought*, Indianapolis, IN: Bobbs-Merrill, pp. 232–39.

Wallis, John J. (1984), 'The birth of old federalism: Financing the New Deal', *Journal of Economic History* **44** (March), 139–59.

Wallis, John J. (1987), 'Employment, politics, and economic recovery during the Great Depression', *Review of Economics and Statistics* **49** (August), 516–20.

Wallis, John J. (1989), 'Employment in the Great Depression: New data and hypothesis', *Explorations in Economic History* **26** (January), 45–72.

Wallis, John J. (1991), 'The political economy of New Deal fiscal federalism', *Economic Inquiry* **29** (July), 510–24.

Watkins, T. H. (1993), *The Great Depression: America in the 1930s*, Boston: Little, Brown and Company.

Whatley, Warren C. (1983), 'Labor for the picking: The New Deal in the South', *Journal of Economic History* **43** (December), 905–29.

Williams, Raburn (1994), *The Politics of Boom and Bust in Twentieth-Century America*, Minneapolis-St. Paul: West Publishing Co.

Winberry, John J. and David M. Jones (1973), 'The rise and decline of the miracle vine: Kudzu in the southern landscape', *Southern Geographer* **13** (November), 61–70.

Wright, Gavin (1974), 'The political economy of New Deal spending: An econometric analysis', *Review of Economics and Statistics* **56** (February), 30–38.

Wright, Gavin (1986), *Old South, New South*, New York: Basic Books.

Zinn, Howard (ed.) (1966), *New Deal Thought*, Indianapolis, IN: Bobbs-Merrill.

Index

Abt, John 19
Agricultural Adjustment Act (1933) 18
  acreage reduction and monetary
    issues 46
  benefits from 50
  Emergency Farm Mortgage Act
    (Title II) 47
  intent and programs developed under
    39–41
Agricultural Adjustment Act (1938)
  intent of 41
  programs to control supply of farm
    commodities 42–4
Agricultural Adjustment
    Administration (AAA) 19–20
Agricultural Adjustment Agency
    (AAA)
  crop-reduction scheme 39–41
  Federal Surplus Relief Corporation
    under 40
  function of 39–40
Agricultural sector
  analysis of relief to using
    disaggregated data 3, 190–94
  benefits under New Deal 30–31
  Commodity Credit Corporation
    programs 41–4
  under New Deal legislative
    provisions 39–65
  political mobilization (1920s) 38
  pre-Depression and Depression
    performance 37–8
  priorities of New Deal subsidies
    (Anderson and Tollison) 174
  priorities of subsidies and benefits
    using aggregated data 187
  see also farm policy, New Deal;
    sharecroppers; tenant farmers
Alexander, Will 59
Alston, Lee 50

Anderson, Gary M. 2, 172–5, 180, 181
Arnold, Thurman 19
Arrington, Leonard xiii–xiv, 145,
    155–6, 225
Bankhead Bill (1937) 59
Bankhead Cotton Control Act (1934)
    41
Bankhead, John 55, 56, 59
Bankhead, Tallulah 114
banking system
  during Great Depression 9–10
  RFC loans to and preferred stock
    purchases from 71–2
Banks for Cooperatives
  Central Bank of 48
  under Farm Credit Administration 47
Barber, William J. 187
Barkley, Alben 121
Bator, Francis M. 161
benefits
  FDR as beneficiary of New Deal
    162
  for industrial and agricultural sectors
    under New Deal 30–31
  uneven distribution of funding under
    AAA 50–52
Bernstein, Barton J. 16, 25, 27, 30, 31,
    33, 50, 68, 69, 77, 125–6
Biles, Roger 125, 212–13
Birdseye, Clarence 125
Bittlingmayer, George 79
Black, Hugo 68, 74, 97, 212
boondoggling 114, 116
Bureau of Public Roads 94, 101
Bureau of Reclamation
  used in First New Deal programs 70
Byrnes Committee 107, 111
Byrnes, James 204
Cain, Louis 9
Cannon, Clarence 97